Dear Friend of tap:

Good lock - love of this form (with roots in London

Musical theatre!

I hope you enjoy my "tome" - the photos, the vintage DVD.

Sincerely Jane Goldberg

Shoot Me While I'm Happy

MEMORIES FROM THE TAP GODDESS
OF THE LOWER EAST SIDE

Shoot Me While I'm Happy

MEMORIES FROM THE TAP GODDESS OF THE LOWER EAST SIDE

by
Jane Goldberg

WITH FOREWORD BY THE LATE
GREGORY HINES

WOODSHED PRODUCTIONS, NEW YORK

Request for permission to make copies of any part of the work
should be mailed to the following address:
Woodshed Productions
310 Greenwich St., New York, NY 10013-2711
woodshedproductions@yahoo.com
www.janegoldberg.org

Library of Congress Cataloging-in-Publication Data
Goldberg, Jane. Shoot Me While I'm Happy:
Memories from the Tap Goddess of the Lower East Side/Jane Goldberg.—1st ed. p. cm.
ISBN 978-0-9801546-0-3 (Paperback)
ISBN 978-0-9801546-1-0 (Hardcover)
1. Entertainment—Pop Culture—Tap Dancing.   2. Memoir/Humor.
3. Social History/Essay.   4. Jazz/Music

Text set in Adobe Caslon
Cover design by Arthur Goldberg and Kathi Georges
Interior design by Kathi Georges

Printed in the United States of America
First edition
E D

In loving memory

of

Gregory Hines (1946–2003)

and

Jackie Raven (1951–2002),

two tap dancers who could

make me laugh out loud

and

to my very dear friend,

Audrey Simons

and

her parents

Marilyn and Jim

who

believe in me

The New York Tap Fringe Festival brings you

BACK BY POPULAR DEMAND!
Her First World Wide Tour!

And with a little help from her friends

Sold Out Shows!
(MAYBE)

JANE GOLDBERG
IN
BELLY TAP FOR WORLD PEACE!

At The Blue Mountain Gallery
530 W. 25th St., 4th Floor (Betw 10 & 11, Very Fringey)
Weekends in November: Fri - Sun, Nov 4-6, 11-13, 18-20, 8 PM
Suggested Donation: $15-$25

Table of Contents

Foreword by Gregory Hines

Jane Goldberg, aka: "The Tap Goddess of The Lower East Side," and I go way back. It was 1979, and tap dancing, after enduring a virtual disappearance from the popular scene for almost 15 years, was in the embryonic stages of a revival.

I was tap dancing for Broadway audiences in the musical tribute to the legendary composer Eubie Blake, "Eubie," and being heralded as a major cog in the new Tap Revival. Jane, in addition to tap dancing herself, was putting on tap shows and workshops around Manhattan, and bringing many of the Grand Masters of the art like, Charles Cookie Cook, Harriet Brown, Buster Brown, Honi Coles, Sandman Sims, and John Bubbles to the attention of an audience that was suddenly not only aware of tap dancing, but growing hungry for its true history.

Well, after meeting and spending some time "talking tap" with Jane, I realized that if I was a cog in the revival wheel, Jane was rapidly becoming the wheel itself.

Since our first meeting, Jane and I have forged a relationship that, while loving, and deeply rooted in our mutual passion for all things tap dancing, can often be extremely difficult and confrontational (to the point where at times, we wouldn't speak to each other for long periods at a time). Yet, it's continued to be one of the most real, important, and nourishing friendships I've ever been a part of. I've never met anyone in tap dancing who brings more intelligence, love, and an intense desire to move the art form forward than Jane Goldberg. Her extensive knowledge of tap's history has bested me on more occasions than I care to recount (and I've been in the art for 52 years), and her vision for its future is profoundly risky and creative. In a typical "Talking Tap" session with Jane, she can be opinionated, stubborn, funny, insightful, and relentless in making her points. I suppose she'd say the same about me. I hope so!

When Jane told me she was (finally) going to put all her notes and tapes from all her years in the art together into a book, I was thrilled and nervous at the same time. I was thrilled because I've long held the belief that if she put all her experiences as a tap dancer, her interviews with the dancers themselves, and all the research she's put in together, she would have a wonderful account of what the tap life is all about, from the deep and true inside of the art. But I was nervous because I wondered if she would write about how intense our relationship is. How would I come off in the book?

Jane didn't give me much time to think about it because soon after she broke the news to me that she was, in fact, going to put her story into a book, she asked me if I would write this foreword, and gave me her manuscript to read. That's so Jane.

Well, I read the book, promptly agreed to write the foreword for her, and I'm happy I did. Because this book is not only one of the most enjoyable reads on tap (and all its assorted characters) I've ever experienced, but the bottom line here is that Jane *did it*. She did it and did it beautifully. Anyone who loves the art of tap dancing, or even has a passing interest in it, will get hooked on it all the more. She put it all down in her own inimitable style, and in so doing, made all of us who wear tap shoes and love the art, proud.

Thanks Jane. I love you. ■

Introduction

This is *not* a history of tap dancing.

It is a personal story of what it was like tracking down, studying and performing with some of the tap greats during the 1970s and '80s and then creating my own take on the art. The writer Molly McQuade once told me the contemporary history of tap dancing is the history of individual dancers. We don't have a vaudeville circuit or nightclub booking agents to set up our gigs. It has been up to each of us to forge ahead, inventing our own venues, performances, and stories.

For the most part, tap has been passed down orally and aurally, voice to voice, feet to feet, sound to sound. In 1973, '30s dresses, brass beds, and Twyla Tharp dances were all the rage. I began going to movie revival houses to see the Fred Astaire–Ginger Rogers musicals. Tap, it seemed to me, was the most direct route to finding a partner like Astaire.

It's been almost forty years since the Summer of Love. Journalist Todd Gitlin writes about nostalgia meaning homesickness, how the celebration of the past becomes a way to express opposition in the present. When I was taking up tap, like my '60s cohorts, I didn't view it nostalgically. We were searching for something genuine, at a time when that something—tap dancing—was nowhere to be found.

I was a journalist coming off the anti-war movement writing about Cesar Chavez's lettuce boycott and women's issues. The most profound influence on my life at that time was my professor from Boston University, Howard Zinn, who told me, "If you can't liberate the world, you must liberate the ground upon which you stand."

I forever gave up my rollers, let my hair go naturally curly again, and looked up "tap" in the Boston yellow pages. Soon I liberated the ground upon which I stood and began to study tap dancing. ∎

The Great American Tap Rap

"It's just one big old foot after the other."
—Mumble, the penguin, in the movie *Happy Feet*

"Tap is not the kind of thing people get into because they can make a fortune doing it or because everybody's doing it. People get into it and they fall in love with it and they have to do it."
—Gregory Hines to Megan Haungs
Details Magazine

"In a way, tap dancing is like an elaborate joke about walking. All you can ever do is move from one foot to the next. No matter how dazzling a step is, it's still a step. It's a very humble art form, being all in the feet, but then, it's also an exalted one. It's so much more glorious than walking around."
—Maggie Lewis
The Christian Science Monitor

"It's a buck dancer's choice, my friend, better take my advice."
—From "Uncle John's Band"
The Grateful Dead

"Tap dancing is the scourge of the devil today, bequeathed to us by St. Vitus."
—Ted Shawn, modern dance pioneer

"That's what I like about tap dancing. It's like playing the banjo. You don't have to answer to anybody. It's up to you . . . it's just: How good can you get?"
—Steve Martin, *Rolling Stone Magazine* interview

Beginnings and a . . . "Homegoing"

When I was little, my mother told me it was very important to marry a good dancer. She didn't mean a modern dancer or a ballet dancer. She meant a ballroom dancer. She definitely did not mean a hoofer.

Tap was the first kind of dancing she had me study. I still remember my first time step, "stomp, hop, fah-lap ball change—stomp, hop, fah-lap ball change go the feet, while I sing, one together two-and-half, three seventy-five, five!"

I was four years old in 1952 when I put on my first pair of Mary Jane black patent leather shoes and went to study with Miss Maxine—not Ms. Maxine, but Miss Maxine. She was a former Rockette who taught in one of those second-floor dancing school studios that also offered toe tap, acrobatics, and jazz. At the end of the year recital, I wore a short red feather cape and a white leotard with my bare legs and feet inside silver Minnie Mouse shoes. During our chorus line finale, my best friend Sheryl Langsner, stricken with stage fright, crossed in front of me, and ran for her life.

My tapping days came to a halt one year later when my fashion-conscious mother decided that modern dance was the way to go. I didn't even think about tap again until I was twenty-five years old and the Fred Astaire and Ginger Rogers movies started appearing at a few Boston art houses, a local library, and the Museum of Fine Arts.

Reading an issue of *Newsweek* in my basement apartment in Cambridge, Massachusetts, I came across a glowing review by Jack Kroll of critic Arlene Croce's *The Fred Astaire and Ginger Rogers Book*. In the first paragraph of the review, Kroll had been unsuccessfully trying to convince his blind date how Gene Kelly couldn't even begin to compare to Fred. In Croce, Kroll found total articulation of this truism and a million other reasons why the Fred and Ginger musicals were so terrific. Kroll's review convinced me to buy Croce's book and I immediately started going to whichever of the dancing duo's movies I could find.

I'm getting ready for my first tap recital with Miss, not Ms. Maxine, 1952.

Seeing Fred and Ginger movies in 1972 was a true revelation. I could find a dance partner like him.

I had to beg my way into a screening of *Carefree*, one of the last films they did together, at the Museum of Fine Arts. It was a members-only event, and I wasn't a member. The audience proved full of fans and we all guffawed as Astaire, playing a psychoanalyst, danced a Highland Fling on the golf green while simultaneously teeing off a hundred balls with different clubs, singing, and playing a harmonica. In one duet with Ginger, they leap across tiger lilies in a pond and end with a kiss. This was the only movie where Fred and Ginger ever kissed! They didn't have to: Their dances said it all.

Carefree is also the film in which Fred and Ginger do "The Yam," which starts out with the two dancing on a country club floor. The crowd of guests spontaneously starts yam-strutting behind them as they travel out of the building, onto a brick path, around the club, and eventually back onto the ballroom floor. Fred, of course, has already tossed Ginger onto stuffed chairs and furniture by the time they return, and, for the grand finale, has lifted and flown her around the room.

By the end of the film, I found myself yam-strutting up the aisles and down the tomb-like steps of the Museum of Fine Arts. What Arlene Croce's writing instilled in me right from the get go, and what Fred and Ginger confirmed on screen, was that tap dancing was romantic when they danced together. Their flirtatious tap duets made me swoon. I wanted a partner just like Fred after watching those movies. That's when I went to the yellow pages and looked up tap.

"It's very important to marry a good dancer."

In the last two years of her life, my mother was in the Hebrew Home for the Aged in Rockville, Maryland, with a sweet kind of early dementia. Mom, known to all as Molly, repeatedly sang a tune from her early youth. It went: "I've got a toothache, a gum ball, a belly ache, I've got a toothache, a dimple on my chin!" She sang the word "chin," and touched her own chin hard with her index finger, exaggerating the word as if to punctuate the Big Ending. She taught me The Highland fling and the Irish jig, both as solo kinds of dancing. We did the Charleston together and I wore one of her chemise skirts as my whole dress. How romantic can it be, though, dancing with your own mother?

Molly Goldberg, (not the '40s and '50s radio and television personality Molly Goldberg) née Goldstein, had once been an Apache dancer who gave up a blooming career getting thrown across the floor in that kind of sadomasochistic style for work in a World War II munitions factory. Later, she met my father and immediately began dancing with him at various Atlantic City nightclubs. Back then, it seemed every couple met to the rhythms of big band music and everyone knew how to ballroom dance.

Even with her Parkinson's hands and compromised memory, Mom sat in the long line of wheel-chaired old timers at the nursing home, shook her finger at me, and for

©CHANGING TIMES TAP ARCHIVE

Mother Molly Goldberg: She gave up a blooming dance career to work in a World War II munitions factory.

the last time told me she wished I'd gotten married to a good dancer. I didn't comment. I didn't want to disappoint my mother, who kept kosher and was practically Orthodox, by reminding her I had met a lot of fantastic dancers, all gentlemanly black hoofers at least twice my age. That fact would have all but sent her right to the grave.

"It's very important to marry a good dancer."

That was obvious to me just watching my parents dance together. They could really go. They did a mean Charleston. I often got to watch them do it at numerous parties in the basement of our Silver Spring, Maryland, home, sweating, swinging, and kicking in a fast tempo. When my father took my mother in his arms, he had this totally determined hard-core look on his face, no kidding around. I became their opening act, performing my little choreographies to "The Green Door" and Peggy Lee's version of "We are Siamese" from Disney's *Lady and the Tramp*. The three of us put on a show at every opportunity.

My mom dressed me exactly like her in matching mother/daughter outfits she sewed from Singer patterns. She created all the costumes for my modern dance concerts when I was little and broke her sewing machine on the sparkles and glitter while stitching the entire cast of guppy outfits for *Pinocchio*. As I grew up, together we went through her blue and green period, her purple period, her mohair sweater period, Molly

"Just Molly and me" in matching outfits Mom sewed from Singer Patterns (1953).

forever trying to make me in her own image. When I left home, she began sewing matching tops and pants for my father and her.

I learned to ballroom dance when I was eight because Arthur, my brother, needed to practice his cotillion lessons with someone. I became my brother's guinea pig as we jitterbugged in the basement to "At the Hop" and "Peggy Sue." Dancing with him was better than his surprise attacks on me and my friends at my slumber parties. Arthur never got over my being born.

When we stopped practicing his lessons, I would still often dance alone in the basement, to Nat King Cole's "Dance Ballerina, Dance" or "Come Softly to

No Kidding Around—My parents did a mean Charleston, and I was their opening act at parties in Silver Spring, Maryland.

I'm the lead guppy in Pinnochio, *1953: Mom switches me to modern dance during The Great Tap Drought, which lasted into the '70s.*

Me." I would cha-cha-cha to the latter and daydream for hours and hours about the boy who would whisk me off my feet, the great dancer I was going to meet, the man I would marry. This unrealized fantasy has stayed with me all my life.

After working as a muckraking journalist/listings editor for one year at *Boston After Dark*, an alternative weekly newspaper, I quit my job and flew to a Greek island to dance. It was a time you could fly practically free everywhere with "youth fare." I had an epiphany while playing catch with a young Greek kid on the island of Paros in the Cyclades, and suddenly saw my whole life in a grain of sand. I knew I would have to dance, that dancing was my life.

I had a journalism and dance background, the kind I needed to become a major conduit in a field where its practitioners had gone underground, or, as we say in tap, "hung up their shoes." I ferreted out a lot of the remaining tap dancing stars of yesteryear, studied with them, and performed with them. We helped re-introduce tap to American and European audiences. I produced and wrote about these remaining masters. Tap dancing became the perfect cause for a cause-oriented person like me. I could still be an agent of change—the tapping reporter. What a beat!

When I looked up "tap" in search of my Fred Astaire, I found Stanley Brown and made do. His was the only studio listed in Boston that offered tap dancing. A year after I learned to tap, I moved to the Big Apple, still looking for *him*.

Nothing in New York City promised romance when I arrived. My first full time living situation was in Soho in a huge, unfinished, unfurnished loft I was to share with three other unemployed artists. The entire roommate situation, from the start, was one big fat mess. Julie, a close girlfriend, and I began leaving mean little notes to each other on top of our dining room table—the only piece of furniture in the loft when I arrived.

Another roommate's mother was killed in the late autumn and we had to deal with that. Her boyfriend—John Lurie of the downtown band The Lounge Lizards, was our fourth roommate. John made matters worse for me. My father told me my reputation would be forever *"besmirched"* even though the "guy" wasn't even *my* boyfriend. That he was "shacked up" with one of my roommates was bad enough in my dad's opinion. I might have come out of the "free love" generation, but my father did not.

Brother Arthur visited me in my new home early on with his second wife, Fruitcake, and he built me a loft bed surrounded by sheetrock walls. High ceilings were probably the only thing I enjoyed about loft living that year. Arthur fortressed me in my little room like "Queen Jane, Approximately."

In fact, when I went out to get some privacy my first month in New York, all the flatiron buildings, tall and ominous, looked just like mine, yet there was nothing comfortingly familiar about any of them. I had left tree-green Cambridge, food co-ops, and boyfriends for something vaguely involving "dance," and I wasn't sure I knew what any of it meant.

"It's very important to marry a good dancer."

I did meet a partner of sorts early on at a party in the loft. Stewart Alter also loved the Fred and Ginger movies, understood rhythm, and always knew where the beat was no matter where it landed. A Queens native, he helped me adjust to New York that first year as he listened to me freak out about my living situation practically every day on the phone.

Stewart was an original. He had studied painting with one of Hans Hoffman's disciples and knew about tap's potential, its abstraction, too. He and his wife Daisy Edmondson eventually wrote a lot of my shows including, *The Depression's Back and So Is Tap*; *Old, New, Borrowed, and Bluesy*; *The Tapping Talk Show*; *Sole Sisters* (featuring tap's Grandes Dames and Prima Tapperinas); and *Shoot Me While I'm Happy*, the latter performed at The Goodman Theatre in Chicago. Stewart and I also collaborated on a dance/poem called "The Neighbor," a take-off on Edgar Allan Poe's "The Raven" about a writer living next door to a noisy hoofer.

I was "art" dance. Gregory was "showbiz." It was fun to argue with him.

By 1975, my second year in New York, I had found some of the old hoofers, got a decent place to study and live, and by the end of the '70s, I was in full swing, carving my niche, living the tap life.

That's about the time I met Gregory Hines.

I had gone backstage during a rehearsal of a Broadway revue, "Black Broadway" at Town Hall looking for John Bubbles, one of the big stars of black vaudeville, and instead met Gregory, sitting on the floor, right in front of me, his legs stretched out in a wide V. We said hello. He told me his wife Pam Koslow had told him about "this hip white chick tapping with some of the old hoofers downtown." Both Gregory and I were wearing glasses; we discovered we were both having a hard time with contact lenses.

Gregory Hines became a huge part of my psyche. We were sole brother and sister, talking tap over the course of twenty-five years. He was my muse, the one to whom I could sing my fantasies, my yearnings for a partner. We often argued with each other about all things tap. Gregory was a visionary and let me enter his life as a close friend and chronicler.

"I want to tap for the people, as corny as that sounds, Jane."

He said this once when we were living across the street from each other during the 1980s. We were walking down West 11th St. toward the Hudson River and our respective dwellings—his swankerola loft, my one-room hovel. He succeeded like no one else in re-introducing tap into the mainstream through movies, Broadway shows, club and television appearances. He did benefits for everything and everyone.

My background was a far cry from show business. I was art-dance. When I arrived in New York, I went strictly downtown, rolling on floors with Simone Forti and other postmodern experimentalists. I admired the composer/singer/choreographer, Meredith Monk, and took a workshop with her. Meredith urged me to start teaching tap and became one of my first students. She sent a lot of her chorus of singers and dancers from *Quarry*, one of her important performance "operas" then playing at the experimental theater company La Mama, ETC. to my Bleecker Street basement living loft to study with me.

Gregory was showbiz. He and his older brother Maurice, Jr. spent their childhood on the road as The Hines Kids earning a living for their family. Later their father, who played drums, joined the act, and Hines, Hines and Dad became headliners at the tail end of the glory days of "the business," when nightclubs and live entertainment still prevailed. Gregory was the link between old showbiz and the upcoming "Age of Aquarius" tap.

Where Gregory idolized Sammy Davis, Jr., I idolized Isadora Duncan. Gregory was exactly two years older than I and defined tap in terms of the Challenge, the Champ, being the best, competition. I felt tap was a "sensibility." Gregory was commercial, practical, all about tap dancers making a living at tap. I was anti-commercial, performance art, left wing, romantic, (although I still wanted to make a living at it).

Gregory was Broadway, Hollywood, and television. I was Marxist School, topical anti-war tap, anti-diet conference, Belly Tap for World Peace. But we both came of age in the '60s, grew up during the Civil Rights movement, and lived through

Drummer Barry Saperstein with Gregory in their hippie years. They remained best friends until the end.

the Sexual Revolution. Gregory felt ego was the most important thing you could have to survive in show business and I was always struggling with mine.

"It's very important to marry a good dancer."

Twenty-five years into our complex friendship, I sat in Gregory's Venice Beach home, pouring my heart out to him as usual. It was July 2003, just a month before his death from a liver-pancreatic type of cancer. I knew it was our last talking-tap session and he knew it, too, but I didn't want to believe it.

"Jane, you know when you're going to start having fun in life?"

I was expecting something deep and profound, thoughtful and heartfelt.

"When you buy a Mac."

My mouth hung open for a minute as I attempted to digest his words. I couldn't even say anything; I was caught totally off guard. I knew he was a "Mac-person"—one of those Mac-crazed fanatics, those totally insane Mac-steins. Still, I hadn't expected him to Mac me right then.

I finally answered back, asking if he could get me a good deal, and he said, no, I'd have to buy one in New York, where I could get technical support. He then walked me all the way up a lot of stairs, walking that slow, endless, halting, depressing cancer walk. I followed him up the hundreds of stairs so he could show me his new G4 model, just out, with the joy of a parent introducing a friend to his newborn baby.

That was Gregory. He was full of surprises and I miss him like crazy. I think about him a ton and I loved him so much. A triple threat, a cross-over artist, he always remained true to tap.

Only three years earlier—just after his mother Alma had died—Gregory sent me an e-mail.

"When I turned 50, I felt reflective, but nowhere near as reflective as I have since my mother's homegoing. There are moments where I just can't believe her life is over . . . and I find myself seeing images of her from many different periods of her life . . ."

The word "homegoing" reminds me of how the old school hoofers would always yell to their musicians, "I'm going home!" or "Take me home!" when they wanted to end their dances. Still the essence of health and athleticism at fifty-six, Gregory "went home" at fifty-seven, catching everyone off guard, possibly even himself. Gregory Hines lived for the "now," and told me in our last conversation, "You know the 'hippie rule'? Everything that's real is right now. There ain't nothing real about what's gone down before, ain't nothing real about what's supposed to come next . . . This is what's real, right now!"

Although we indulged in a long, intimate, far-ranging e-mail relationship, one thing we never shared was his passion for Macintosh computers. ∎

Greg and me after a master class he taught at New York University, 1992.

Years Ago It Was Heel and Toe

February 1974: I'm going to try out New York City for a month. When I visited Julie, my roommate from Cambridge, who had moved there to dance the year before, she told me I'd always feel like I was missing the boat if I didn't try it.

I'm scared.

The only time I had ever spent in New York was in my early teens when my parents and I drove up from Maryland. We stayed at the Edison Hotel in midtown and saw Broadway musicals. Even if the shows were sold-out, my father always managed to get a ticket to one.

I particularly remember seeing Gwen Verdon in *Sweet Charity* and wanting to be her, red hair messed up in a bun of sorts, with that left arm akimbo, her back to the audience, in her famous Bob Fosse pose that's on the record album. I still hum, *"If they could see me now, that little gang of mine,"* when I'm feeling really good about myself, even if Gwen did play a prostitute. No one had a throaty warble like Gwen. I also remember looking into the windows of the rehearsal studios and seeing dancing girls kicking high. I wanted to be one of them, or better yet, a Peter Gennaro dancer on the Perry Como show.

New York City also meant shopping in these crowded bins at Klein's Department Store in Union Square, going to the Lower East Side, so my mother could buy mohair to knit sweaters (cheaper wool on Grand St. than in Maryland) and my dad could eat fresh baked bialys and hot dogs at Katz's Deli. I stood in front of Gus' Pickles and eagerly awaited the Jets and Sharks to appear, snapping their fingers, and starting a rumble. My mother had taken me to see the movie *West Side Story* on my fourteenth birthday and apparently it had made a big impression.

Master and Pupil: That's Chuck Green in the wings of The Brooklyn Academy of Music, and I'm trying to get in a step or two, 1979.

February 1974: It's cold cold cold. I rent a room for a month at sixty dollars from a friend's stepfather who lives alone on the Upper West Side. Harry's an old anarchist/communist abstract-expressionist painter and soon has me going to movies like *Lenin's Mother* and *Stalin's Uncle* and calls me a "late bloomer" since I am kicking around, a little directionless. He tells me that everything important happens between Lincoln Center and Columbia University. I don't mind Harry's communist leanings, because I pride myself on being a pinko, too. Still, I am geared more toward Greenwich Village.

On a particularly freezing day, *Village Voice* dance critic Deborah Jowitt, my dance-writing mentor, is walking with me down Christopher St. in Greenwich Village. She hands me a flyer promoting an event called *Mama J and her Tap Happenings*. Even though I am gung ho about dance journalism, Deborah also knows of my ever-intensifying tap habit. I decide to check it out.

Upon encountering those four black tapping men clad in business suits and bow ties, telling jokes as they dance in the basement of St. John the Apostle on Columbus Ave at 59th St., I know *immediately* I want to join them and "get their feet." They play such beautiful rhythms, those feet, and boy do they have a lot to say to me.

Chuck Green "Taking the A Train," his signature song he performed at most of the shows I saw him in.

Tap Happenings of 1969. From left: Raymond Kaalund, Leticia Jay, Sondra Gibson, Bert Gibson (in front), Chuck Green, Tony White, Jerry Ames, Sandman Sims.

First out, John T. MacPhee, from Atlantic City, who starts, "Ladies and Gentlemen, I'm the World's Greatest Tap Dancer—Rhythm is *MY* business. You know, years ago it was heel and toe. We did this for a living."

He proceeds to show us a few tap steps, hardly leaving the floor. He doesn't do the kind of stuff people try to do when they hear you're a tap dancer—some kind of stupid imitation of jerky feet, going in all directions. No, MacPhee is smooth, svelte. Black tux, on lean legs, he is way too dressy for this basement, this musty dirty linoleum floor, but I don't care. My eyes are on the prized feet. They are illuminating.

MacPhee plays emcee for the occasion and introduces Raymond Kaalund who acts a little tipsy on the floor. But it is just an act—a drunken hoofer. When he picks up a jump rope and shuffles to the tune "Perdido" with the rope going backwards, he doesn't miss a beat.

Rhythm Red, the next dancer introduced, is more inward, even shy. He has on white buck shoes and a white wrinkled cotton suit. He does a soft shoe, slow and mellow, not the kind you see Bob Hope do with the exaggerated kicks and expressions. Unlike the two before him, he doesn't speak.

Then MacPhee brings out Chuck Green, who floats over a taped recording of "Take the A Train." Chorus after chorus, he never repeats a step, and what steps they are! With each step Green emphasizes, he is almost invisibly telling us he is about to do something *killer*. He drops his heels down in the oddest, most wonderful places and turns on them. That's right, his *heels!* Just his *heels!* He isn't doing comedy or joking at all or anything Chaplinesque when he dances. And his feet are *GIGANTIC!*

I could do this, I think to myself. That's how confident this heavenly man makes me feel. Chuck Green mesmerizes the audience into stillness, watchfulness, serenity. He is spiritual, otherworldly, doing some kind of sleight of foot.

MacPhee then gets all four of the dancers in a half circle facing us and each charges out one at a time in a "battle of the taps" one by one, each coming out with a step that outdoes the last man. It's a lot of fun for the audience, although at that point I have no inclination to join any of them. I both love and hate the competition. Leticia Jay rounds out the bill, a zaftig woman dressed in flowing pants and gypsy earrings. She shows us what she calls "exotic dancing." Her gyrations appear somewhat out of place after the tappers. Little do I realize hers are the brains behind this revue, as well as the Tap Happenings of the late '60s at the Hotel Dixie in midtown.

After the show, the dancers linger, schmooze, give autographs. I run up to Chuck Green and ask him for lessons right on the spot. He gets Leticia to set up a time for me to meet with him and I go back to Harry's apartment in a daze, completely wowed by the thrill of the feet. It's different than the romancing of Fred and Ginger, but I'm not even thinking of them when I go to sleep that night. I'm thinking feet. I want those "feet!"

—~~~—

With the old school of tap dancers, a lesson is a "session," and it sometimes lasts a few hours, as Green's sessions did. You didn't rent a studio space back then or study in a classroom. I already had fallen in love with tap dancing and thought I was pretty adept at my Boston teacher Stanley Brown's routines, but Chuck Green raised the art to a whole other intricate level.

We take up a little corner of a big basement in a tenement building right across the street from Lincoln Center for the Performing Arts. Leticia Jay sits nearby in an old, uncomfortable looking metal folding chair, watching us intently. I use my recorder to tape these sessions. Chuck can't break any of his steps down for me. After awhile, I wonder if he has ever broken down his material for anyone. Maybe he's never taught, period. No matter how many times he repeats his tricky steps, I can't get even one of them. I begin to realize quickly this is a listener's dance. Like Green, the other Tap Happening hoofers didn't rely on arms and torso to get them through their show.

I am usually so fleet of feet and fast on the trigger when it came to picking up steps. I come away with a tape full of Chuck going, "Uh uh, no that's not it," me rattling off what I thought he meant, and then him doing the step again. Finally I put on my journalistic cap and begin asking where he learned to tap, where he was from, that kind of thing.

Chuck was born in Peachtree, Georgia, and moved briefly to Atlanta where he began performing outside Lucille Lashay's record store.

"I used to dance on sidewalks—did little cute things to get people to throw money. I'd put bottle tops on the bottom of my feet to make the sound. See, people didn't know, and they'd ask, 'now how the heck did he make such a sweet sound like that?'"

He ran away to New York as just a kid where he met Nat Nazzaro, an agent who represented many of the headliners of black show business, including one of the most popular acts, Buck and Bubbles. (A lot of little hoofers ran away in those days; Bill Bojangles Robinson did, too, to make his fortune).

Nazzaro came up with the idea of having Chuck and his young partner Chuckles run on stage to copy Buck and Bubbles' routines. He coached the two boys, taught them how to tell jokes onstage like Buck and Bubbles, and changed their act from Shorty and Slim to Chuck and Chuckles.

I was getting somewhat confused as Chuck was telling me all this—Chuck, Chuckles, Buck, Bubbles? I knew nothing about black vaudeville at this point and Chuck still seemed a little otherworldly, poetic, as he reeled off his story. One thing I was to learn quickly: Not only did each hoofer have a story, usually incredible, but he'd know everyone else's story, too. They were all well-versed in their histories, give or take a zillion facts.

CHANGING TIMES TAP ARCHIVE

Buck and Bubbles: Buck Washington and John Bubbles—stars of black vaudeville.

Stanley Brown Studio of Rhythm, with Stanley (left arrow) and guest instructor Bill Bojangles Robinson (right arrow). You can tell everyone in this photo was asked to give the Bill Robinson stage exit salute with the right hand. The boy in the front right with the tie seems resolute in holding his own ground.

Chuck credited Bubbles with putting tap in what he called the "the jazz bracket." He told me he learned steps from Bubbles at John Bubbles' house, where he was staying, although Bubbles didn't want him to know his style, his steps.

"Like, Bubbles would do a step just once and say, you got one chance. He was a creator. They called him 'the father of rhythm.'"

Bubbles' sister taught Chuck a way of tricking Bubbles into teaching him.

"His sister told me, 'I know his ways. You should say, you didn't do that. That ain't the way you did it.' And Bubbles would say, 'You can't tell me what I didn't do.' So I'd tell him to repeat something. Finally, one day he laughed and said, 'If you want me to teach you, just ask. And you don't have to call me "Uncle" anymore.'"

I still wasn't sure, though, how the information was transmitted. Did the steps have names like "shuffle," "flap," "riff," names I'd learned when I studied with Stanley? Or were they passed on rhythmically the way Chuck was doing with me, just scatting, yap, yap, be de de de, de de de bop, not even counting? Was Chuck a much faster study than I? How long did it take *him* to get the great master's routines down?

The new style of tap dancing Chuck said Bubbles invented was a real eye-opener for me because of its ties to jazz music. Before Bubbles, it was all up on the toes with Bill Bojangles Robinson as the forerunner of that style.

"Bubbles created different sounds and different times and he started dropping his heels. You could get a more floating quality, like a leaf coming off the top of a tree. It changed the quality of the sound, gave it tonation. Up on the toes you had a bobbing kind of quality. Where there used to be no sound, Bubbles dropped his heels, in turns, things like that.

"Tap really *is* jazz itself," he professed. "It's like a person walking and then they say 'I think I'll walk a little faster,' and so they walk faster. They say, 'I'll run a bit.' Tap dancing was here before jazz, though. In the old times, slaves used to take their shoes off, and dance for the master family. They'd make sound with their feet."

Chuck always sounded so poetic. My favorite of his responses was when I asked him how he started on his own and he replied, "My own is still coming. I'm getting a new thing now."

Here, this wonderful old hoofer, easily in his sixties but looking older than Old Man Time was *still getting his sound*. Maybe he was just talking in metaphors. In any case, he exuded mystery, passion, solemnity. His words gave me hope. Possibility. I left my session with him baffled, but not defeated.

———

Stanley Brown, my Boston "tapologist," had also given me Henry LeTang's name to look up. Unlike the four guys I saw at the church, Henry had a dance studio in the same building on West 47th St. as the old Jazz Museum, once a New York institution that occasionally presented hoofers in performance.

Henry proceeds to give me some steps to "Blue Skies," which he plays on his old piano.

We talk a little about Stanley and the tragic story of a young dancer named Pete Petersen who has just been killed in a plane crash. I'd seen Pete dance and made a point of finding out more about him. He was a young white man who could tap "black." Henry had taught Pete, liked him a lot.

I also visit Jerry Ames' studio. I learn that he had appeared as the only white dancer in the very first '60s revival of the *Tap Happenings* that I'd read about in a review by Marcia Siegel, another of my journalistic mentors. Jerry Ames has a beautiful balletic style, somewhat reminiscent of Paul Draper, the ballet tap dancer.

At Henry LeTang's, where I'm left to my own devices, it isn't very much fun woodshedding, practicing alone in a room. I'm not yet ready to woodshed, not advanced enough to get my own sound by practicing alone. Henry doesn't seem that interested, and maybe he is too busy, coming and then vanishing quickly to the next studio where I can hear another tapper through the walls. I feel like a number, not an individual—a

Sans cigarette: I'll remember Henry with cigarette hanging from the side of his mouth while he was teaching me "Blue Skies."

contrast to how I felt working with Chuck Green. Only later will I find out that Henry LeTang was responsible for building the Hines Brothers' act.

——————

I was surprised at how attracted I was to tap dancing, at first glance such an old ancient lost forgotten art, though actually it was none of those. It had just gone temporarily underground. It wasn't that old, not like ballet. The little girls in Mary Janes never really stopped tapping. Nor did the hoofers; they were still doing benefits, having great shows up in Harlem and other scattered venues.

It was odd, because I was usually drawn to the new. Choreographer Twyla Tharp was my dance idol at the time and I wanted to be a Twyla dancer. Marcia Siegel took me to see her *Deuce Coupe,* the rage of that year's dance season. It combined classical ballet performed by members of the Joffrey Ballet Company while Tharp's own wiggly, shrugging, topsy-turvy modern dancers did their thing. Twyla also hired teens from the Bronx to spray colorful graffiti on the backdrop while Beach Boys tunes blasted away.

It was her *The Bix Pieces,* however, that originally made me a Tharpophile. In that dance suite, she even taps a little—a standard time-step early on—while a narrator recites Tharp's childhood memories of her father, to whom she dedicates the dance. Borrowing from vaudeville, batons are thrown from the wings in quick succession, and she keeps missing them until they all pile up onstage. I loved her humor and the deadpan nonchalance she displayed as she missed each catch. I loved how structured the piece was, how unnostalgic, even though it so beautifully evoked the past. I loved her dancers—Sara Rudner, Rosemarie Wright, Kenneth Rinker, Isabella Garcia Lorca.

I wrote up the dance for my terrific editor at the time, Jon Lehman of the *Quincy Patriot Ledger,* where I was paid $10 a shot for dance reviews. He accepted a piece on the hoofers, too.

—※—

Back in Boston, I studied the pictures on Stanley's walls—autographed photos of John Bubbles, Bill Bojangles Robinson, other great tap dancers. Stanley could tell something had changed in me: I was even more excited to study tap in those half-hour lessons, more eager to learn about the lore.

It was during that period that Stanley told me the difference between the closed style of hoofing I'd just seen in the basement of the church—hoofing that wouldn't sell, the feet too close to the floor—and his open style, like that of Gene Kelly and Fred Astaire, the style that traveled the space, used the arms, the whole body.

That closed style sure sold it to me!

I told Stanley the names of some of the acts I'd heard about from Chuck Green, acts with names like Moke and Poke; The Three Chocolateers; The Businessmen of Rhythm; Pete, Peaches and Duke; Tip, Tap, and Toe; Stump and Stumpy; The Dancing Demons; Buck and Bubbles; Chuck and Chuckles; Snake Hips Tucker; Groundhog. Stanley could see I had found the gold. He began to open up even more about his own past with his act, The Brazilian Nuts.

I invited Stanley and our little class of four to dinner at my apartment. It was a big honor to have Stanley over because you never saw him outside of his

Mass. Ave. studio. He held court that hot summer night in my pad in Central Square, Cambridge.

As we ate chicken and rice, he told us about his days with Burns and Allen, all the spots his act toured, places like Australia, New Zealand, Turkey. Stanley Brown's philosophy for making it in show business was clear: "You can't just tap." You had to study voice, ballet, and jazz dancing, too. This was during the time of the drought.

This is how I remember Stanley Brown: at his traps, accompanying our class of four doing his routines.

The only time I recall Stanley bringing the "real" world into our classes was when the Broadway musical *Seesaw* came through town. Tommy Tune was starring in the national run and Stanley stopped everything to teach us the time step—a standard every hoofer knows. The show came and went and none of us tried out for it. Stanley never even told us this was the standard time step. It sure was different from his lyrical style.

Stanley talked about the limited number of opportunities for black people when he was a performer. You were a Pullman porter, a shoeshine boy, an elevator operator, *or* an entertainer. As one of The Brazilian Nuts, he traveled everywhere, but at home he "trembled" when he saw the greats like Honi Coles and Pete Nugent on the stage. He told us he had something else to offer, though. He could play the congas. He didn't like traveling with women because they could get pregnant on the road. Then what do you do?

He described working with Jack Benny. Benny wasn't stingy, contrary to the image he set on radio. Stanley told us it was TV that spoiled it for tap dancing because people could stay at home for their entertainment. They stopped going out as much.

Stanley also told us how he "wept uncontrollably" when Bill Robinson died. "It killed me when I saw him and he couldn't walk," he told us. "We didn't make any money in those days, but it was a family. Everybody was close. The beauty of vaudeville and show business is that you knew everybody."

As Stanley talked into the night, I began to wonder what happened to tap, an obsession that would take hold of me for the next fifteen or so years. This was a new cause for my cause-oriented personality. Once upon a time it was muckraking about the Cesar Chavez lettuce boycott. Now it was digging up stories about what killed tap.

<hr>

With her black hair pulled back in a ponytail, dark eye-lined eyes, piercing New York Bronx accent, able to balance on one leg like a stork, Claire Mallardi couldn't help but make an impression on me. She was my modern dance teacher at the humongous wooden-floored Radcliffe Gym. She lived on Boylston St. in the Back Bay and helped me overcome my fear of leaving my life in Cambridge. At some point, she told me, all dancers had to live in New York if they were serious about dance.

She was always late to class, but worth the wait, her back to us as we began her ritual warm-up, spreading our arms out wide, prayerful almost, while David Maxwell's live blues bounced off the piano in front of us. Claire made me understand how I could combine my political thoughts in college with modern dance vocabulary. I joined her classes as an outsider, biking over the BU Bridge to Harvard Square. As I sank into a plié, rising taller, I could feel some kind of

Claire Mallardi was a night owl, bewildered by people who actually got up in the morning. "What do they do *with all those hours?"*

contradiction taking place, some kind of Marxist dialectic moving up and down in my body. At least it seemed so when I was just twenty-one.

She adored the Fred and Ginger movies, too, tried hoofing a little back in her youth, and helped me choreograph my first tap dance, a conceptual piece set to voice-overs of Stanley Brown, Henry LeTang, and Chuck Green talking about what I could do with tap dancing, circa 1973. I called the dance *Years Ago It was Heel and Toe,* quoting John T. MacPhee, and did some numbers I deemed to be "white tap" and "black tap."

Claire was a night owl, and when you were invited over to her apartment, it was *always* an all-nighter. Her six cats crept quietly around the apartment, appearing, disappearing, sleeping, leaping, indifferent to our endless conversation. Claire had an amazing rock collection from Santa Fe and other southwestern places, and each of the rocks was carefully placed in its own little home. Like her cats, Claire was so much a creature of the night that she was bewildered by people who actually got up in the morning. "What do they *do* with all those hours?" she'd exclaim in disbelief.

As the summer rolled by, I was getting more focused on moving. In a sense, this new mission replaced "The Movement" of my anti-war days. When I informed one Boston buddy that I planned to abandon the tree-lined streets of Cambridge for Manhattan, he accused me of moving to New York to "make it"—such an uncool thing to do, so unhip in my countercultural circles.

So, on August 9, 1974, the summer of Watergate, I finally left Beantown. President Nixon was waving his defiant farewell as he boarded the helicopter that hot humid morning. In the afternoon, I squooshed myself into my neighbor Wayne's Volkswagen bug, my bicycle hooked up on the round little back, my typewriter, suitcase, and tap shoes inside. Wayne was going to his brother's in Westchester and offered to drop me off at my new home on West Broadway, New York City.

Autumn, 1974: After seeing the work of avant-garde director Robert Wilson, I decided I wanted to be part of his artistic constellation. I began hanging out with his choreographic associate, Andy DeGroat, for whom the art of spinning (dervish spinning, not Rumpelstiltskin spinning) was essential. Whirling like a dervish wasn't exactly my calling, but it seemed that in those circles one had to "spin" to feel a part of the downtown dance community in New York City back then. I liked the idea of being part of a community and Robert Wilson ran a loft space right near where I lived on Spring Street called "Byrd Hoffman School of the Birds." You could go there every Thursday night and spin to your hearts' content. Or roll on the floor, do anything you wanted to do really in the way of movement. It was a free-for-all.

I got a part time job typing for modern dance choreographer Rod Rodgers. The best part of that job, if I woke up early enough, was going to Rod's studio at 7 a.m. to woodshed on his West 12th Street floor. Rod was "pro-tap"—he never had a problem with my ruining his floor with my tap shoes. This was a time when all the floors were starting to "Soho-ize," get refinished and shiny, with a veneer that screamed: "No tapping on me!" Rod would sometimes come in early, too, and he'd hear me practicing. At 9 a.m., I'd transfer my rhythms from the floor to the typewriter.

I was determined to find someone to study with, so every week for six months I would call the other name Stanley gave me besides Henry LeTang's—Charles Honi Coles. He lived in East Elmhurst, Queens, and I still remember his phone number: TW 8-0156, no 718 area code back then. His wife Marion usually answered the phone and inevitably told me Honi Coles wasn't there and to try again later. I was persistent and called every week for months until one day he *was* there and I asked him for lessons, telling him about my studies with Stanley Brown.

He didn't sound too eager, but reluctantly agreed to meet me at Jerry LeRoy's, a rehearsal studio at 8th Ave. and 46th St. I didn't know at the time he'd almost

"Queen Jane, Approximately," me holding court in white dress with then boyfriend Neil Katz, to my left at the top of the heap. Neil owned the used clothing store where we all posed for this vintage shot by photographer Lee Post. Neil provided me with my first Ginger knockoffs, circa 1973. Mexican dresses and headscarves were the rage then. Marlene Clauss on left with the great smile, sitting in front of the baby, now owns The Great Eastern Trading Company, a vintage clothing store in Central Square, Cambridge, Mass.

Honi Coles—he was tall tall tall, thin thin thin, handsome handsome handsome.

"hung up his shoes," and stopped dancing. I didn't even know he was considered "the fastest feet in show business."

Honi Coles was totally amazing to look at and made me forget immediately about the millions of stairs I had to climb to get up to Jerry LeRoy's studios. He was tall tall tall, thin thin thin, handsome handsome handsome, with a mustache and wearing all grey—top to bottom. He was older, distinguished, like someone out of a detective movie—the hero, not the bad guy. Lean. Hungry. Looking for something. Like one of Claire's cats. Maybe looking for some good clean feet, special feet. I looked down at mine in their beat-up patent leather and sighed.

The studio was filthy; the floor was uneven, but the whole place reeked of atmosphere and showbiz as I showed Honi Coles what little I knew. For once I was shy. Honi said a little tentatively, "Well, you've got some feet," and I told him I could round up three other students who wanted to learn tap and we could pay him $3.50 each, the same thing we paid for our other dance classes.

He had a good laugh over that offer and took down the directions to Pat Catterson's Soho loft, where we planned to meet on Monday afternoons. I headed back downtown on my trusty bike. Watching Honi leave Jerry LeRoy's, I noticed him crossing the street with a group of other men heading over to a Blarney Stone's. I didn't realize then that they were all great veteran tap dancers from famous black acts, gearing up to rehearse for their annual Copasetics Ball. ∎

Bicycle built for one. West Village, circa 1983.

The Copasetics Ball

"Everything's Copasetic"—a popular expression of the 1940s,

(coined by Bill Bojangles Robinson), meaning everything is OK.

The Copasetics were a fraternity dedicated to Bojangles' memory.

I t was pouring the night I went to my first Copasetics affair at the Manhattan Ballroom in midtown. A Harry Belafonte look-alike, who told me his name was Frank Goldberg, was at the door selling tickets. When I told him I was "press" coming to cover the event, he gave me a hard time, said they didn't have "press" at their shindigs. I had never met a black Goldberg before and tried to flirt with him a little, asking if we weren't long lost cousins. Finally, I dropped the name Honi Coles and he let me through the doors.

An alien from another planet couldn't have felt more ill at ease than I did when I entered the huge, dark, chandeliered ballroom. There were about twenty-five round tables jam-packed with people whooping it up over a smorgasbord of chicken, fish cakes, booze, and from what I could tell, lots of plates of deviled eggs. I spotted a table of the only white people in the room and gravitated toward them.

Two of the people, tappers Brenda Bufalino, and her student, Dorothy Anderson (now Wasserman), were seated with their friends and we all eyed each other suspiciously after some cursory introductions. We hardly said a word and being the only whites in the crowded noisy room didn't create a friendly atmosphere or bind us together. Still, we were all trying to feel the groove of the rollicking scene that was surrounding us.

In fact, I was so uncomfortable, I got up and began to wander around hoping my alienation would go away sooner or later. It did. I finally met a man at one of the tables who welcomed me into his jovial crowd. He was Albert Gibson and he was with his wife Sondra. They had an extra chair near them and I took it. I explained that I was a budding tap dancer and Mr. Gibson told me he was a not

Bill Bojangles Robinson in a classic publicity shot on the stairs.

so budding one. In fact, he told me he'd grown up in vaudeville and was born right into that proverbial suitcase, on the road from his infancy. His claim to fame was in the now defunct act The Three Chocolateers. He told me he was inventor of a dance craze called "Peckin" and it was in an Ozzie and Harriet Nelson movie.

Sondra, too, was a dancer, once winner of the 1938 Harvest Moon Ball, a contest for ballroom dancers. As we talked, she pointed out Sugar Sullivan, another lindy-hopper, who was on the dance floor swinging to the big band led by a drummer with the single name Tito. Sondra also pointed out the comedian and swing champ Norma Miller, lindy-hopping with Frankie Manning, and all of them had once been regulars at the Savoy Ballroom in its heyday in the 1930s when Chick Webb and Count Basie led the Battles of the Bands.

Come to think of it, Sondra did look familiar to me and I recalled her face from an old film clip I'd seen up at filmmaker/dancer Mura Dehn's apartment in Washington Heights when I had just moved to New York. Mura Dehn was a Russian-Jewish free spirit who had fallen in love with jazz and followed her dreams from Russia to New York, where she gravitated to the Savoy Ballroom and made amazing footage of that famous Harlem night spot. Mura had beautiful white hair pulled back into a ballet bun and was an entrepreneur having taken the Copasetics to Africa on a State Department tour in 1969.

When I had gone up to Mura's, she showed me how to do the Black Bottom and the Big Apple on my visit. She wanted to steer me into her passion, which was the ballroom jazz dancing, and I enjoyed it. But tap was my love, not hers. Still

The Three Chocolateers: Paul Black, Eddie West, and Bert Gibson.

New Paltz: Three Copes on the dance floor, left to right in mirror: Ernest Brownie Brown, Leslie Bubba Gaines, James Buster Brown.

the two dance styles evolved together in Mura's heyday. She served me cottage cheese for lunch and told me how fattening raisins were. She asked me what I thought of Jimmy Carter who was running for President. She was married to a man everyone loved, called, "Captain."

A teeny bit of history: In 1949 a group of five black entertainers banded together and invited friends to join in to commemorate Bill "Bojangles" Robinson, who had just died the year before. Robinson was loved and admired by just about everyone in show business, not only tap dancers. He coined the expression, "Everything's Copasetic" or everything's all right, A-OK.

The word "copasetic" itself, (also spelled copacetic) is derived from the Yiddish "copa Seder," everything is in order, according to William Safire in his weekly column in *The New York Times Magazine*. I know a lot of the black acts worked in the Jewish Catskills during their working days, and Honi Coles knew a lot more Yiddish than I did.

I suspect they'd rather it be their word than the Jews' word, though. I'll give it to them. They made it popular, after all. It's a true 1940s expression, and I love the word, it just rolls off your tongue—copasetic! Like tap, even its expressions go in and out of popularity. I still get some big smiles of recognition in the subway when I wear my "Everything's Copasetic" t-shirt. Definitely a hipster's word.

The club, once thirty-eight strong now has two of its original members remaining, Ernest Brownie Brown in Chicago, of the act Cook and Brown and my ol' Uncle in Harlem, Frank Goldberg of Harry Belafonte look-alike fame. The Copes once held regular Monday night meetings at Frank Goldberg's gorgeous seven-room tastefully decorated apartment in Harlem with original paintings hanging all over

A rehearsal in Brooklyn: Dizzy Gillespie (in front) was an original Copasetic. Joining him, left to right: Bubba Gaines, Buster Brown, Ernest Brownie Brown.

by Chocolateer Eddie West, including one West did of The Copasetics club (which I now own, pictured on page 36).

Frank also had an intricate valuable electric train set that actually ran. His father worked on the trains as a Pullman porter. When they say, "those were the good ol' days," that all seems true when you see pictures of the Copasetics gatherings. We all smile for pictures, but back then those snapshots of old black Harlem are reminiscent of a very different era. Billy Strayhorn, Duke Ellington's alter ego, who rarely got any credit for the Ellington music, was President of the Copasetics. He loved the tap fraternity of dancers and wrote a lot of their material. They were definitely a group known for doing benefits.

The Copasetics meetings were all male, and there was a female counterpart called The Copatites. It's hard to find out anything about them. Talk about a minority of a minority. The male Copes hosted an annual Easter Breakfast, summer boat ride, the autumn Ball, and visits up to Peg Leg Bates' Country Club, the first black-owned and run country club, in Kerhonkson, upstate New York.

The Copasetics were these ideal hosts, watching over their tables, making sure all their friends were taken care of. Friends, in turn, bought $2.00 "boosters" and you could spend as much as a full page ad to get yourself in The Copasetic Booster Book. Even though most of the Copasetics and their audience had moved out of Harlem and now lived in The Bronx, Queens, and Brooklyn, you felt like you had entered the heart of The Harlem Renaissance when you attended any of their affairs.

It was just about midnight and I was still gung-ho learning about all the people at the ball, when there was a hush in the huge, noisy and getting noisier ballroom. Gip told me the show was about to begin!

With a huge flourish, the curtain to the big stage at the far end of the room opened and out walked the tall, suave, elegant very, very long-legged Honi Coles, the man who had just agreed to give me lessons. He wore a red, white, and blue jacket and white pants and talked right to this in-crowd shouting, "Is everybody happy!" à la Ted Lewis. Then, from the far right side of the stage a whole band of men in the same jackets and white pants as Coles' sauntered on the stage walking in a circle as Honi cajoled the audience, "If you can walk, you can dance." The dance indeed was called "The Walk-Around."

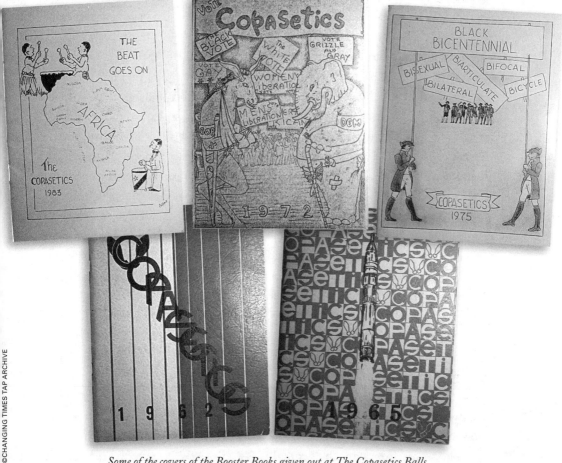

Some of the covers of the Booster Books given out at The Copasetics Balls.

Honi called them off by name, "Cookie," "Brownie", "Louie", "Phace", "Buster," "Emory," "Chink," "Bubba," "LeRoy." They walked slowly around in a circle and every eight musical bars; they'd add another sound so that by the time they faced the audience in a line they sounded like a symphony. Without missing a beat after the applause had died down, Honi joined them on the diagonal as they began to sing, "I'll be down to get you in a taxi, honey, better be ready 'bout half past eight." This began their number "Dark Town Strutters Ball" and they all did strut, right in unison, kicking their legs low à la The Rockettes.

But these guys were no Rockettes. There was a swagger to each of their walks full of personality, individuality, and all very patriotic looking in harmony with the Bicentennial-themed 1976 gala.

I was lapping it up because it was all one glorious surprise to me, to see so many more tap veterans, a different group from the men in the church basement I'd seen a few months earlier. The Copasetics were more sophisticated, less down home in this ballroom. But it could have been just the difference of a church basement and the hoopla of a dressy formal ball. The Copasetics had more routines they'd worked out together where the dancers in the basement came out as complete individuals.

I'd soon find out, though, that The Copasetics all had their individual self-expressions from their former acts. It seemed like they were cast together as a matter of survival. After all, they were all coming up from underground for some fresh air and a chance to get their shoes back on. Later, I also learned the Copasetics were fairly exclusive in who they let in. I mean, it *was* a fraternity. They needed business people and social status people, not only tap dancers to legitimize themselves and take care of business. Dizzy Gillespie was an original Copasetic.

As these gentlemen suavely strolled off the stage, one stayed behind and Gip told me he was Bubba Gaines, formerly of The Aristocrats of Dance and he was going to do his specialty number tapping to the song "Perdido" while jumping rope. Another rope jumping tapper! My first was Raymond Kaalund, back at the church. Bubba Gaines sped up, triple timing his former time as the band played, "Happy Days Are Here Again." Gip told me the names of other songs, ones I didn't recognize. He even hummed and scatted along with the band while the dancers performed.

Then Mr. Gibson let out a huge whoop as Honi Coles announced the next package: Bert Gibson's Gibson Girls. This certainly seemed like a harking back to some other era as the multigenerational ladies glided on the stage in sequined silver helmeted hats and woven silver fringed skirts that shook and swayed over their bright red unitards and silver high-heeled tap shoes. Gip proudly sang the words from our table while his Gibson Girls, seemingly hearing him

"Can You Pull It?" Bert Gibson's Gibson Girls, including Ellyn Long (third from right; Jackie Raven, second from right).

from afar, followed his singing instructions. It was a dance they'd learned from him called, "Can You Pull It," that started out "Not now, I'll tell you when, de dum de dum . . ."

Each Gibson girl got to do a little solo at the end of the refrain, "Can you pull it, YEAH!" looking very sexy. That dance began to give the ballroom a raucous hilarity by 2 a.m. That's when the stage show finally ended, but the whole audience seemed to want more. No one was in any hurry to leave.

Despite my Weight Watcher's diet, I was famished and started eating some of the deviled eggs and chicken as I made the rounds at a lot of the tables, picking up leftovers, and in the course making new acquaintances. People were eager to feed me.

As the night (morning) loosened up, I, too, began to work the room. Everyone was doing it by now, leaving their tables, dancing, eating, drinking. It was a nice kind of anarchy. No longer an alien, I asked one of the Copasetics, Buster Brown, to dance and he knew a lot of jitterbug steps, a lot more than I did with my brother in our basement in Silver Spring, Md. This wasn't Fred Astaire, but it still felt like a partner was not far from reality.

PAINTING BY CHOCOLATEER EDDIE WEST, COURTESY OF CHANGING TIMES TAP ARCHIVE

Some of the original Copasetics in painting (l to r): Sitting: Frank Goldberg, Billy Eckstein (reading), Leroy Myers. Behind the piano in the back: Roy Branker. In front of piano to the right with sheet music: Billy Strayhorn (President of The Copasetics). Next to the piano, profile, talking: Charles Cookie Cook. In back: Lewis Brown; Paul Black in front right of Lewis Brown. (The unfinished Copasetic with white face): "Youngblood," Peg Leg Bates, Chink Collins, Henry Phace Roberts (sitting), Milt Larkin (behind Phace standing), Cholly Atkins (drink in hand), the painter of this picture, Eddie West (drink in hand), Johnny Rocket (sitting on right couch), Francis Goldberg (Frank Goldberg's twin brother,) Emory Evans (right end of couch). In front: Charles Honi Coles (standing, left profile, talking to Pete Nugent, Ernest Brownie Brown in the middle, Pete Nugent (on right with cigarette). This painting hangs in my living room!

"If you can walk, you can dance!": The Copasetics beginning "The Walk-Around," later known as "The Coles Stroll."

By 4 a.m., I'd had a few drinks, too, and even had a dance with the sexy Harry Belafonte look-alike, Frank Goldberg. I went back to Gibson's table and as I was getting ready to leave, he proudly showed me The Copasetics' booster book and pointed out pictures of The Chocolateers, the comedy tap act he formed with Paul Black and Eddie West. They had done knee drops from balconies, he told me, and I figured that was why he was using a cane.

The booster book was full of pictures of the men I'd just seen dance, with their families, or in their old acts. There were also a few quotes like "Thanks for the Buggy Ride," and "Sally Does Your Dog Bite" which were actually tapping time steps done to those words. Uncanny expressions were how these guys often taught the steps. Both expressions were on Charles Cookie Cook's page. Gip told me it cost $2.00 to give a "boost" to one at The Copasetics Ball; that's how they paid for the room. I vowed I'd be a real booster for him at the next year's ball. ■

Tap Daddies . . .

This was the fun part: finding the hoofers, tracking them down (not easy), hanging with them, interviewing them, studying with them, making tap happen again. Getting it down and moving it forward. The following pages are some "vignettes," sketches of some of my mentors and some of the lessons I learned.

CHARLES HONI COLES
The Fastest Feet in Show Business

It was *Jazz Fest*, 1987, in New Orleans. Honi Coles had been hired to dance at the New Orleans Jazz & Heritage Festival. I hadn't seen him in a long time, since his stroke, and he'd aged a lot. Still, he seemed like the old Honi, bringing tap to the masses.

He only had to do two gigs, but the Festival organizers didn't make it easy for him. His first show was on some patch of slate, not even part of the main festival, which happened inside the famous NOLA racetrack. His gig was early evening, too, when people were resting, eating dinner, gearing up for the night music on the famous New Orleans club scene.

Honi decided to sit out most of his set because the musicians were pretty mediocre. He did his "Walk-Around" dance, now called the "Coles Stroll," the Shim Sham (our one chorus of the tap national anthem), and a little improvisational tap across the slate. I, for one, didn't blame him at all for not dancing much. With a crummy floor, and an audience wandering in and out whenever they felt like it, it was hard to get any decent attention for his act. Honi was as contemporary a man as I'd ever known in tap or otherwise, and though 76 at the time, was hardly a relic. He deserved more respect.

The next day, his second gig, felt like some kind of mandatory community outreach. My girlfriend, Cher Bertram, a New Orleans native, drove us to the edge of the black section of the city to see Honi work in one of the high schools. Even

Honi Coles, circa 1983, getting down to the basics. You had to repeat the step 'til you got it down. He always sang "Tea for Two" when he taught me, but Honi was anything but a nostalgic figure.

Cher had a tough time finding the venue. She astutely remarked that although the festival organizers were force-feeding tap-dancing to kids, they were making it physically unavailable to the vast majority of an audience who might have appreciated it more at the renowned New Orleans Jazz and Heritage Festival.

Honi, more than any of the hoofers I knew, was into promulgating our art to the masses. He was a man of the streets, but could also hang with the elite. He was elegant, the kind of man who looked great in a top hat and tails. Still, I could see him doing this gig out of the goodness of his heart, without any cachet attached to it.

It was a pure lesson in stamina and dedication, watching him work that auditorium filled with these rowdy kids. Honi commanded respect, even under the worst possible conditions. Just as he could talk "street" in Harlem, so he could talk the unruly high school students' language. He asked how many in the crowd of five hundred had ever heard of tap, and only about seven raised their hands.

When he asked for volunteers for the "Shim Sham," I jumped up to join my teacher. He showed me a lot of respect in front of everyone, telling the kids I was a great historian, and that I owned a tap archive. (I wondered how they could process "tap archive," when most didn't even know what tap was.) He told them I was, "by the way, a good tapper in her own right."

I felt very exposed—aside from another dance history buff, Cheryl Willis, also from NOLA and my pal, Cher, I was the only white person in that auditorium. Honi then asked Cheryl Willis and me to join him in the "B.S. Chorus." I hardly knew this familiar tap routine and had never performed it, but I faked it by watching Honi do the moves. All the while I kept thinking that these kids would probably never have been exposed to live tap if he hadn't visited them in person.

———

Honi loved to tell the story of how he got his speed. His fellow dancers in the Miller Brothers act had given him a raw deal; so, he left New York and returned to his native town, Philadelphia. He rehearsed for a year in the room that he lived in, removing all the furniture so he had as much space to dance as possible. "The landlady was just like my mother," he told me. "I was more her son than her own two sons, one of whom I went to school with. I rehearsed in that room one solid year, all day every day.

"At the time I didn't drink. Alcohol meant nothing to me. And when I came out of that room, my feet were the fastest feet in show business. I've never claimed to be the best dancer in the business, but I've always claimed that I had the fastest feet in the business at that time."

I once asked him what he thought was his biggest contribution to the art and he replied, "Speed. Pure and simple. That's my only claim to fame." And yet, what he was most renowned for when it came to Honi lore, was his slow-tempo soft shoe with Cholly Atkins. Honi and Cholly were one of the first acts to appear on color television on The Gary Moore show.

— ∞ —

For two years, 1975–76, Honi took the subway to Pat Catterson's loft in Soho from his home in East Elmhurst, Queens, to give four of us lessons. For those couple of hours each Monday afternoon, he mesmerized our little class with his dancing. He'd always "perform" a little for us, which was mind-blowing enough. Then he'd get right into the session, showing us logical rhythms that we repeated over and over while he hummed "Tea for Two." At the time I thought the song so old-fashioned, so clichéd. I don't anymore.

Honi danced with his back to us, his long legs and feet spelling out exactly what he wanted. He reminded me of a Riverboat gambler with his distinguished look.

— ∞ —

I was deeply touched when a couple years before he died, he and his wife, Marion, took a very long and expensive cab ride from their Queens home to my downtown Manhattan apartment to attend a Passover Seder. It was expensive not only for the distance from East Elmhurst to Tribeca, but because there was so much traffic. It seemed everyone was having a Seder in Manhattan to go to that night.

Having frequently played the Borscht Belt, Honi knew a lot about us Jews, especially how to speak Yiddish. He was even cast in the part as the emcee in the poignant movie, Dirty Dancing, which took place at a Catskills resort in the early '60s.

Honi seemed to enjoy my crowded living room full of people and the Seder led by an actual cantor who could sing a lot of the Hebrew. Honi acted fatherly to me that night, perhaps because his daughter, Isabel, and I were the same age, and this was a family gathering. Honi and Marion stayed after all my other guests left and we watched some videos. He had had his second stroke by then and was now using videotapes of his dancing to show at festivals and teaching gigs. When I walked him and Marion to the elevator of my building, he told me he was relieved I had finally found an apartment in Manhattan, "a place where you can ride your bike around the Village." He knew all too well about New York City rents.

Although all my tap daddies were savvy in giving me showbiz tips, Honi was more so, especially when it came to comedy. He himself liked and performed comedy bits in the celebrated act he developed with Cholly Atkins.

Honi told me about "back caps," comeback lines I'd need when responding to hecklers. When I told him about the Jewish Sisterhood luncheon I'd performed at where no one was paying any attention to my act, Honi sagely noted, "Never perform while people are eating. Food comes before everything else, even show business."

PAUL DRAPER
Ballet Tap and Floor Dancing

Fresh off the heels of a workshop with Twyla Tharp in Washington, D.C., I drove with another tap enthusiast, Stephanie Mattfeld, to Pittsburgh at the end of the summer of 1974, to meet Paul Draper. My modern dance teacher, Claire Mallardi, had loved Draper's dancing—it combined ballet with tap and classical music. I'd postponed studying with him because I thought Twyla was going to be more tap-oriented and improvisational. But I was wrong. Every wiggle the woman did was counted and choreographed.

Paul Draper was friendly and told us we could rent a dorm room at Carnegie Mellon University where he was teaching. He looked to be in his late sixties, very lanky, with thinning white hair. When we finally landed in one of the classrooms to talk with him, it was hard to miss his stutter. He was one articulate man, nonetheless, and let us look in on one of his tap classes.

Draper told us he had wanted to be a ballet dancer but didn't start early enough. He figured out a way to realize his love of ballet by creating a ballet/tap barre, adding the tap sound to every plié, tendu, battement—all the ballet vocabulary. You could hear every move you made.

Like a lot of the old school tappers I would study with in my formative years, Draper was primarily self-taught. Unlike most of them, he was a white dancer, upper class, and into a whole other bag stylistically. Paul Draper loved to be up on the toes. He even danced on a pedestal as part of a gimmick. "Ballet was an expansion, a development," he told Stef and me. "If I were going to advance at all, I would have to develop the work into a more expansive theater of operations—a bigger canvas. Ballet seemed the most available way of expanding."

Draper's performances with his partner, the virtuoso harmonica player, Larry Adler, were a hot ticket on the New York nightclub circuit. The swanky Persian Room alone paid Draper $75,000 a year. They started each show as solo acts and then joined forces for their finale, taking audience requests at the end of their show. During the '50s, however, both performers were black-listed during the McCarthy era for their liberal politics. Draper stopped performing in New York and found a teaching job in Carnegie Mellon's renowned theatre department. Larry Adler moved to England.

—⁓—

Always eager to show off what I could do in the shoes, even at the incredibly early stage I was at, I showed Paul Draper all the rhythms I had learned from Stanley Brown and Honi Coles.

Paul Draper popularized a form using ballet and tap rudiments.

He wasn't impressed with what he called my "floor dancing." Honi Coles had told me that floor dancing referred to wings, knee drops, Russian dancing, knee falls, but I never did any of those kinds of things. Draper's definition of floor dancing was "not ever being off one foot and never being up in the air." With floor dancing, the dancer was almost always on both feet by Draper's terms. "Even a time step has to be more active," he told us. "A time step has a hop. There is one dancer, Jimmy Slyde, who stays on the floor, but moves a lot more than the average floor dancer." I told him the hoofers, other "floor dancers," I'd seen in the church basement hit me emotionally, right in the gut.

"What they do is fun," he said. "It's entertainment. It hasn't really got much to do with dancing, but it's undeniably fun. I don't mean to knock it. It isn't going to go any place, it hasn't got a basis. The first exercise we did in class today has more emotional content in it than six hours of the stuff you just showed me." Somehow I knew I wasn't getting a compliment right then.

Draper loved Bill Robinson's dancing: "I've never seen or heard anybody in his league. He could do slaps and make you cry. He didn't do that many steps, but what he did was impeccable. I've never heard anybody make the sounds he made. It was totally unlike anything I'd do, but in its own way it was absolutely superb. It was unique, thoughtful, but it wasn't anything you ever could learn. It was his own style; it was so much of a higher order. It was in that hoofer genre, but it was that genre, developed. He never lifted a leg, but you wouldn't have wanted him to. It was lovely."

I went to study with Paul Draper at the University of Maryland the next summer and quit halfway through the course. To me, combining tap with ballet was forced, artificial. It didn't swing. Well, I didn't swing. I could hear the transitions in jazz with the tap, but I never heard them when I combined tap with the ballet barre. They just stopped and started, suddenly.

Later that summer, I caught up with Draper at Carnegie Hall. He and Larry Adler had reunited in a benefit concert for The Harpsichord Society. As I stood in line with several of his disciples, among them other teachers of mine, Jerry Ames and Bob Audy, I heard a familiar stutter. "You flew the coop!" Draper exclaimed. He was surprised to see me after my sudden disappearance.

———

Paul Draper did offer some good advice about my shoes, which I took: "See if you can get lighter taps on your shoes. If not, go to some friendly shoemaker. You have to get a friendly one and get him to thin those (taps) down. They are a little 'thumpety-thump.' Your shoes should help you. Get him to put rubber next to the tap. Its main function is that you don't feel the tap on your shoes. It's all the same level. Tell the shoe man you'd like the shoe to fit as if you've worn it a year. Learning how it feels is what matters."

SANDMAN SIMS
Each One, Teach One

Albert Gibson had given me Sandman Sims' phone number at The Copasetics Ball and fortunately I kept it.

When Honi Coles began getting work again (the national tour of *Bubbling Brown Sugar*), I was still gung-ho to keep studying the real thing.

I was living on the extreme east end of Bleecker Street at the time, a basement one of my first pupils, Meredith Monk, turned me onto. It was a huge space in what is now called Noho, between the Bowery and Lafayette Streets. In 1976 the block was full of dancers, painters, drummers, printers, book makers, The War Resister's league (which is still there on the corner of Bleecker and

Sandman Sims: In the silky white shirt that billowed when he performed.

"Standing on the corner" (almost) outside my gated basement "castle" on Bleecker Street, 1976.

Lafayette), the original Yippies and zillions of Bowery drunks waiving their way to the soup kitchen on the block. Aaron, the pie thrower, could be seen handling the next pie he was going to throw in some "capitalist pig's" face. Two huge wonderful way pre-gentrification hardware stores stood on the Bowery end of the block. One of them sold antique fly-fishing hooks. I had gates that I locked every night so that no one would disturb me or fall down the stairs into my pad.

My 21 Bleecker Street basement was truly très bohème back then; prior to my living there, it had been an after hours club and I heard someone got shot there. That didn't scare me. It was only $130 a month. It was such a steal that I didn't mind paying the parking tickets Sandman accrued for illegally parking on Bleecker Street each time he came for a session. I could tap whenever my muse struck and no neighbors complained about the noise. A carpenter friend of mine built a sprung plywood floor and laid masonite on top of the wood. That's where my lessons with Sandman began, although they moved in all locations of the loft by the end of our six months of battling it out.

We were both arguers, fighters, Aquarians. He loved yelling at me and I loved yelling back.

His real name was Howard Sims, but everyone called him Sandman. He was brash, provocative, but he didn't offend me in the least. I could handle his cantankerous personality as he broke down steps for me. He worked with me on the paddle & roll, which dance critic Mindy Aloff described in *The New Yorker* as "the name of a step that makes you look as if you were walking through jello in motorized shoes." I once danced for two hours straight while Sandman clapped time. He always got on the floor to dance with me. He taught me a lot about time and how to hold it down when someone was taking a solo.

Sandman once suggested we do an act together where I could be Shirley Temple to his Bill Bojangles Robinson. I was already thirty, a little late for Shirley. Sandman told me I had to learn to build on foundation steps if I was going to improvise, that foundation steps thrived on the rhythm and your feet could then tell the story. I'd heard the audience sometimes call out, "Feet, talk to me," but I didn't know what story I was supposed to tell yet.

"You're dancing like a little black boy," Sandman screamed in delight once. I was really going at it, improvising, tapping fast, too. Sandman always stocked up on California sand, a place he spent a lot of time in, visiting relatives. He claimed California sand had the best sound. Once when he didn't have his sand, he worked on sugar. It didn't have that toothbrush sound to it at all. Sandman, never taught the sand to anyone, least of all me, because he could tell I wanted to do things, go places. I could understand his keeping his specialty dance to himself, but Sandman alienated a lot of his fellow hoofers by telling everyone he invented sand. Oral history.

I used to think Sandman's favorite saying "Each one, teach one," at the end of a session was something coined until I went to his memorial in 2003 at the Apollo Theatre and learned it was the name of a Harlem educational organization. At that memorial—whose highlights included Savion Glover sneaking a pair of tap shoes in the coffin—I learned so much about Sandman that I hadn't known—that he was active in the community, that he staved off race riots in Harlem, that he was a very sports-minded man whom kids looked up to. After learning so much about Sandman at the funeral, I realized how lucky I had been to have had him come down for private sessions at $6 a pop. It was obviously not about the money when it came to his eaching and teaching.

CHOLLY ATKINS
The Man Who Moved Motown

Finding the hoofers in the early stages felt like detective work. Honi told me his old partner, Cholly Atkins, lived in Las Vegas and I jumped at the chance to meet him. In the fall of 1975, I accompanied my father on one of his gambling junkets there. My dad loved the Vegas nightlife of comedians and blackjack, of cheap steaks, and warm swimming pools in the cold weather. My mother often tagged along, knitting and showing off the watches she sold for Hadassah.

I'd read in Marshall and Jean Stearns' book, *Jazz Dance, The Story of American Vernacular Dance,* that all tap dancers had specialties and Cholly's was a "scoot-out" step done with some wings. I didn't know what that even looked like and hoped Cholly would show it to me. Cholly was a perfectionist, however, hadn't tapped in eleven years, and didn't want to show off anything. Strangely enough, though he hung up his tap shoes, he was one of the only old school hoofers to continue making a living in dance during the Drought.

Cholly Atkins, Honi Coles (with Jo Jones on drums) doing the famous scoot step popularized by Bill Bojangles Robinson.

He had to pick up and move from New York to Detroit, but he became part of the Berry Gordy Motown machine. Cholly created what he called "Vocal Choreography" and was able to teach famous singing groups like *The Temptations*, *Gladys Knight and the Pips*, and Aretha Franklin how to get on and offstage, and move in a minimalist unison style, while singing.

"See, tap is very technical," he told me, explaining its disappearance. "It's far more difficult than most people realize. It takes time to develop. With television and shows today, there's very little rehearsal time. We're living in an instant age."

He sensed my keen interest in tap, so he took me to meet his friend Maceo Anderson, of the original Four Step Brothers. Cholly drove me to Maceo's dance studio and I did Honi's version of the Shim Sham. Maceo called me a "hoofer's hoofer." He told me he charged Ann Margaret $1,000 for that dance. Wow, what a bargain I got.

Of his act with Honi, Cholly said they got together after the war and stayed together for eighteen years. "We weren't spring chickens when we first got together, remember. We were thirty-two and thirty-four. We began talking more, inserting more comedy. That type of change is a gradual process. It first has got to be done quietly, changing your act. You have a reputation, an image. If people expect to see you dance and all of a sudden you're singing, those things have to become process. At the same time, you're still dancing. We were trying to cultivate and be respected as more than just hoofers because hoofers were one step up from chorus girls pay-wise and the sense of value . . . it was the same with Bill Robinson. He became a great talker."

Joe Glaser, their agent during the 1940s, told Coles and Atkins they were way ahead of their time. They were a cut above other acts in the way they dressed and handled themselves onstage. In spite of the speed with which both of them could tap, they were known for a very slow soft shoe done in total precision, performed to the song "Taking a Chance on Love."

I felt like a conduit for the old school when I asked Cholly if he wanted to say anything to my then teacher Cookie. Cholly spoke into my tape recorder: "Hey Buck Dancer, you sent me a real hoofer!" I returned to New York and played the tape for Cookie and Honi. They had been out of touch with their Copasetic brother.

JIMMY SLYDE
The Basics and Zen Tap

In the spring of 1982, I had promised myself a real present: sessions with Jimmy Slyde. I made arrangements to drive up to Boston and study with him later in the summer. Jimmy Slyde was the premier product of the Stanley Brown Studio of Rhythm, but that wasn't why I was going.

Slyde was of the bebop school. He was as good as it got in the swing department. Slyde covered a lot of space when he danced. Like many improvisationalists who danced to bebop, Slyde never had a routine. He did have pocket steps galore, steps he'd pull right out of his pocket when he needed to make an impression. He was a smooth operator on the floor and played the melodies of tunes, not just the rhythm.

When I first heard about him, he was known as "Jimmy Slyde of Boston," had lived in Paris, and Los Angeles, but more recently, he had returned to Hanson, Massachusetts, a distant suburb of Boston, to look after his parents, Lillian and Pops.

Slyde didn't want to teach back then in the traditional sense of holding sessions and breaking down steps. He didn't like the idea of anyone saying they'd "studied" with him when they'd been with him only a week or two or he'd given a master class. He was much more like the traditional Indian guru. He felt that if you took on a student, that person would become your protégé, the dancer to whom you'd bequeath your material.

People who knew Slyde then, knew that, apart from tap dancing, golf was his other love. I learned this the hard way. My first lesson with him was scheduled on a perfect golf day. I ended up waiting hours for him to return from the links. Often I'd arrive to see him practicing his putting on the rug.

Slyde wanted to see what I knew, so I went through a lot of my hardest stuff, which consisted mostly of the routines I'd worked on with Cookie Cook. I went through many time steps and dances—anything I could think of to impress him.

The next thing I knew, I was doing shuffles for hours. *Only shuffles.* I'd do that the whole lesson—for three hours. As he listened, he would punctuate my rhythms with an "uh huh" or "uh uh" according to whether I hit it right. Even with my mistakes, he punctuated in time. As we discussed the distinction between a flap, what a "fah-lap," or a "slap" sounded like, he got so impatient that he literally spat these terms out.

I was skeptical. He was not interested in any of my routines, or hard steps. He slowed me down to the basic sounds of brushes, shuffles, slaps, and cramp rolls. Was this why I had driven all the way up to Boston to study with my idol, Jimmy Slyde? I wanted steps and routines.

Steve Condos watches Jimmy Slyde at the Boulder, CO. Great Tap Reunion, 1986.

Our second session took place in the evening. This time, he turned off the studio lights and listened to me in the dark. He kept his eyes closed the entire lesson. Brush, shuffle, slap, riff, went my feet over and over again. Brush, shuffle, slap, riff. I'd speak the steps as I did them. Stanley called steps and sounds by name, and Jimmy Slyde followed suit. The entire three hours were brush, shuf-*fle* with the accent on "fle," slap, riff. I even had to break those four sounds down into miniscule bites. No rhythm at all. Well, no steps, anyway. Lots of repetition. For the first time, I was slowed down to a near halt.

Slyde surprised me. None of my other teachers—Cookie, Bubba, Honi—called out names of steps. It was all about singing or scatting the rhythm. You might stop and ask them what they were doing, and they'd show you. Words like "shuffle" or "flap" or "riff" just never came out of their mouths in any of my lessons. This was old school. This was the "real thing." This was authentic. They also had expressions for their specialty steps like "pulling trenches," "over the top," or "falling off the log"—all steps developed during World War II. It appeared there were vast differences in how people taught tap.

By my third and last session, I had graduated to a cramp roll, four little sounds, jumping up and landing toe-toe-heel-heel, to let the four sounds all blend together. I was a good candidate for Slyde's detail to precision at a time when I was still gathering steps. There was supposed to be a precise and different sound to every shuffle and slap they produced.

It was all very meditative, very Zen, Slyde sitting there in the dark, paying close attention to the sounds, saying practically nothing. It turned out to be a very spiritual experience.

———

Later at his home in Hanson, I brought the Baby Laurence album at a time when people still used turntables regularly. His mother took me out to her garden and showed me the peas she was growing. Pops sat in the living room, quiet and observant. When I was ready to leave, Slyde followed me in his car in the late afternoon to make sure I was driving in the right direction to Martha's Vineyard. After arriving on The Vineyard, I began to practice what he preached. I stayed with a friend at her rental house in Gay Head at the tip of the island, still run and owned by Native Americans. I was bewildered by those three sessions. What had I learned?

When my friend left the house, I practiced those minute sounds, the sounds of the basics—brush, shuffle, slap, riff—trying to hear the difference in every sound. In the starkness and quietude of Gay Head, for the first time, I was hearing single notes, not just rhythm. It gave me new respect for detail, paying attention to my every sound, to notice tonation and nuance.

Leon Collins, "That Dancing Dynamo."

LEON COLLINS
My Dining Room Step

Muhammad Ali is not the only one who made a point of being The Greatest. The old school tap dancers also had an obsession with being the best. Listening to Leon Collins, you might think he was still in the ring.

"When I see a cutting session, I measure myself up with the other dancers to see who I'll take on," he told me during a private session I had with him in Boston, where he lived and taught. "I won't go into my trick of bags (sic) unless they get bad," he grinned as he slid and spun fast along his dining room corridor. "And then I'll take on all of them. Starting with Chuck Green. *Starting* with him!" The tap Challenge might last for weeks and take the contestants all around the country to do battle.

Leon was considered by many of the great masters "on the other side of the coin," meaning he transcended the swing rhythms popular in the '30s and '40s to get to the complex sounds of bebop. He was from Chicago and known as *"That Dancing Dynamo."* Fletcher Henderson carried Leon on a lot of his big band gigs. His unique sound was the most important thing to him. "It's what made Charlie Parker different from other alto players. You'll see a lot of people doing the same steps, but they're not going to be getting the same sound."

I used to love watching Leon fine-tune his taps with his little screwdriver as he talked about jazz and Baby Laurence, the dancer everyone idolized. Some of his students had set up a studio for him, first in South Boston, then in Brookline, Massachusetts, called "Tapper's Paradise." I'd heard he was so bummed by the Great Tap Drought, he not only hung up his shoes, but when his old friend and partner, Buster Brown, came up to visit and jam with him, he wouldn't dance.

The first time I formally set up a session was on a freezing January morning. We met in the South End at a men's social club Leon had booked to rehearse in. The building was tightly locked up. The door was bolted; it was after all, New Year's Day—a holiday. Not to disappoint me, Leon drove me to where he lived in Roxbury and we commenced to dance.

I had a ball listening to his analogies to boxing. "Ali has a lot of fancy footwork," he said, in his dining room. "But Joe Louis was the real stalker. He took his time and had even more style. See tap is fast, reflexes, ankles. It helps you get out of the way."

I got one of my most favorite, most-used steps from Leon that day. It had a military feel with lots of heelwork, ending up in a swinging slide. He made up routines to thirty-two-bar choruses for his students all the time. But I really loved his takes on nursery rhymes and tunes like "Who's Afraid of the Big Bad Wolf?"

The only way I ever remembered that favorite was to tape record it. I would force myself to get the rhythms and exact footwork as soon as I got back to New York. But at some point on the tape, I was laughing too hard and having too much fun watching Leon getting into his "trick of bags" right there on his dining room floor to absorb any more than one great step.

Leon danced in a gig I did at Harvard University in the late '70s, and he stole the show with his superb technique and musicality. Cookie and Bubba were also performing with me on that occasion, and instantly recognized Leon's genius. They stepped aside and paid homage. They also invited Leon to be an honorary Copasetic.

I took him to Vienna, Austria, accompanied by his main squeeze, Joan Hill, who played classical music for him. Leon had to adapt to the classics because they were Joan's forte. He did a great job with "The Flight of the Bumble Bee," one of his signature pieces. Still, he swung the classics hard. In Vienna, he was pronounced the "Bach of Tap," with standing ovations all week, performing in a white suit, white tap shoes, beard and bald head. (He'd finally stopped wearing a toupée, which sometimes slipped when he turned a flip). His scholarly looking face always broke out into a huge happy smile when he'd hit a particularly hard step.

©PHOTO BY L. BARRY HETHERINGTON

Leon Collins—The Bach of Tap.

"David Danced": That's Bunny Briggs in one of his sudden, accented *"halts."* He was Duke Ellington's choice for the Sacred Concerts.

BUNNY BRIGGS
Pretty Music and Fingernails

One day, looking at the newspaper, I noticed an ad for Lionel Hampton and his Orchestra at The Rainbow Room in Rockefeller Center. Underneath in small letters was "featuring Bunny Briggs."

WOW! I thought. I'd heard and read about Bunny Briggs in the Stearns' book *Jazz Dance*, and how he played the original "David" in Duke Ellington's Sacred Concert, "Come Sunday." The song has the lyric, *"He danced before the Lord with all his might."* I even heard a recording of Bunny's dancing in it, but had never seen Bunny live, didn't even know that he still *was* alive. I immediately called my buddies Brenda Bufalino and Dorothy Wasserman (then, Anderson) who I knew would love to see him. They drove in from New Paltz, in upstate New York, to catch his act with me.

It was as magical as we'd all imagined, with Bunny doing his own unique brand of paddling and *continuation*, something he said he invented. In continuation there were no breaks, and the bar-line "continued" past the standard six bars and a break.

When the musicians played a break, Bunny would keep on going. Around the same time, Honi Coles also claimed credit for continuation and it wouldn't surprise me if the two simultaneously had been "inventing" it in separate studios. Some tap dancers wanted to experiment in the new world of bebop in the '40s. The two were among others who decided to extend the melody line into sixteen and thirty-two bars, rather than stay confined to the six bars of the same step and rhythm with the two bar break. Like Honi, Bunny was able to switch into the complexities of bebop, although many great tappers stayed within the music of Ellington, Basie, and others of the big band swing era.

As part of his act at The Rainbow Room, Bunny mimed opening up an umbrella, looking to see if it was raining and then closing it. He also did the Susie-Q, Big Apple, and Charleston, all popular social dances of the time. He had doe eyes that were always open and wide and an impish mouth. He often punctuated his tap "sentences" with a look of surprise, and made exaggerated gulps and breaths, as if he was about to choke on something. Lionel Hampton got a huge kick watching Bunny. Hampton was loyal to tap dancers in general, and got them work whenever he could, even during the Drought. He never minded playing background to them.

The show felt improvisational as chorus after chorus of "The Very Thought of You" filled the air. As gentle as he was, Bunny Briggs had powerful, hard accented sounds and clean feet. He also sang Ellington's "It Don't Mean a Thing" and scatted "*zowwwwwweeeeeeee, weeeeeeeee, zeeeeeee*" into the mike. It was a very different kind of scat than I'd ever heard from jazz singers.

Dorothy, Brenda and I went backstage and told Bunny people were getting interested in tap again. I brought my Stearns book for him to sign, right on his photograph in the book. Brenda congratulated me for staying on the case—finding tap dancers we thought had hung up their shoes and were possibly gone forever. I was proud I'd spotted that ad in the paper. Bunny Briggs was about to go on a cruise ship gig. We could have missed him.

—⁓—

I caught Bunny's act anywhere I could and a few years later found him performing at the Brooklyn Academy of Music. When I went backstage with Steve Watson, another writer, we found Bunny washing his socks out in the sink in his dressing room.

"You know, it's great getting all the applause, but then the curtain's down and it's just time to come back and wash out your socks, before the perspiration gets all through them," he told us. "After performing, I feel so high, so up, that I can't sleep. I just walk around a lot, smoke about ten cigarettes, watch the late, late show. I hum a lot. I don't go off to sleep until about 7 a.m."

Bunny was eager to talk to us. "The dance when I started was the Charleston, so I just elaborated. Which I'm still doing today. No taps then. I didn't put taps on until I saw Bill Robinson. That's when I wanted to be a tap dancer. Before, the Charleston was my famous thing. Putting the hands on the hip and just shake, and then do the Charleston."

The first time I had interviewed Bunny, he told me that his idea of a great performance was having a couple sitting in the audience, relaxed, the man's arm around his date, loose and very cool. He *HATED* it hot. He hated the words "Hot Feet." P.S. Bunny only began "teaching" his moves on a regular basis when he went into a retirement facility in Vegas (where he is now). I studied Bunny very closely from backstage every chance I could get before his retirement.

I was always amazed how much the musicians he was playing with, no matter who they were, loved playing with him, keeping up with him, even though it seemed like he was repeating his act the way many of the acts often repeated themselves, changing little in their routines. He was one of the improvisationalists for sure. He was always in the now, even with all his "Bunny" moves, and never to be taken for granted. He had a good laugh at me when, as producer for him for my first time, I asked him to do ten minutes. He did half an hour. Cookie held me back from bringing out the hook during our first show together, *Old New Borrowed and Bluesy*, because he was going overtime. He was going over! That's what was important. I was glad to learn showbiz "etiquette" from backstage, from the pros.

"I saw tap dancers before, but they were doing something in the norm," Bunny explained during a lull in his laundering. "They'd dance fast and do a split or a flip, but I never saw a dancer come out calm and just dance pretty. I never saw that before. The others were always dancing fast, you know, c'mon get hot. Bill Robinson just came out there and *shoo bup de bup be doo bup do bup be dop*, that kind of thing. It was just pretty. He didn't exert himself. He didn't do no splits or flip over or drop on his knees. He had a pretty suit on, and when he walked off, he was still neat and clean. That's what attracted me to him. No perspiration."

I knew Bunny was Duke Ellington's favorite tap dancer, but I didn't know about the TV variety show host Ed Sullivan, as one of his greatest admirers.

"I was his favorite dancer," Bunny explained. "He'd have me on his show just about every other week. But one thing used to drive me crazy. He'd stand on the side of the stage, you see; he always wanted to watch, and then he'd clap his hands and say, 'Come on, Bunny, get hot.' After about two years, I worked up the confidence to say, 'Please, Mr. Sullivan. I'd appreciate it if you didn't tell me to 'get hot' during my act.' Well, he apologized up and down. And never hired me again. I was replaced by 'Little Buck,' now a landlord in Brooklyn."

There seemed to be only one thing Bunny Briggs regretted in our short conversation with him. He would never forget when Bill Robinson came knocking at his door asking Bunny's mother permission to let Bunny come on the road and work with him. "I was really young and my mother wouldn't let me go. I wouldn't be having such a hard time now, if she had let me go. The only way I can get work now is for a superstar to put me in his show."

Bunny told us how he had made money by hanging out in front of the Cotton Club when he was very small. "I would also open the door for people coming in. Well, I'm a little devious at times. I thought to myself, what about those cars in the back? They be lined up, one two, three, four five, six, on down the line. So, I decided to make some money opening up the second and third doors. I would open up the door and say 'Welcome to the Cotton Club.' And they'd laugh and give me a dollar. When the doorman saw that, he would run me down to 5th Ave. He could never catch me, though. That's how my name was 'Bunny.' My grandmother called me 'The Rabbit.' BAM! I'm gone. Bernard was my christening name. It was 'Rabbit' at first and that evolved to 'Bunny.'"

When I was putting together the 1980 *By Word of Foot* festival, I decided Bunny had to be part of it. It turned out he was just about to leave on a cruise ship gig.

©CHANGING TIMES TAP ARCHIVE

Bunny Briggs, and groomed nails.

He literally signed the contract to teach at the festival minutes before the ship left the port.

He looked so hip the day he showed all the Festival participants what continuation in tap was all about. He wore mustard colored slacks, a black and white checkered jacket, and sunglasses. Gregory Hines, then just breaking into the movies as an actor/dancer, took his class. Bunny had been one of Gregory's main influences growing up.

Bunny demonstrated his act to the students, his burning cigarette in hand. The students were seated on the Village Gate floor in a semi-circle, glued to Bunny's every word, as he told them how important it was to be put together well. "That's including your fingernails," he said. "Nails are very important, you've got to have nice fingernails," he said. Everyone looked at Bunny's fingernails after that remark. At the end of his last class, Bunny invited Gregory to join him in a spontaneous improvisation, and, as pianist Jim Roberts played a melancholy "Green Dolphin Street," the first thing Gregory did was hold his hands out to Bunny, presumably so his old teacher could check out his fingernails.

———

Years later, in 2004, I had read an amazing interview with Bunny by Alana Radecki in my *On Tap* newsletter. Bunny sounded so animated, I had to go visit him myself. When I arrived in the hot dry air of Las Vegas, in a rehab home, Bunny was lying in his bed in bathrobe and slippers, reading the Bible. Though eighty-three at the time, his memory was as clear as if it was yesterday when he talked about his years in tap.

"I like pretty music," he said. "When I come on, I want you to sit back and relax and say, 'Oh, I bet I could do that.' I want it to look easy. I'm a romantic dancer." I brought him clear fingernail polish and did his nails during my short visit.

He also talked about his competition: Baby Laurence and Teddy Hale.

"Baby Laurence and Teddy Hale and I were what you call 'friendly enemies,'" Bunny said. "Baby, when he danced, forget it. And Teddy Hale, too. I was up there with them, and there was no other people when you mentioned tap dancing. We loved each other—we were brought up together as children—but everyone pitted us against each other. We never got together, which I'm sorry now. . . . Back then I didn't want no part of them, because they were great dancers and they'd take away from me. I was a star, too, and if I got with them I was afraid they'd show me up."

He even talked about his favorite female tap mastress, admitting to loving Ann Miller. "Ann could tap you to death! I'm sorry. When dancers get together, they have their likes and dislikes. Ann Miller could whip Eleanor Powell. She did a step and she was coming up to the screen and she looked right dead at the screen and it looked like she was looking right at me. And gave that seduction look and hitting them taps together. It was just amazing how she did that."

Bunny got up after I did his nails and began moving around a little, his IV tied to him. He showed me what a flam was, something Gregory had loved to see Bunny do, and Bunny could still get the hard double sound out there, even in bedroom slippers.

I told him I was calling my book, "Shoot Me While I'm Happy."

"That title has no class to it, no class, whatsoever. Shoot each other to death," he groaned.

"You're taking it too literally," I said, surprised by his strong reaction.

"I am," he said.

"Well, don't," I replied.

"You've got to," Bunny shot back. "People right away think 'shoot shoot shoot.' Take my advice," he said, "because I'm older than you are and I know what goes and *that's* out. It's old timey, and it's nothing." I asked him where the expression came from and he conceded, "It came from tap dancers so you're on the right road."

I liked the title but didn't push it. I thought it captured some essence for me.

He also didn't care for *Rhythm & Schmooze*, when I did part of my act for him.

"Stop talking!" he shouted, not realizing that talking while I was tapping *was* my act. I guessed he didn't know the word "schmooze." But the next day, he told me to add rap and hip-hop music to my schmoozing and tapping, to make it more contemporary, with the times. I was touched.

From my first meeting with Bunny Briggs until my visit to Las Vegas, I always knew how much religion meant to him. Reading the Bible wasn't something he just did to pass the time. He always talked about God.

Queens, N.Y., 1979: Tap Daddies in action. Marion Coles is the only "Mommy" here. I'm on right.

STEVE CONDOS
Transcendental Tap

The news that Steve Condos had died right after a performance in France with his tap shoes still on was très dramatique! I heard he said, "I feel great," took his bows, walked downstairs to his dressing room, had a massive heart attack and died. No one could put Humpty together again! (Although Steve was too cool to be considered Humpty Dumpty.) Another tap dancer on the bill, Sarah Petronio, I heard, tried to give him mouth to mouth resuscitation. What a way to go!

An early shot of Steve Condos; in his last years his feet rarely left the floor.

I could just see him practicing to "a whole side of a record album" as he used to tell his students. He practiced a lot, rarely stopping on his little floor in Hollywood, Florida, unless his devoted wife, Lorraine, interrupted him for something. Steve was never waiting for any second act to happen.

The way Steve Condos died was significant to me, because he always seemed to be in some transcendental plane, even on earth, a state he exhibited all the time when he danced. He didn't have to click his heels three times to get over the rainbow. He could do a lot more with his heels than click them. Even with his thick boxer's body, he was going to lift off the ground into a kind of trance/dance. I wasn't the only one who felt Steve was more at home in the heavens than here on earth. In the movie *About Tap*, director George T. Nirenberg has a blue starry background behind Steve as he dances and talks about what tap means to him. Steve was so focused, looking down, staying in one spot—that's right—one spot, and built his dancing up gradually like a Phillip Glass composition. Steve's face had a look of total serenity and peace of mind when he danced.

It's interesting, and a bit ironic to watch some of the wonderful young black lions like Savion Glover, Marshall Davis, Jr., Derek Grant, and Jason Samuels Smith start with Steve's rudiments as warm-ups in their own classes. Steve—a white, Greek-American dancer—had developed pedagogy for the rhythm tap dancing. His patterns were contagious and he'd always tell you where you could go with them to get even more sound out of your feet. These dancers studied Steve's rudiments, which were enough to get them started in the development of their own warm-up steps.

The reason was that Steve considered himself a drummer, a musical purist, who never had to leave the spot he was on. His concerns were strictly about sound and tonation.

My first tap experience with Steve was listening to an interview he gave the late Trina Marx, a young hoofer. He sounded so positive and enthusiastic that I invited him to teach at one of my By Word of Foot festivals in 1982. I had only read a little about him in the Stearns book, but it was his positivity that made me want to hire him.

Steve started out in showbiz at Philadelphia's Standard Theatre, a traditionally black vaudeville house. His father ran a grocery store nearby and the black dancers who appeared on that stage influenced him and his two brothers.

More than any of the old hoofers, Steve could relate to drummers the best, and in fact, he worked a lot with Buddy Rich and other drummers in the big bands. Of big bands, he sometimes had complaints even though he considered himself a musician of sorts. "I couldn't say they're playing too loud because all these guys were my friends. They went out to groove me so much they forgot that I'm a tap dancer and that people have to *hear* me.

"Instead of playing soft, they're swinging like mad and here I am trying to tap and my legs were so tired. I didn't want to hurt their feelings but in the meantime they're knocking me out. I said 'the hell with tap dancing,' and I reverted to what I used to call 'hot dancing' when I was a kid in the streets, which is now modern jazz.

"After the concert was over, drummer Davy Tuff got the whole band together and he says 'I'm ashamed of you guys. Here's your friend, here's *our* friend, Steve Condos, his first time out as a *single* and you guys are out there blowing your brains out.' All the musicians' faces dropped. 'This guy does things with his feet people want to hear. They don't want your loudness.'"

"I said, 'that's alright, it's alright.' So each one came up to me and said, 'Hey Steve, rough time.' The next concert, the next night, boy, you could hear a pin drop."

—⁓—

Although I never had any "privates" with Steve, I'd take his classes at some of the early tap festivals I got to. I loved his warm-up, but I also liked the videotape that was made of him, because I'm a slow learner and I could hear every sound and not worry like I did in person about not getting the material. There was something nice and gradual about it, but the best thing was Steve's untiring enthusiasm.

He's also the only hoofer who ever sent me money when I was fundraising for the first rendition of *Sole Sisters*. I was very surprised. I'd always paid the guys, never gotten any money from them. Steve seemed to "get it," get something about producing tap in the '80s. He got the essence that the teacher/student relationship and the future of tap could be perceived as a two-way street.

EDDIE BROWN
Patience and Humility

"No, honey, watch it again. Drop that heel! Do it again. There you are! Can you dig it! Eddie Brown then goes over to his sister-in-law's piano in a seedy part of Oakland, California, and plays, "On a Clear Day."

Eddie Brown meets me at the BART train in San Francisco. It's 1979 and I heard about him through Camden Richman, a drop-dead gorgeous woman tapper of my generation who lives in Oakland, and "discovered" Eddie for the rest of us.

Our first session lasts all afternoon and into the evening with Eddie Brown being extremely patient and forgiving as he tinkers away at the piano while I try to remember his steps. I love what he does with his heels. He drops them

Eddie Brown: "Can you dig it?" He called his style "Scientific Rhythm."

in the strangest places, in the middle of a step, places I'd never ever think to drop them.

"BREAK!" he shouts as I putter around on the floor. "When I say 'heel,' Janie, *that's what I want!*"

"I have to do it slow," I say to Eddie.

He replies, "That's OK. That's the way we're gonna do it." I'm dropping my heels everywhere except where they belong. He drops a heel here and there, like someone adding that crucial ingredient to round out the recipe. You insert the heels. I rarely see that kind of craftsmanship anymore, that stitching together. I really have to bend down a lot to see what Eddie's heels are doing. He is the master tailor.

I sure like that Eddie Brown. He is thin as can be, light and gangly, as plain as his name. He drinks a lot, but is never ever a mean drunk. Just sad, sometimes, if you catch him sitting down by himself. He doesn't ever reminisce to me about how great the golden age of tap was or anything like that. He was pretty into the now.

<center>~~~</center>

Just to get a break, two bars of rhythm, was a two-hour ordeal for me.

"I stopped dancing that hard rhythm, Janie," he tells me. His "hard" rhythm refers to jumping up in the air a lot and doing numerous tricks. "My tongue was hanging out of my mouth and my heart was about to drop out, you understand, Janie? I used to do that old shit, but there had to be a better way. There's got to be a better way, I said to myself. Now double it up on the left side. I dream about this step but it doesn't make any sense. Nothing hard. It's just unbalanced."

Wow, to dream about steps. That was beautiful to me. I was glad he wasn't doing a lot of jumping anymore—my knee arthritis was just starting to kick in.

"Ah, Janie, it ain't nothing," he says when he delivers his nerve taps, where the ball of the foot is tapping a mile a second on the wood like a little fluttering hummingbird.

I make a song request, "Once In Awhile," which he hammers out as best he can. He gets the melody and, thankfully, it's slow. I like the old soft shoe.

"See, all the dancers are different. Everybody does his own thing. I try to do your thing. I steal that, and that's good. If you go somewhere and work and you do a step like someone else's today, they have you blackballed. They do! There's not enough work for anyone to get blackballed. You can't do nobody else's steps. That's a drag. That's an honor, too. It's one thing to pay someone for his step and another to rip him off."

I ask him how he feels about getting ripped off or having steps "stolen."

"If *you* can do it, it's not mine. It's not Eddie's anymore, honey. I've had my day. I've been doing this jive dancing for fifty years.

"*Look*," he says after a big pause, "I'll show anybody anything I do. You see that I never dance a routine. That's the reason I can't remember anything. I make it up out there. It just comes to me. When I walk offstage, I don't remember what I did back there."

At a West Coast evening of tap, I caught a rare cutting session between Eddie and Leon Collins. It was the first time I saw Eddie in a competitive framework. It happened over two evenings. Leon Collins, also quite a "heel man," blew into town and Eddie wasn't prepared for this dancer. Didn't know him. Leon *whipped* Eddie. *Clobbered* him. Followed him, too. Eddie was out in the first round. It was the end of the first night's show when that happened. Eddie didn't look happy in the final Shim Sham with the whole cast. He was just off his mark.

It was the first time I was exposed to a *serious* cutting session in tap. The others often look staged like professional wrestling. You could see it in their eyes. Leon had that Challenge mentality anyway. I didn't know if Eddie had one.

Still, he could take on the Challenge if he thought something was being taken away from him and *something was*. The next night he was sober as could be, and this time, it was all-out war. It wasn't one of those, "you take eight and I'll take eight bars." Each did his own solo, but it was clearly a competition as to who was topping the other. There was no loose camaraderie here at all. Nothing easygoing, Eddie Brown was in no mood to be challenged on *his* coast. This was his turf and he meant to hold onto it.

Although Leon was in top form and could blow any of the dancers off the floor, especially in an onstage battle, Eddie had figured out how to even up the score. He was the total gentleman in the classroom, but like Leon, he knew how to take out his bag of tricks when it got bad. He took them out and won.

TONY WHITE
The Lone Hoofer

Tony White never belonged to any of the teams, factions, clubs. He was a loner. He often did one man shows at Cami Hall, a venue right across the street from Carnegie Hall, where he tapped, recited his own poetry, and played guitar.

He was also a loving teacher. My favorite time step is still the one he taught me which I use now with my Eddie Brown break. He also taught me how to paddle & roll by repeating the words "Mom and Daddy, Mom and Daddy," as he took me by the hand and we paddled and rolled up and down the wooden floor together. Sandman gave me combinations, but Tony White, who was also of the black hoofer genre, broke it down. Even my little Indian students in Ahmedebad loved to say "Mom and Daddy" as they worked on their rudiments.

"Mom" (dig your heel) "and" (brush), "Da" (ball of the foot) "Dy" (land on whole foot) and then you go to the other foot and say the same thing. It can be done with a lot of different accents. It just depends on what part of the foot you want to hit harder. The "paddle" refers to two shuffles (brush forward, brush back), and you combine that with the roll into infinite combinations. It's one of my favorite things to do on the floor.

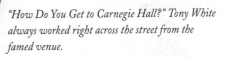

"How Do You Get to Carnegie Hall?" Tony White always worked right across the street from the famed venue.

CARNELL LYONS
King of the Paddle & Roll

Carnell Lyons was one of the original "Businessmen of Rhythm" out of Kansas City, the act that twirled trays as they tapped. The Businessmen traveled the black nightclub circuit in the '30s and '40s. In 1940, Carnell came to New York, bringing his own version of the new style of tap, the "paddle & roll,"—that invisible rocking heel to toe that makes the dancer look like he's ice skating or gliding across the stage.

After World War II, Carnell never returned from Europe like his buddies. He became an expat, doing his acrobatic flash act during the tap drought. He and his partners were soon playing to standing room only crowds. He set up shop in West Berlin and fell in love with a tall blond contortionist whom he helped escape over the wall.

He seemed as happy to greet me at the airport in Berlin, in the spring of 1984, as I was to meet him. I'd just spent a month alone trying to set up gigs in Paris. Carnell had read some of my articles and had organized a gig for me teaching his students.

He also arranged lodging for me with his friend Andy with whom I ended up sharing a bed. I was pretty game back then in my thirties. I had a sore throat after traveling a month in Paris, trying to get an agent for my company. Carnell called his beautiful wife "Mama" and asked her to get me some warm water to gargle with as he lowered the volume on the television. We watched some tap footage—I was surprised to see a few of my own bootlegged shows among his tapes—and talked shop. He was eager to find out about all his buddies back home.

Carnell knew there was a big revival going on back in the States and he himself was teaching his famous brand of paddling all over Germany. He talked about an old act he remembered called "Motorcycle and his Side Car" (Carnell pronounced cycle, "sickle") who were great eccentric dancers. He talked about all the agents, with names like Pransky and Beckman and Charlie Rapp and inquired if they were still around. They had booked his act into the Catskills, other venues.

"That scene is over," I told him not wanting to spell out the "not-for-profit" world of apostate modern dancers and an assortment of other backgrounds who, like myself, had formed companies to preserve, promote, perform the art. I felt like I had so much to share with Carnell, about the future. So, I showed him a couple of my steps on Andy's living room wooden floor.

Carnell Lyons—he got us gigs and "crash pads" in Europe.

"You're doing some old steps I haven't seen in a long time," he laughed in recognition.

—∿∿—

I asked him why he never came back to the States like his buddies.

"Nothing was happening in the States," he said. "Stump and Stumpy, me and the Businessmen, we was all in Frankfurt working for military bases, officers' clubs." Carnell and his act also did a film with John Bubbles in Europe, with *real* mountains in the background in 1956. "That scene took six weeks, we was on set for three months because the weather was so bad." I got to see a version of the film at Andy's and I loved teaching Carnell's students the next day. They were more tuned in to tap's history than even a lot of the dancers back in the States. But they were afraid to improvise back in 1984.

Carnell eventually became *the* renowned hoofer abroad. Today tap is global and there are many Europeans and Americans tapping in Europe. That is largely due to Carnell's early influence. His tap classes were extremely intimate as if with each step you were learning to walk for the first time. Like some of the others, he always took you by the hand. I loved that.

The seventy-fifth birthday homage to Carnell set up by one of his protégées, Jackie Shue, at Sweetwater's, a nightclub on 10th Ave., was one of the happiest hoofer occasions I've ever attended.

I can still see Carnell holding court in his tux and derby as dancer after dancer spontaneously took the stage and tapped, recalling the generosity of the man who became our European contact, who got us gigs and a place to crash. Despite too many hip transplants, Carnell got up himself, bent over his six-foot frame, and tapped with his two protégés, Tap and Tray, Kurt Albert and Klaus Bleis.

Carnell Lyons had a bittersweet relationship to America, but at the end, many finally came to know who the "King of the Paddle & Roll" really was.

LESLIE BUBBA GAINES
Jump Ropes and Old Jokes

"If you keep encouraging me like that, I'll completely destroy myself," Leslie Bubba Gaines would tell his audiences every time he goes out there to do his jump rope/tap act. I watched Bubba from backstage do his jump rope act a million times and I never got sick of it. Just the jokes which I never "got." He knew it, too. We laughed about that, my not getting his jokes, but I never found them funny. He wanted me to laugh and I just couldn't. I liked that Bubba told jokes though, to catch his breath between dance numbers.

He was easygoing, after a few drinks. He was always willing to talk about his USO tours with Alberta Hunter and how he danced for Hitler, though I have no idea how that was possible. He kept to himself, but if you asked him questions, which I often did, he liked to talk. He was a regular trouper in my Changing Times Tap tours for a few years.

What impressed me most about him was that he practiced consistently, even when he wasn't working. Maybe it was part of his boxing ethic, because pre-tap, Bubba was a boxer. He was good friends with Jerry LeRoy, who ran the studio at 46th and 8th Ave., and Bubba was always in one of the big rooms practicing. In his late sixties, he was still going strong and it was great to watch him woodshedding like that. Tap was his practice, not only something he did when he had a gig.

"PIE" —— "HUTCH" —— "BUBBLE"
THE ARISTROCRATS OF DANCING~

Bubba said he had to have the ropes because people couldn't appreciate just rhythm. He learned the ropes in the South, and worked the tent and circus circuit with his partners, Bloody Hutch and Pie. They formed "The Three Dukes, The Aristocrats of Dancing." (On the previous page, "Bubba" is called "Bubble.")

━━◦◦◦◦━━

I always called my grandmothers "Bubba," so I didn't know it was also a Southern name, like Bill Clinton was also called Bubba, right? Anyway, Bubba went to the Hoofer's club a lot, a room owned by a man named Lonnie Hicks who just adored tap dancers and put a piano in the room and kept the whole club open 24/7. Tap dancers came into that back room and laid down their "irons" (taps) and beat the boards. Anyone who wanted to, could dance there, and sometimes the big stars like Bill Bojangles Robinson and John W. Bubbles would show up, too.

"If we didn't have a piano player, we'd just hum to ourselves. Musicians came in sometimes. We just went in if we felt like it. We used to pick nights when there wasn't nobody there, or go at three or four o'clock in the afternoon. When you wanted to work out, it was open twenty-four hours, that club. Gambling happened all night, too, and people shot pool all day. During the Depression, a lot of guys slept in the room. Redd Foxx did. Those were the days of ambition, getting off the streets, going somewhere."

I loved Bubba's delicate, stylistically pure and clean feet, as he did his triple time step with flying wings. I also was thrilled, and I don't use that word often, when audiences responded to Bubba's up-tempo jumping rope routine. He'd start slow to the tune "Perdido," in a nice easy tempo. And then he'd go into double time. There was a secret to how to jump rope and tap at the same time. The only other hoofer I'd seen do it was Raymond Kaalund in the church basement.

━━◦◦◦◦━━

Bubba never missed skipping the ropes when I featured him in my little revues, and my favorite part of his act was when he threw his rope off to the side after his last

"Off to the races, down the runway . . ." Bubba always shouted that right before he went into double-time with his ropes.

Leslie Bubba Gaines, Charles Cookie Cook, and me practicing "The Suitcase Dance," from Bubba's old act. Bubba always said, "It's so easy when you know how."

jump, and ran to the front of the stage to shake hands with the front row; he was all sweaty and smiling. That was just great to see, how everyone wanted to touch the old jump rope tapper. He could really milk his age, too.

My most special learning experience from him was when he decided to give Cookie and me one of the Three Dukes routines. We learned the great hoppy fun syncopated synchronized rhythms in what I called "The Suitcase Dance" on little 2' by 2' "suitcases" my manager David Taylor built. In the original act, the Three Dukes would saunter offstage with their regular top hats and walk right back on with top hats made of wood. They tapped on their wooden tops.

My one regret about Bubba is that I never laughed at any of his jokes. I tried faking it for awhile, but he was onto me; he knew I didn't get them. He had a great delivery, though. Here are the lyrics to the song we did the suitcase dance to:

> *Give me a neck of some old bottle*
> *Give me the arm from some old chair*
> *Give me a leg from some old table*
> *And from a horse, I'll take some hair*
> *And then I'll put them all together*
> *With the aid of string and glue*
> *And I'll get more love from that silly old dummy*
> *Than I ever got from you.*

ALBERT GIP GIBSON
"Peckin'" and Syncopation Galore

Like a rooster with his head chopped off, Gip's neck jerks back and forth as he sings, "Well, you talk about the Truckin' when the Peckin' is new, Boy! That's the dance that you should do. You get way low to the floor and then you pecka-pecka-pecka-pecka-pecka some more!"

Inventor of the social dance "Peckin," Gip is so syncopated when he sings and dances, you're always thrown off guard by his unusual timing. A former member of The Three Chocolateers, he told me "If young people don't carry it on, there won't be anything but walking left. It takes sense to do dancing."

One might argue Gip's own *sense*-ability. Part of his act was jumping from a balcony into knee drops. Towards the end of his life, he used a cane because of his gangrene. He had to have one leg amputated and was then confined to a wheelchair. His wife Sondra said, "His doctor couldn't believe it when Gip told him knee drops were part of what he did for a living."

©CHANGING TIMES TAP ARCHIVE

Albert Gip Gibson with Jackie Raven standing behind him—even in a wheelchair his humor and imagination prevailed.

Gip was born in that proverbial suitcase on the road and came from a showbiz family; he knew the ropes from day one. He'd also take on Challenges and would travel the distance to take on any hoofer. He even took on the champ, John Bubbles, and I heard he won!

Sondra was also a dancer, a former Harvest Moon Champion. She earned her reputation as one of the great Whitey's Lindy Hoppers, and was tossed in every conceivable direction by her partners at the Savoy Ballroom, *Home of the Happy Feet*. When she and Gip worked together at the end of their lives, they wore matching outfits (like my parents) and were known as The Mad Gibsons. The late Jackie Raven, and Neil Applebaum, of the company, *New York City Tapworks*, had a lot to do with reviving Gip's career by featuring him in one of their shows, called *Subway Series*.

Gip was in charge of the Copasetics Ball shows in that event's final years. He conducted and choreographed from his wheelchair. His head was always bopping around. Even though he no longer had use of his legs, to me, Gip was still *dancing* with his voice, never landing on the one, always off the beat.

He taught me a version of "Me and My Shadow" in his tiny apartment in the Bronx. I still have it on tape. This was the dance Ted Lewis made famous with Teddy Hale, the tap dancer, as Lewis' shadow. Gip sat in his chair in the poorly lit room, singing "yak a dac a de da-boop a dah dah dah," as I tried to imitate his voice with my voice and then my feet. I always liked to sing the "arrangement" before I tried it.

It was the "cross-over" step where your feet literally crossed over one another. We were going to perform it one day. His imagination, however, totally outran the reality of the times.

I consider Gip very responsible for my own success, because when he joined my show one drunken evening when Cookie and I were up at his apartment in 1977, Gip added the true *showmanship* factor that made it go from lecture-demonstration into a night of wonderful entertainment and fun.

PEG LEG BATES
80 at the Roosevelt Baths, 87 in NYC, 90 at The Nevele

I was looking forward to seeing Peg Leg Bates on his eighty-seventh birthday at the Fashion Institute of Technology on West 27th St. I'd last spent time with him on his eightieth birthday. I was at Yaddo, the artist colony, and caught sight of his van with his logo saying "Peg Leg Bates Country Club" parked in front of the Roosevelt Baths in Saratoga Springs.

Sure enough, he was under two steamy white towels and his head was wrapped in one. A staff member at the baths told me Peg Leg came to get his steam, sauna, massage, and healthy spring water soak every week and he'd be happy and surprised to see me on his birthday. And he was. They brought in some cupcakes and we sang "Happy Birthday." He told me he'd never seen anything like my talking and tapping act and that made me feel great!

This birthday, number eighty-seven, at Fashion Institute of Technology (FIT) was going to be great because FIT had one of the best wooden floors to tap dance on. An hour before the celebration, I got a call, one of those sudden emergencies. Tap dancer Harold Nicholas didn't feel well, and I was asked to sub for him on the panel and talk about Peg Leg's art. I was honored, of course; I didn't even have to change my clothes. I was ready.

Highlights of the event: Seeing Peg Leg live. The audience watched clips of his appearances on The Ed Sullivan Show. Chuck Green looked frail, but could still really go! He didn't jump anymore during "Take the A Train," but his rhythms still rippled throughout his entire frame. He was completely bald and looked oddly fashionable, with the times. I'll never forget Traci Mann's singing a new version of "Peg O' My Heart" and soft shoeing it in high heels and flaming red dress, leading a chorus line of young women tappers.

My favorite celebration of Peg was his ninetieth birthday at the Hotel Nevele. Spelled backward, The Nevele is "eleven" after the eleven brothers rumored to have run this Catskills landmark. Buster Brown told me about the event and said I should be there, but didn't offer a ride. I had to scramble for one and finally landed up with Carl Schlesinger, a seventy-ish-year-old man in charge of The New York Committee to Celebrate National Tap Dance Day. I'd known him on the scene for years and he tapped a bit himself. We once went to see Jackie Mason together. Carl's a connoisseur of Borscht Belt humor.

Peg Leg Bates was the most frequent hoofer on The Ed Sullivan Show.

———

Also at the celebration was Fay Ray, one of the dance grandes dames of jazz, who later joined The Silver Belles and is a highlight of the featured documentary, *Been Rich All My Life*. She and I were both dressed completely inappropriately for the event—she in some green sweat pants with white lines up the sides and jacket, a sports outfit you'd wear to the gym, and me in a green and white flowery dress that showed too much cleavage in spite of my having two pins strapped across the front to "hold me in." It was a summer dress, and though it was warm outside, it was still the wrong thing to wear in autumn. The event turned out to be more of a black tie, sequined affair. Although it started in the daytime, it ended well past the midnight hour.

In fact, it felt like some big Jewish celebration up there, some bar or bat mitzvah or Jewish wedding, but it wasn't at all. It was a gorgeous Sunday, and of course, the autumn leaves were a great incentive for getting on the New York Thruway on Columbus Day Weekend. We actually had little traffic, and the leaves were indeed wonderful.

Living in NYC surrounded by concrete buildings, I'm happy to see any trees, anywhere.

———

It was kind of goofy that I was in that summery Florida dress, but the weather was goofy, too, so hot in the sun. You didn't know what you were supposed to be wearing. I saw soon, in the company of three other tapsters on the ride, that all were in gloomy New York black and variations of it. I had on my bird hat, a wonderful (to me) nest of a chapeaux with seemingly alive quails attached all around it, and my curls peaking through the nesting center, which Buster told me to take off as soon as I arrived. He almost caused me to lose my appetite.

It came right back once I saw the spread up there. The "early" food was sliced turkey—thick slices, mind you, ham, knishes (potatoes, just the way my mother used to make, small, hand designed), fresh diced vegetables that sat lonely with their Russian dressing nearby, cheeses, pigs in the blanket (kosher of course), stuffed mushrooms, Greek spinach pies. Needless to say, I was stuffed, truly stuffed, by the time dinner was even served. There was also some big, big ice sculpture carved in the shape of a peg leg!

At dinner we got to watch a slide show of all of Peg Leg's old pictures, and it was lucky I was sitting with the Copes and Fay Ray because even Ms. Black Culture here didn't know most of the performers by face or name. It was hard to concentrate on the food, which consisted of a choice of salmon (rich and heavy), stuffed chicken, or prime ribs. I chose the chicken and that came with a nice salad, and spinach cut in this big square.

I couldn't eat the meal, except the salad, but of course I could eat the dessert:

cake, not very good, but I always have room for my sweet tooth. Meanwhile there were pronouncements by the Mayor of Kerhonkson, where Peg set up the first black-owned country club. I saw one big, handsome black man at the next table with the end of a rib in his mouth and wondered who he was. He turned out to be the chef of fifteen years at Peg's country club.

Peg's daughter Melody organized this gig. It was supposed to involve anyone who was still alive in show business that Peg had worked with. They were coming in from wherever they were in the country to pay tribute in song and dance. Melody was going to put together a scrapbook that would show a photo of that personality in his/her heyday and then the live performer/present time. One person who didn't show was Jerry Lewis who had had six peg legs built for the "monoped master" (a student thesis I read once, conferred that title upon him).

Performers had come in from Boston, California, Missouri, Michigan, and New York to pay their respects. Sitting in that nightclub, I thought of Billy Crystal's "Mr. Saturday Night" and how it evoked a bygone era I'd always longed to be a part of, or at least witness to.

A black comic who had worked at Peg Leg's country club made my night in his scathing act. It reminded me of my father's cutting kind of humor, mean but funny, unless you're the object of the sarcasm. Like hearing the comic Mal Z. Lawrence, live.

CHANGING TIMES TAP ARCHIVE

Peg Leg Bates' ninetieth Birthday Invitation.

Melody put together a little show within a show, casting herself as Peg's daughter, cleaning up after the show, and reminiscing about the great night of her father's ninetieth. It was very ambitious theater, considering that the performers had no rehearsal time.

Dianne Walker was particularly brilliant that night, doing some terrific Latin rhythm; she's truly one of our great tappers today—the musicians got a kick out of her and it reminded me of the days when those most musical of dancers Bunny and Leon would have a ball, just playing with the musicians.

The pianist, Frank Owens, was a pleasure to listen to and watch just because he's such a dancer's musician. He *always* gives the dancers what they need.

Part of the show was a video of Peg Leg scrapping through his scrapbook, so he must have been in on this, even on some level. We'd keep hearing about the Resnicks, this old "multimillionaire" family and how they took care of Peg Leg. There were lots of whites in the audience, none on the stage, and I got the sense of Peg Leg's community, the people who supported him in Kerhonkson.

I was impressed by seeing *"THE"* Jerry LeRoy, of Jerry's LeRoy Rehearsal Halls, dancing in a movie with his ice skates on top of a suitcase. Dianne Walker made the gigantic mistake of asking Peg Leg if he had anything to say after the already hugely long night. *He went on and on.* I love Peg Leg, but, boy, could that guy talk! I don't think I got home until 4 a.m. We were all so sleepy and quiet on the way back, no chitchat about how great the event was.

I wished I had stayed the night at the hotel to be in line for all the hors d'oeuvres again the next morning. And maybe take a swim, even have a shvitz.

LON CHANEY, JR.
Another Contender for King of the Paddle & Roll

Like others in the family of tap, I came to respect Lon Chaney, Jr., tap's heavy weight champ, after the '60s revival times. In *The Original Hoofers,* or *Black & Blue,* or *Tap Happenings,* Lon never seemed to change his routine. We all had memorized "Perdido" to which he played his Paddle & Roll; we knew all the climaxes, what to expect.

What I didn't realize was what high standards Lon had for himself when he did that dance. It was his "work song" and like any classic it's how well you play it, not that you've been playing it for years. We often don't think of the hoofers as performing the classics. Rather we think of them and their "routines."

In fact, Chaney always danced "Perdido" differently and he knew when he was performing it well and when he was out of shape with it, which inspired me. Savion Glover was also inspired to become a hoofer through Lon Chaney's influence. He even named his own son, Chaney. ■

©CHANGING TIMES TAP ARCHIVE

Lon Chaney, Jr.: Once a boxer, he also aimed for
perfection when he danced his work song, "Perdido."

As of this writing, Jimmy Slyde, 80, passed away May 16, 2008. The only mentors living that I wrote about in Tap Daddies... And a Few Mommies are Bunny Briggs, Marion Coles, and Mable Lee. Harold Cromer (pictured on p. 188) was just given an honorary doctorate from Bloomfield College, N.J., and Charles Cook's partner, Ernest Brownie Brown, in his 90's, lives in Chicago.

Some obits that I had published of John Bubbles, Honi Coles, Cookie Cook, James Stump Cross, Carnell Lyons, Sandman Sims, and Henry LeTang, are in old issues of The Village Voice, and Dance Magazine.

...and a Few Mommies

FRANCES NEALY
From Show Girl to Movie Extra

Frances Nealy was my closest sole sister of the old school. I'd first met her in the early '80s when we both happened to be visiting Bubbles. After that, when I went out to California, I always stayed with her in her little apartment in West Hollywood. Frances even gave up her bedroom to accommodate me and a jazz dj dude I had hooked up with at the San Francisco Tap Festival; she slept on her living room couch! And she could roll a perfect joint while driving her car, too!

I loved her huge laugh when she talked about tap dancing.

"AHHHHH—HHHA—HHHAAAAA!!!!!!" she'd shout. "Tap dancing *has to be* something groovy, 'cause this is the *ONLY ART FORM, the ONLY, ONLY ART FORM, WHERE* YOU GO, YOU GO, YOU GO, AHHHHH! HA! HA! HA! HA! HAAAAAAAAA! I could do this tap dancing all day *every day* if they paid me to do it."

We tapped a lot at the Hollywood and Vine studio she rented for teaching and rehearsing. She was constantly auditioning for something. Like Gregory and Cookie Cook, she always had her television on, checking out who was making commercials, who was appearing on sitcoms, who was just appearing! She herself played extras—maids in lots of movies. She wasn't too happy about those roles—even the one she scored in *Ghostbusters*—but those roles paid the rent. This was the '80s though, and she deserved better.

I have fond memories of Frances spending a lot of time sitting in front of one of those huge magnifying mirrors, doing her hair and makeup each morning, telling me stories while she readied herself for that day's audition. There was no trouper like Frances Nealy. She danced well into her eighties. Her true love was tap and it was a big deal for her when she came east for the first time in 1986 to appear in *The New Sole Sisters*. She almost didn't come, because she thought the East Coast women in the 1985 edition of *Sole Sisters* could dance better and she was

Frances Nealy was known as "the female Bill Robinson" with her stair dance.

Frances said, "When tap came back, the women didn't."

more than a little bit intimidated. The next year and rendition of the show, she did come and Frances turned out to know a lot of the moves in Marion Coles' *For Dancers Only* already. Those female chorus lines! East Coast, West Coast—they shared a lot of the same great moves.

Frances performed her *Female Bill Robinson* act, sang, and told funny (sometimes blue) jokes. You knew you were in the hands of a great pro. She carried her own set of stairs that folded up neatly and proved easy to move around.

At 68, she was still slim as could be, with sleek hair and not a single wrinkle on her gorgeous very dark black face. That skin tone had prevented her from getting work in places like The Cotton Club, where "high yaller" girls—those with a lighter skin tone—might find a place in the chorus line. This time around, she felt that it was gender, not skin color, that was setting up road blocks.

"When tap came back, the women didn't," she told me. But she was always something of a cockeyed optimist, still hopeful about opening for some nightclub show out west.

"You'll see," she'd tell me. "There was a time when everyone was wearing ruffles on their shirts. Now, suddenly, ruffles are back. Some people don't change or care, so for fifty years ruffles are out and I'm not even aware they *were out* and I'm still wearing my ruffles on up to the time that ruffles have come back. I don't care what the styles are. I paid $50 for this shirt, and I'm going to wear it right on up until it's back in style."

MARION COLES
"For Dancers Only"

Marion Coles is choreographing a new dance for our upcoming all women's tap show, *Sole Sisters*. She's in the original 1985 version of the show, the one I produced at The Greenwich House in the West Village.

We have an issue. Sarah Safford is about seven months pregnant, and wants to stay in dancing shape. Marion decides we'll perform her new dance sitting down, for Sarah's sake. The guys have a "chair dance." We needed one! Marion is practical. She begins to pull out her "pocket steps" and choreograph.

She pulls out a great tune, "How Am I to Know", which later would become the tune for one of the big bank commercials on television. (It's always interesting to see how old jazz standards return to pop culture.) Marion is making up a soft shoe that Mable Lee will later embellish with her throaty voice. Our friend and compatriot, Beverly Wasser (née Rolfsmeyer), is also in the dance.

Marion is the woman who answered the phone way back in 1974 when I was calling Honi, her husband, for lessons. She never said anything about being a dancer herself. She had such a sweet soft voice on the phone.

©CHANGING TIMES TAP ARCHIVE

Marion Coles taught me "Watch What Happens" for a show at Dance Theater Workshop, NYC, circa 1979.

In the '70s, a lot of us budding hoofers were influenced by the women's movement and it wasn't strange to wonder about women in tap, especially since most of our teachers were older black men. Marion had started out as a ballroom dancer, but, like Frances, told me her first love was tap dancing. Her first ballroom partner taught Marion her first tap steps. To earn money they performed Spanish dancing, the Waltz, the Fox Trot, and the new Lindy Hop.

As a chorine in Restina Banks' A-1 chorus, she had to learn a smattering of everything—ballroom, ballet, swing. She and the rest of the chorus learned a stair dance directly from Bill Bojangles, who taught them everything but his main spot. The chorus line of women, all over the black vaudeville circuit, often did four shows a day, and had to learn new shows every week, unlike the men who could keep doing the same routines.

"Tap was considered a man's dance," Marion told me flat out one day when I was talking to her about the possibility of an all-women's tap show. "The best tappers were men, the women didn't do it . . . the men must have originated it; the women weren't out there tapping. I mean, it went way back, like Marshall [Stearns, the jazz historian] said—back to the Louisiana days."

I began working with Marion in the late 1970s when I started putting on shows on a regular basis. We performed a piece to the tune "Watch What Happens." One landmark day, she decided to teach us a particularly special gem from the A-1 chorus repertoire, "For Dancers Only." Jimmy Lunceford wrote the music for the dance, but as Marion tells it, the music didn't "fit" the dance, so Sy Oliver rewrote the arrangement. Because the dance was made up before the music, the dance and music were called, "For Dancers Only."

That's one of the few tap dances of the '30s where the dance was composed *before* the music. Although Marion was pretty much a homebody when I met her, taking care of her mom, Nana, she got back into dance when the revival was going strong.

She was always very with it, modern, studious, looking down as she concentrated on the combination, and refreshingly laid back. I was really glad for Marion when *Been Rich All My Life*, a documentary about the chorus line dancers in which Marion was the featured choreographer, was a hit. She's no longer only "Honi Coles' wife."

On a woman's panel once, Marion professed her love for the chorus line, *staying* in the chorus, dancing with others, collaborating, and learning new stuff. Unlike the guys, Marion would actually learn new steps from me! Holding down the end of the line, she came into her own totally as a dancer, and in her late eighties, too!

Mable Lee: the essence of longevity and style with one of her present collaborators, Tony Waag, on floor (circa 2005).

MABLE,
"As in Table"

Mable M. Lee was the first black female tap dancer from the old school I ever saw dance live. I had seen her on video in Leticia Jay's *Tap Happenings* at the Hotel Dixie. But live, Mable is a major flirt, a vamp vamping, the Mae West of black tap.

In the '40s in Europe, she was known as a soubrette, a female singer/dancer who stood out so much in the chorus line that she eventually appeared solo in front of the line. In 1947 she starred at the London Palladium for 18 months, with one of England's greatest comedians, Tommy Trinder. Mable appears just as active now in her eighties, performing sly, funny duets with The New York City Tap Festival's producer, Tony Waag.

It's almost as if she's the star again, only now she is the dance director as well. In works like "Lulu's Back in Town" and "I'm an Old Cowhand." Mable has created an inimitable brand of funny, sexy song and dances. In "Lulu," after Mable sings a few of the choruses, two dance lines of young female hoofers (all individualists in their non-Mable hours) suddenly appear singing the song down the aisles. They're all in heels—a requirement for the Mable Lee style—tight skirts or dresses, with lots of leg showing. You almost feel like their next tune will be, "I Enjoy Being a Girl." Mable looks upon them like a mother hen.

Mable M. Lee: "If you've got gorgeous legs, you've got 'em" (circa 1950s).

It gets even raunchier when she slinks in front of her girls in "I'm an Old Cowhand." She slithers in front of the line while the "cowgirls" in the chorus, low slung belts around their hips, make the most of the "wiggle room" Mable has given them in her choreography. She's one of the only old school dancers left who can still pass on the elements of a fun but exacting style of vintage showbiz.

On a blustery day in 2004, Mable came to my apartment and we spoke a little about the difficult subject of envy.

"It becomes a sore, an ulcer," she said. "And you shouldn't let that happen to you. If I have done something wrong, or you have a problem with me, you should call me up. Don't fire me or ignore me.

"Look, if you're pretty, you're pretty. If you've got gorgeous hair, you've got gorgeous hair. If you've got gorgeous legs, you've got them. But God gave me something, too. So, I don't have to be envious of what you have."

Well, that's a nice idealistic way of thinking, I thought, as Mable got up and started to do a few steps on the little three-by-three tap floor I had in the living room, just in case she felt like dancing.

"I hate auditions, because I don't like the stone faces," she told me. "But most every time I've gone and done an audition, I have been called back three or four times. One time I was sure I got the part. It was *Anchors Away* and I went home screaming and hollering, 'Momma, O, Momma, I got it!' But then they stood up and . . . guess who got it? Thelma Carpenter. Now I was, you know, all riled up and just knew I had it, but Thelma Carpenter got it. She got it because at the time she had a name. I was not known. I have lost a lot of things because I was not known. If you have someone known, they can bring in the money. But I didn't hate Thelma Carpenter. Me and her became—you see that bicycle you have in your hallway?— We would ride through the Village just like you do. Have fun and all that.

"We became friends, but what I'm trying to say is, you don't hold evilness and hate because somebody got a part and you didn't. Because if you're going to keep doing that all your life, you're never going to be anything."

I asked Mable if it bothered her that I, a white woman, was working with "the guys" at a time when she herself wasn't working.

"It didn't bother me," Mable said. "I was doing my own thing."

It turns out Mable *was* working. "I was singing and dancing in places. It didn't bother me about the boys dancing and I was very happy that they were dancing because there was a lot of them wasn't working and I *was* working."

I was always under the impression during the late '70s that even if there was some work out there again, there wasn't a lot, certainly not enough to make a living. Mable Lee actually had stayed active as a cast member in the national tour of *Bubbling Brown Sugar* starring Honi Coles, followed by the bus and truck company of that same show. She then left the bus and truck company and went on to another show.

Mable seems to have no performer's ego when you hear her talk about tap history. At a memorial for four major and minor players in our small tribe—Tony White, Bubba Gaines, Chuck Green, and Harriet Brown—Mable reeled off, like some hip chronicler, all the tap happenings past and present. I was mesmerized by her rendition, which sounded totally accurate. Hers was a fabulous rundown and gave me even more respect for this special entertainer. ■

John Bubbles—Stage Father

J ohn Bubbles was staying with an old girlfriend, Laurie Catrell, who had once danced in the chorus line at the Cotton Club. Both of them were in wheelchairs when I arrived at her apartment way uptown on Riverside Drive. I ran around the apartment, answering the phone, doing errands for them while conversing with Bubbles.

He was wearing big sneakers, a short-sleeved light blue shirt, and had beautiful white hair, shaved very close to his head. Even though it was freezing cold outside, Bubbles looked like he had just breezed in from Inglewood, California, where he lived.

Marshall and Jeanne Stearns' book *Jazz Dance*, the Bible for tap dancers during our revival, covered how John Bubbles had created a new style by dropping his heels, adding more syncopation, and putting tap into the jazz bracket. I was eager to learn how he did that, and I asked him if he knew he was developing a new style at the time.

"Of course," he replied. "I wanted to make it complicated, so I put more taps in and changed the rhythm and timing. The other dancers used to sit four deep in the front of the theatre at Loews State watching me, trying to steal my steps. I changed my steps four times, and I did each one four different ways so they couldn't catch it."

Bubbles kept his audience in mind, too. "I figured out how to do a dance so the audience wouldn't stop applauding. I hated for them to applaud, then stop, then applaud, then stop, so I made a dance all in changing tempos. I'd finish one step; they'd applaud, then I'd change the time, they'd still be applauding, and when I was finished, I'd be dancing 2/4 gallop tempo triple time and they would still be applauding long after I've left the stage. That idea knocked my brains out."

I asked him if it was always about competition and challenging the next dancer. "My whole life was based on that—the Challenge against the other fellow."

John W. Bubbles, known as "the father of rhythm." He influenced a whole generation, putting tap into the jazz bracket.

Eubie and Bubbles: Rare shot of Eubie Blake and John Bubbles backstage at Black Broadway, *1979, a show produced by jazz impresario George Wein.*

I asked him why.

"Don't ask me that," he scolded me. "It's how I got recognized. It's how everyone got recognized. It don't look like a Challenge, but that's what it is. If you like Peggy Lee better than Frank Sinatra, that's a compete (sic). I was competing as a singer since I was nine years old in amateur contests. I won first prize eight straight nights until no one would work if I went on."

As he reminisced, Bubbles revealed much of what competition meant during the golden days of tap. It started as soon as he began to dance. "I already knew how to turn, so I walked into the Hoofers' Club and did my turn and was booed out. I went to California and when I came back, I was a dancer. I had everything. I went back to the club and ran everybody out. I practiced day and night under theaters, and backstage. It's funny when I think about it—to think what they had over me and booed me out and I came back and they can't do nothing I'm doing. I'm doing double over-the-tops, triple back slides . . . everything you can think to dance because I got crazy with practicing when they do that to me."

I'd heard about the renowned Hoofers Club, a room in Harlem that was turned over to dancers where you could stay up tapping all night. That's how dancers got so good—watching, listening, and one-upping each other at times.

I had also seen Bubbles' fabulous "Shine" number, which he danced and sang in the movie *Cabin in the Sky*.

"Some people have complained that the song 'Shine' put the Negro down," I said. "Did you think so?" I used the word "negro" instead of "black" because I had been reading Stearns. The Stearns had published their book in 1966, and had used the word "negro" to define African-Americans. I also knew "negro" was the word Bubbles most identified with and he was extremely race conscious in all his conversations.

"How could they put the negro down?" he responded impatiently. "The words to that song are beautiful." He sang some of the lyrics in his natural soprano: *"What is there about me/that makes me feel well-dressed?"* You could almost feel him drifting; his eyes wandered back to the time when he played the part of "Shine" in the movie. It was so beautiful to hear him sing, sitting there in his wheelchair.

I learned that Bubbles had become paralyzed after a severe stroke that apparently occurred just after he had appeared along with Judy Garland on the *Tonight Show*. He didn't want to elaborate on that trauma, but it sounded as if the stroke's effects were first apparent upon his waking up the next morning. The stroke seemed to have come out of nowhere, and it stopped John Bubbles from participating fully in our tap revival.

I told him I was studying with Cookie Cook and that we had a class of four meeting weekly. He couldn't conceive of four of us in the same room learning the same step from one person. No one *taught* his "recipes." Dancers in Bubbles' era either taught themselves or "stole." I showed him a step I'd learned from his protégé, Chuck Green. Bubbles was not impressed.

"What are you going to do with *that* step? Get him to show you a routine."

"But Chuck's a perfectionist," I protested. "He corrected me the whole hour until I got the right sound on that one step. Besides, I don't catch it that quick."

Bubbles told me how he taught Fred Astaire for $400 an hour but Astaire was a slow learner, himself, and had to get all his steps from Marilyn Miller. I had never heard of Marilyn Miller. I thought Bubbles meant the famous tapper Ann Miller, until I read up on Marilyn Miller. She was much more of a stage performer than a film personality.

I had read in several books how Astaire had been taken up to Harlem to see Bubbles dance. Hermes Pan, his dance director, had grown up in New Orleans, where he was exposed to the black style of tap in the '20s. Astaire's dancing was great, but he only showed the basics when he danced, steps you could break down and learn off a video or television. What could Fred possibly glean from Bubbles in just a few sessions? With Bubbles' heels syncopating all over the place, what could Astaire have picked up?

What could my fantasy Fred Astaire possibly have thought of Bubbles as a teacher? John Bubbles wasn't doing basics, on screen, onstage, or anywhere else. Bubbles didn't use words like *"shuffles," "flaps,"* combinations you could get right off the screen. Did Bubbles have more patience as a young man than he did when I got to him in his eighties?

"He was such a nice guy, I didn't want to teach him for an hour without him getting anything," he said of Fred. "The way I teach, it would take four hours because of how I unravel it. It takes time. I wanted to see some results. I gave him some heely-toe cramps, stomps, heely-toe turns, cramp rolls."

Suddenly I saw myself with Fred Astaire in the same camp of slow learners. Only, I was getting a bargain. I had paid Chuck Green only fifty dollars for an hour-long private lesson.

"People are interested in seeing tap again," I told Bubbles. "Look at *Ain't Misbehavin'* on Broadway. They should put tap in it," I complained. "Some of the stars wear tap shoes, but they don't tap. And Fats Waller worked with tap dancers all the time."

"That show is good enough like it is," Bubbles disagreed angrily. "Besides, who they gonna get to execute it? Nobody's around. Honi Coles probably isn't interested and Chuck Green wouldn't fit. You've got to get someone who can tap dance to the extent of drawing in the public. Each step has to be *just like that.* That was my job. Who else do you know?"

"I guess we need to find another John Bubbles," I replied, retreating into my chair.

"Please don't think like that," the great master told me. "You've got to surpass me, darling. Not just do me, but surpass me."

———

I was so excited by our afternoon visit, I wrote my article for *The Village Voice* immediately, and then sent a letter to Bubbles back in California, thanking him for such a great interview. I was getting ready to do a lecture/demonstration with Cookie Cook and my students, so I sent Bubbles some of my pre-publicity, a black and white photo of Cookie and me standing together.

A week later I got a letter back from him in lovely cursive type on *"From the desk of John Bubbles"* stationery:

> *"Dear Janie,*
> *Just to let you know that I rec'd (sic) your nice letter with contents and photo of you and Cook. And that by-line, "Shoot Me While I'm Happy," which is not up to date. (It's "Pay Me While I'm Able")…And you should use a photo of "Bill Robinson"…P.S. And so you have gypsy in your Soul. Oh well, what more do you need."*

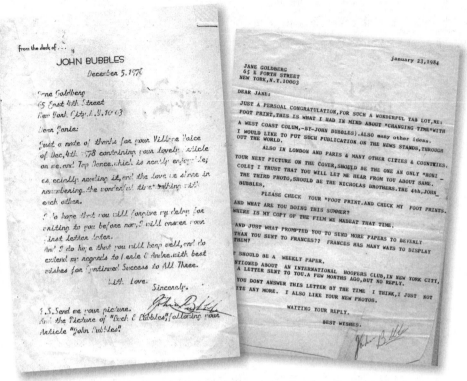

Letters to me from John Bubbles: He typed them from California. (1978, 1984)

I wrote him again, after I'd performed Charles Cook's *Bambalina* dance in a little showcase. He wrote back, addressing me by a new name:

"Dear Jane Allison,
I'm calling you that because you need a better stage name. Goldberg is not a stage name…. I trust that this letter will find you feeling as well as possible as it leaves me feeling fine. I received the other 5x7 Jane Goldberg and Charles Cook photo. Well, it is not good in many respects. 1. The floor just in back of where you are both standing looks very bad; 2. What is the name of the step you are lifting your right foot, over Cook's right foot and holding on to his left arm, and holding a hat in your right hand? How you got bookings from using such a picture is most surprising! There is no class in that photo at all. Excuse please, don't forget you are beginning another year and you are on your way up the ladder. Keep well. John Bubbles. P.S. No matter who you work with, have a good act." (The photo Bubbles is referring to is on my book's back cover.)

I next wrote Bubbles of my problems finding a theater for my impending lecture-demonstration. Everyone I asked was uptight about what tap dancers were going to do to the floor. Elaine Summers, renowned for her cutting-edge mind/body work, was generous with her Soho loft and even gave me a "space grant" when she saw I wasn't going to mess her floor up. Bubbles' response:

> *"Thank you for your every correspondence extended to me. I trust that you have not settled on the idea of quitting dancing which is much too sudden in spite of these off-the-wall crises and prices. There is so little that you should learn about happy tapping being as advanced as you are. I only wish that I was able to coach you just long enough to get you above reproach. Perhaps a revue of six would be better for you commercially, than the two or three you are planning to use. Such as three girls and three boys, twenty to thirty minutes with a few wise cracks at each other. Did you check out Michael's Rehearsal Studios on 8th Ave between 43rd and 44th St.? Mention my name. And what about "In Time" Inc. Dancing School. P.S. And what about Hoofers' International, Inc.? Did you get a manager yet?"*

This was the closest I ever got to having a stage mother. Bubbles really seemed to take an interest in my budding career.

In 1980, I was able to bring John Bubbles to a weeklong festival through my new company, Changing Times Tap. Considering his competitive spirit, it was probably hard for him to sit through all the goings on in a wheelchair. My festival co-producer and publicist, Melinda Mousouris, got Mayor Koch to honor him at

Mayor Ed Koch, Bubbles, and me. Bubbles insulted Koch about the water crisis in Harlem (1980), but accepted a key to the city.

©CHANGING TIMES TAP ARCHIVE

Thumb wrestling in Bubbles' nursing home in Southern California (circa 1983). I couldn't "unravel" his intricate steps, so we made do.

City Hall and Katherine Kramer, also a co-producer, handled the mechanics of getting him up and down any stairs.

A year later, I flew out to California to have Bubbles teach me his twisty-toe turns. I drove a couple hours down the Pacific Coast in a rented car every day for a few weeks to get to his nursing home. He showed me his steps with his fingers. His fingers tapping out the rhythms turned out to be just as intricate as Chuck Green's feet. When I got frustrated with all the finger tapping, we would just thumb wrestle. When he got frustrated with how I didn't get his material, we thumb wrestled some more.

One night I walked into his nursing home room and came upon him reading old fan letters that he kept in a cigar box next to his pillow. He quickly hid the box and asked, "Would you still love me, even if I weren't 'John Bubbles'?"

"Of course," I told him as I helped him into his bed. This was a side of show business I didn't know at all—the need to be loved as a human being, not just as a celebrity, or as an idol for an adoring and aspiring hoofer. ∎

Ginger Rogers—
Dancing is Just Dessert

It looked promising—Ginger Rogers in a new nightclub act at The Waldorf-Astoria, dancing cheek to cheek with four men in "Will You Be My Fred" sweatshirts. It was 1976, Ginger was back into dance and I was going to meet one of my first female role models.

I would tell her how I had yam-strutted out of all ten zillion reruns I saw of her and Fred Astaire. I'd get her to reveal her dance secrets and at the end of our interview, I'd show her a few of my steps and she'd put me in her new act. What went wrong?

I sat nervously in her suite hoping Ginger would float through the doors in her backless feather gown from *Top Hat*, but she walked briskly into the hotel room wearing a brown suit, heavy makeup, and demanding to see my photographer. Was this the woman whose picture dancing beside Fred I had covered with my own and plastered all over my basement walls for inspiration? I had read in numerous interviews that Ginger didn't like to be known for her dancing career, that she yearned to land dramatic roles, "to grow up onstage and get more serious." But wasn't dancing serious?

"I think that if you have an all-around athlete, he won't just want to play tennis," she neatly skirted my first question. "I think he would be dissatisfied being pigeonholed. What do you think?"

I wasn't ready for one of Ginger's renowned retorts.

"Oh, you're a real pioneer in that kind of feeling," I agreed. "But, in your career, you had to concentrate on dance while making those musicals with Astaire. I sensed that later on you were fighting the image of the dancer."

The "tapping reporter" with first female role model, Ginger Rogers, 1976, at her Waldorf-Astoria opening night.

I plastered my face all over Ginger's for inspiration.

"No, I wasn't fighting the image of the dancer. I don't think that if you're a chef who can cook a whole meal, you're going to be satisfied just making desserts."

"And you were more intent on doing dramatic roles, right?"

"If you've made desserts, darling, you have *had* the dessert part of your chef ability. You can always go back and make dessert. But if you could also make beautiful salads and beautiful steaks and beautiful breads, is there anything wrong in wanting to do that?"

True, Ginger had won her Academy Award for a straight acting role in *Kitty Foyle*, but it was dancing in Fred's arms that she romanced the public. Audiences of the Depression loved escaping into the lush settings of those musicals—enough to make Fred and Ginger the third biggest box office after Shirley Temple and Clark Gable. People tend to remember them for their ballroom seduction numbers such as "Night and Day" and "Cheek to Cheek," but I prefer their flirtatious tap conversations, when they were just getting acquainted. It was those syncopated sentences, which made me buy tap shoes and find the hoofers.

I wondered how Ginger had learned to tap, but she didn't seem eager to give that secret away. I settled for a more general question. "What was your favorite kind of dancing?

"*All kinds*. Anything that moved my body and was joyous. My parents used to come home from their jobs and find me dancing in the living room with the other kids in the neighborhood. We'd make up all kinds of romantic dances and memorize them to the music on the Victrola because it was fun. I wasn't the only one who did that."

"It seems that your musicals coming back have something to do with people wanting to dance with each other again," I piped.

"Young people don't know what they've been missing. I have taught a few young men who are sons of friends of mine and they love dancing together. They can't wait to go to the ballroom and they always want to go when I'm in the party 'cause they know we're going to have a good time dancing."

"Is it true that Hermes Pan taught you the dances after he worked them out with Fred?" I'd read that Hermes played Ginger when he was with Fred and Fred when he was with Ginger.

"That's not exactly the fact. Certainly he did, Fred did. We all pitched in. You hear one-sided stories and I'm not going to contradict them. I'm going to do my own book about it one day. I'm not going to give everybody my story." It occurred to me later that nobody could have choreographed the way Ginger slooped her shoulders or arched her back and stayed in Fred's arms the perfect amount of time.

"See, I actually wanted to meet you, so you could show me how to dance. It's been one of my biggest . . . "

"Hang-ups?" she smirked. Ginger the wisecracker had emerged. "Dancing is the most wonderful exercise and discipline."

"I read you never took a class in your life."

"Well, I did. But only for exercise. Of course I do pliés and all that but only for exercise and warm-up. Everyone knows what they need to do to warm up."

I felt hopeful. If I could look like she did in her films without taking any more classes, I'd be in great shape.

"You said dance is three-quarters work and girls have it harder because of all the makeup they wear."

"I believe that, so it's very normal for me to have said it. But it's according to what we're talking about. If we're talking about the kind of dancing I have done in connection with Mr. Astaire, it was harder on me because I had my hair hanging down my back and it would get wet and his hair wouldn't show being wet even when it was. I hated that."

"You mean while you were dancing all the sweat would . . . "

"Of course. And my hair, which would hang curled in the beginning, would get wet and straighten. It didn't stay curled."

"Mine does."

"Well, that's interesting," she said, studying my head. "Your hair isn't long, though."

There I was, raring to launch into my questions about female oppression and we were comparing hairdos. My fantasy of the countless hours Ginger and Fred rehearsed their routines to perfection, uninterrupted, was quickly shattered as she revealed to me how many times they had to stop the cameras because of hair emergencies.

Gamely I went on. I asked her about women in tap.

"Women today are so liberated," she said. "They'd like to kick their sisters right in the rear and I don't think that's nice 'cause they'll go right out and vote for a man when there's a woman who could probably do the job just as well. See, the innate jealousy of the human mind is something you just can't cope with." She launched into a long rap about how companies screw women, and how women should be able to stand up for other women.

When I confessed I had trouble supporting other women in my field even though that was one of my real goals, Ginger began talking about God and turning my thoughts to the Creator. I quickly switched the subject.

"Why do you think the image of 'Fred and Ginger' has remained so popular?" I asked.

"Because there's no other entertaining films like them being made. Those films gave hope and joy. You don't come out of them saying, 'Why did I pay that money to hear those foul words and see that scene about sex that is anti-everything I believe in?'"

"Is it a problem getting older with the image people have retained of you?"

"It doesn't come into my thoughts," she said quickly. "The trouble with the newspaper business is the emphasis is too much on age. The problem is not age. It's limitation and you want to fasten limitation on someone else. What you're saying to me is not new. You're a journalist. I've lived beside ink all my life. "

"But I'm a dancer, too," I protested. "And you know that in dance the emphasis is on image and youth. Boy, my father always says to me if you haven't made it by twenty-two, forget it."

"You tell him to stop limiting you," she said excitedly. "Anyone—male, female, whatever—if they speak of limitation to you about your abilities, you just put your thumbs in your ears and march on!" I was sure Ginger was going to break into "Pick Yourself Up, Dust Yourself Off, and Start All Over Again," but her secretary suddenly walked in to remind her of her dinner appointment.

"Let us have one more minute," I pleaded. I was feeling totally supported. It was *Stage Door* and Ginger and I were about to walk off into the sunset together declaring unequivocal loyalty.

"Limitation isn't a fact. It's a *myth* and you can disprove it," she yelled. "Any time anyone writes anything, says anything, that makes you feel limited . . . "

Ginger wannabe

"Which is what happened to you when you played dramatic parts?"

"And what did I do! What did I do? Did I disprove it?"

I shook my head wildly, feeling a little guilty that I hadn't seen anything but her films with Astaire.

"If I did it, *you* can do it. Of course you can."

Her secretary walked in again and I swooped back to my original purpose.

"Did you know tap is a dying art? I've been trying to track down some of the old original hoofers and learn their routines."

"I love people who tap," she interrupted. "I'm the best audience anyone ever had. When I sit out in the audience, I root and I toot and I'm thrilled and I cry. I went to see *A Chorus Line* and I cried and cried."

"But how did you like the dancing? Certainly the dancing didn't compare to the dancing you did with Fred . . . "

"I don't compare. As Shakespeare said, 'Comparisons are odious.' You're asking me limited questions because your thoughts are limited and until you dispose of them, my girl, those thoughts aren't going to hurt *me*. They're going to hurt *you*. There's an old saying: 'The head that thinks it is the head that hurts.'"

"But they don't make good dancing musicals anymore."

"Oh, we can talk about the 'thens.' But this is *now*. I sing a song about that in my new show. Nothing's ever really going to come back. Don't limit yourself, little angel. Thank you so much."

She got up to leave, but I still had hope. Fumbling with my tape recorder, I blurted, "But I wanted to dance with you."

"Okay, let's see your time step."

Ginger began singing in stop-time while I showed her some of my Honi Coles rhythm tap. Even though I was on a thick carpet with no shoes, I hoped some of it would come through. Down with Fred and Ginger. Up with Ginger and Jane."

This time, her secretary looked irritated as she reminded Ginger she had to go.

"Tap is back! Tap is back!" I shrieked.

"You tell 'em, dear," Ginger said, as she exited the room. "I haven't got the time." ■

Charles Cookie Cook:
"Love Ends in the Classroom"

Cookie once told me, "Love ends in the classroom." Once we were on the road, things got much more hard-edged. Showbiz sucked.

We had been getting closer even as I was traveling around ferreting out other tap greats. I began to get a huge crush on Cook when I watched him work on a video documentary about the Copasetics. I fell hard the moment I saw him perform with his old partner Ernest Brownie Brown. They had worked together as Cook and Brown for decades, headliners in black show business.

I knew Cook as a great teacher, but I didn't know how cool, hip, and swinging he was. His speech was full of non-sequiters and rumbles, lows and highs. Even his words came out syncopated. Six feet tall and lean, a drummer and trumpet player, he was one of the cool cats of the jazz age.

With Sandman gone, I asked—pleaded really—for another "name" from Honi Coles, who had left me and our class of four to go on tour in "Bubbling Brown Sugar," the national tour. Honi reluctantly gave me Cook's phone number and I later realized he liked our little class. It's natural for a teacher to be a little possessive of his students. He'd just given us a big piece of himself, his individual personal style, and wasn't quite ready to give it all up that year in Soho at Pat Catterson's loft.

Cookie got so lost trying to find my Bleecker St. home behind gates, that he called for directions at least three times. The last time was from a bar around the corner, and he eventually entered the basement smelling of alcohol. He carried a silver flask of vodka. I had never been exposed to a drinking man before. We hit it off, in any case, as he corrected Honi's rendition of Honi's own ending of "The Walk-Around," now called "The Coles Stroll." I told Cook about our class in Soho and made arrangements for him to come to Pat's the following week.

Classical Cookie, 1985

I loved standing behind him, watching his hips swing side to side as he came up with songs I'd never heard of, humming them under his breath while he taught us. I loved the concentration each of us brought to class as we patiently waited and doodled along with him, matching sounds to notes, trying out his phrases. A teacher improvising might drive some students crazy. I loved it.

Once you get into someone else's style, you can almost anticipate what rhythms they are going to use next, what patterns they will develop. Each of these old masters had a certain unique way of phrasing, hearing, breaking up time; now and then they dropped their heels or punctuated with their toes. It would be a Honi-ism, or a Cookie-ism, or a Leon-ism, and you'd know it. From the waist down, we were musicians creating music; whatever we did with our upper body was up to each of us.

Jazzers like Cookie didn't mind where we looked or what we did with any part of ourselves. It was about "time," and with only four of us, you could hear yourselves, mistakes and all.

It was always a nice surprise when you were proven wrong in your anticipation of the next step. James Stump Cross, from the comedy/dancing team Stump and Stumpy, told me I had Cookie's "feet" meaning his "feel" for the music he was making with his feet. Sometimes I did and sometimes not. Cookie himself once told me to "stop doing that white time." And I retorted, that it wasn't white, it was Jewish "time."

I was falling in love with him. Or was it his feet? This was the partnership I'd been hoping for ever since seeing Fred and Ginger. If dancing with Charles Cook was that fantasy, it was hardly as I had fantasized. We were standing side by side, not cheek to cheek. Cook was a comedian, so my fantasy adjusted to accommodate that aspect of our personalities. The comedy was rarely deliberate, though, in our odd couple status.

In the summer of 1977, I traveled to a workshop where he was teaching and we had some time to talk about tap dancing. He called me "Stearns, Jr." with all my questions about tap history. I was impressed with how much he knew about everyone, having been raised by his mother in a rooming house where all of black show business had stayed at one time or another. All you had to say was "20/40" and everyone knew that was Cookie's mother's rooming house address.

Our first regular gigs in 1979 were for the Comprehensive Employment Training Act (CETA) program. President Jimmy Carter pushed to have artists get jobs like the Works Progress Administration (WPA) during the Great Depression, when artists were also employed by the government. Five hundred artists from New

Cookie liked mugging onstage and off.

York were chosen from all disciplines and paid $200 a week to produce work. It was grueling competition pitting teachers against students in many cases, all in the quest for a steady paycheck.

I didn't even know Cookie was auditioning for a CETA job, but we were both selected, separately, and became known as the "CETA couple." We were perfect for the multicultural moment at hand: man and woman, old and young, black and white, looking like we were having a ball, tap dancing. We began working at nursing homes, schools, senior centers, libraries, and small theaters throughout New York City's five boroughs. That's when we began spending Christmas together because we always had a gig that day at some lonely nursing home or senior center. We even began exchanging presents. Once he gave me a Nephritides necklace, which I still have. Another time he gave me a used camera with pictures of suburbia exposed on the half-used roll of film inside. I figured it must have been a "hot" camera! And I loved it!

At the midtown church, where we picked up our checks every other week, Cookie would greet me with the chant, "CETA, CETA, pumpkin eatah." He would act very nonchalant, like it was no big deal to get that check. But I knew that this was a huge deal for him, to finally have something steady as a dancer again, to be working. It was certainly a huge deal for me, because it felt like I was going to have the opportunity to tap dance for a living!

Cook and Brown when they were kids, a popular slapstick comedy team.

By then, we had developed a repertoire of numbers, some from his old act of forty years before. The first time I'd seen them perform, I realized tap dancing was only a sliver of their act. He and Brownie had been the forerunners of the two-man comedy dance teams of the 1930s, according to the Stearns book, combining acrobatics with Russian floor dancing, jokes, and knock-about comedy.

I didn't want to be knocked about like Brownie, but I did want to do comedy with Cookie. He saw me as his protégée, not quite the Shirley Temple that Sandman Sims envisioned. I was, after all, thirty years old, not ten. Still, I did enjoy dancing right next to him, doing his old time routines. My favorite was a soft-shoe to "Breezing Along with the Breeze." When he saw that we were being billed together, he taught me "Old Man Time," his and Brownie's opening number, where we stooped over these shortened canes, and stomped along the floor as he sang, "Old Man Time, you're so mean, the meanest man I've ever seen."

Program, 1983: The Depression's Back and So Is Tap *and* Found Sound, *two different shows, same season.*

Cookie began making up new dances for the two of us, too, such as "Let's be Buddies," from the movie *Panama Hattie,* and "The Jitterbug Waltz," composed by Fats Waller from the then current Broadway hit, *Ain't Misbehavin'.* That was his very uncanny old school thinking to cash in on what was popular in culture now. Cookie also had great wisdom for making up dances to rarified jazz tunes like "Dancing on the Ceiling," "It Could Happen to You," and "Jump for Joy." He, himself, began using Jobim's Bossa Nova, "Wave," as his signature dance, always introducing it as "I Remember Hanya." The modern dance pioneer, Hanya

Holm, had worked with him and Brownie on the Broadway show, *Kiss Me Kate*. My own modern dance teacher, Claire Mallardi, had danced with Cookie in that show. What goes around comes around couldn't have been a truer statement.

We also had a neat little bit where I went back to my roots and performed a Hebrew soft shoe to a Friday night prayer, and Cook followed me throwing sand down on the stage and doing his African roots to Cole Porter's "Easy to Love."

In addition to our CETA jobs, I was getting together my first production, a show called *It's About Time: An Evening of Jazz Tap Dancing.*

The story of *It's About Time* is as follows: After persistent calls to the National Endowment for the Arts, I received a $1,800 choreography fellowship to support the project—a lecture-demonstration with my teachers and students. One day Cookie and I went up to The Bronx to visit Bert Gibson—and I told Gip about the impending performance. As the night rolled on and everyone got a little drunk, Cookie announced, "I don't work anywhere without Gip."

I was agreeable and this lec/dem soon took on the trappings of a full-blown show. Gip brought his friend, "Little Jazz" Richardson, to rehearsals. Cookie, Gip and Little Jazz revived material from their old acts. I invited Andrea Levine, another student of Cookie's, and her drummer boyfriend Chris Braun, to join us. They had a great drum/tap duet. Andrea and I had also composed an acapella number and I improvised with my sax playing friend Harvey Ray. Andy Wasserman, who

Cook and I played "The Big Bucks" dancers, the first ones trying to get to the moon, in "The Depression's Back and So Is Tap" at the Riverside Dance Festival, 1983.

©PHOTO BY RAYMOND ROSS

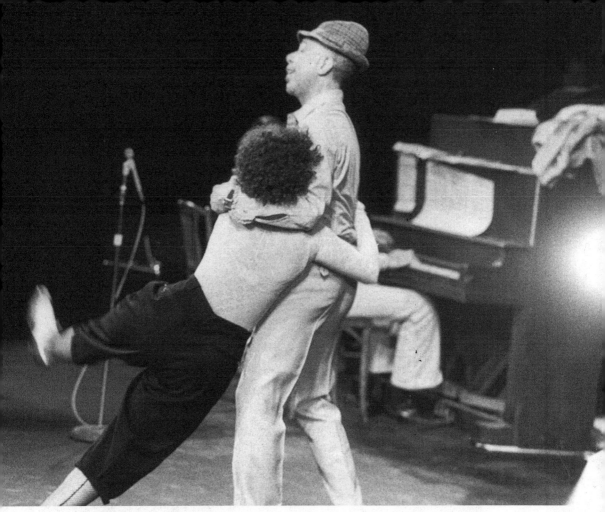

"Me and You": One of Cookie's favorite expressions when he signed off.

knew a lot of the Copasetics tunes, was our piano player. And choreographer Elaine Summers had offered me a space grant to perform in her loft.

I bought my first answering machine and put my home phone number in the press release. *The New York Times* gave me a Friday preview listing, and with my number published in *The Times*, my phone began ringing off the hook. Since my show was billed for only three nights, I set up late shows and still couldn't accommodate everyone who called for reservations. It was funny to see all those well-heeled people from Westchester wandering up and down lower Broadway, looking for a theater, and, if they could get in, finding themselves seated in metal folding chairs or cushions in that funky old fifth floor Soho loft. Composer Nam June Paik walked through a performance once to get to his loft in the back, behind Elaine's.

That little show was a life-changer. Overnight, I was thrust into the world of show business. Here, I had been going around to everybody I could think of, trying to get work for the old masters of tap. Now, I was onstage with them. Jennifer Dunning of *The New York Times* came out with a review headlined "Jane Goldberg Taps with Hoofers" that ended with "Break down the doors if you

Cookie and me at Jacob's Pillow in the Berkshires, 1978. Great floor!

have to" to see my show (see Appendix, page 300). After my brief run at the loft, Joe Papp of The New York Shakespeare Festival called up asking for Cookie and me, as did Max Gordon of The Village Vanguard.

It's About Time was a happening for tap dancing, especially with all the media attention we received. It was downtown, for one thing, a hip Soho cache. Jazz critics came to my show. Nightclub owners and modern dance festivals began calling. Suddenly Cookie and I started touring places like Cincinnati (the chili capital of the world—Cookie loved chili), Seattle, Washington, Washington, D.C., Philadelphia. We played George Wein's Kool Jazz Festival. We were invited to Harvard University, The Goodman Theater in Chicago, and we danced on the steps of Manhattan's Custom House.

Cookie and I were also invited to do *The American Dance Festival* and *Jacob's Pillow* where tap hadn't been performed in eighteen and thirty-seven years respectively. Gip developed a horrible case of gangrene in his legs, so Leslie Bubba Gaines became a regular member of my entourage, which also included Cookie and various younger dancers. I picked up old greats like Ralph Brown, Buster

Brown, Leon Collins, Harold Cromer, and Marion Coles to round out the packages, depending on how much money I could get.

I always told the presenters hiring me, "Hey, I'm not working with twenty-two-year-old modern dancers. I'm working with the tap legends!" I was quickly learning the ropes of agenting. We were now in a different market—the concert stage.

What I didn't count on was taking care of business for Cookie. He was still my teacher, but I soon became his agent/producer. Lots of times things weren't that calculated. Max Gordon of The Vanguard, the premiere venue for jazz, called to have a meeting. When Cookie asked if it was a "B" or an "A" house—a vaudeville term for what kind of venue we'd be playing, I realized Cookie might be living in another era. When he didn't show up for that initial meeting with Max, it began to dawn on me that I was going to be the one taking care of our business. Changing Times Tap Dancing Co., Inc. became my umbrella for writing grants, doing shows, and paying performers. I teetered between the Apollo Theater, the Borscht Belt, and the downtown art scene.

We met our trusty piano player, Jim Roberts, at Macy's when the three of us were working on a small stage set up at the department store and live music was the order of the day. Jim knew "Wave" and could read our charts quickly, no rehearsal. He was great with tap dancers, always acknowledging that they were the headliners. Turns out he had played a few of the early *Tap Happenings* and knew how to play for hoofers.

PHOTO BY PAMELA DUFFY

Promotional photo circa 1983.

The Museum of Modern Art hired us for a reception cocktail party and while we danced, everyone around us got drunk and noisy. Above the din of tinkling glasses and loud voices, Cookie shouted sarcastically, "Jane, are you sure you wanna be in show business?" That same night, as I paid him his fee for the evening, Cookie declared: "Love ends in the classroom." With that sentence, Cookie let me know that our relationship had fundamentally changed. This was no $3.50 a lesson and it wasn't all fun and games anymore. We were no longer carefree in my

Bleecker Street basement or Pat Catterson's airy loft. We were making a living tap dancing. It came at a hefty price.

———

I wasn't emotionally ready for all the business calls, the auditions, the quest for an agent. Success was, as the saying goes, "killing me." Our little ensemble was a crazy quilt of old hoofers and young dancers, not an easy-to-define package, in the late '70s world of Twyla Tharp and Baryshnikov.

Worst of all, Cookie was being pulled in all kinds of directions. He claimed he was getting in trouble with The Copasetics for teaching the younger generation and me their secret recipes, dances like "The Bill Robinson Routine," which Honi Coles often performed solo. There was competition for bookings between my package and The Copasetics. Cookie was also good at pitting his young female protégées against each other, a legacy that made the young women back then even more competitive with each other than we needed to be. It seems the smaller the field, the more the competition.

I rose to the occasion. One summer, American University hired Cookie and me for a month to teach and perform. Cookie usually flipped out the night before a show or gig, telling me the money was funny. Even with a signed contract, he felt he deserved more. He was a pain in the butt to do business with and his partner, Brownie, it turned out was even worse, as I found out later in our Goodman Theatre gig.

Why? Was it years of being ripped off by all those agents or just a terrible sense of how to take care of business? Cook accused me of making more than he was at the AU (American University). I still wasn't savvy enough about running

August 1981, Lincoln Center Out-of-Doors.

PHOTO BY SARA WELLS

"CETA CETA Pumpkin Eatah." We were the CETA "couple" in 1979.

a nonprofit and was paying him the same as I was getting. Eventually, he realized that, in fact, I was getting less money than he, despite my brokering the deal. To "apologize" he took me to Georgetown, and bought me a beige quilted skirt and pink pastel top, not my colors at all. I let him pick them out, always eager to smoke the peace pipe with my temperamental teacher.

Despite his contrariness, the great thing about Cookie was his consistent creativity. He didn't rely on his old act or old routines, as was true of most of the hoofers of his era. And he was always creating new work. He was also always game for a fresh experience, whether reciting and tapping to Shakespeare in producer/director Ken Rubenstein's offbeat theater pieces or attending performance artist Blondell Cumming's piece on menstruation and Eric Bogosian's early character sketches in lower Manhattan.

I always felt secure dancing beside him, in synch with his routines and rhythms. He taught me the etiquette of backstage manners, too, how to let guest artists take their time if they were going over with the audience, and still keep my show tight. Only when we'd arrive at some of the college campuses to perform, and there were no bars or drinking holes visible, did his insecurities mount. And

Performing our first duet at La Meri's Cape Cod festival, 1977.

when he'd been drinking before a gig, it was a drag onstage. He'd lose control, miss steps, get sarcastic toward me in front of an audience. That didn't happen often, but when it did, I was always taken by surprise, and would muddle through his mood, hoping for the best.

⟿

Cookie loved the writing my friend Stewart Alter did for him. Stewart could write lyrics to fit Cook's curmudgeonly on and offstage personality. I loved his writing, too, especially his titles: "The Depression's Back and So Is Tap," "Old,

New, Borrowed, and Bluesy" which defined the humor and fun of tap. I called two of my revues *Shoot Me While I'm Happy*. That last name was a line Cookie always shouted during the break of the third step of the Shim Sham, the dance at the end of the show. To me, that line said it all.

—⁓—

I never had so much fun with any of my tap daddies as I did when I was tap dancing next to Charles Cookie Cook. Our collaboration lasted over six years. All tensions would disappear once the lights hit. He even started addressing me slyly, as his "partner." The stage was the place where he could feel the power of his choreography, be funny, and share his good humor.

I never developed the hard shell I needed with him, though I could play hardball with a lot of other people along the way. I never got used to his outbursts and mood changes around show time. I thought that's what show business was about—temperamental outbursts and a strange dichotomy of fun and total pain. Here was someone I cared so much about—he was *why* I was dancing in front of audiences, so I believed—and then he would treat me like I was always ripping him off.

I last visited Cookie in his apartment at 125th Street right near the A train, just before he died in 1991. I was showing him some new political material, set to some of Cookie's steps. My then partner, Sarah Safford, had made up a ditty to "Bei Mir Bist Du Schön," and called it "Dear Mr. Hussein," but Cookie could only see the steps. He began making a few changes and improving the routine immediately. Always the teacher. ■

Interlude: My Tap Addiction

By now, I had reached a point in my career where anyone looking at me could plainly see I was addicted to tap dancing. Being addicted to tap dancing was a whole lot healthier than being addicted to chocolate, nicotine, alcohol, and unavailable guys. At least with tap, it was a healthy physical addiction and there was even a shot at keeping the weight off. I was obsessed about having a dancer's body even though I have a naturally zaftig frame.

With tap, body type wasn't as important as in other forms of dance. When I stood behind the hoofers, getting their steps, watching their feet, imitating their sounds, they were listening, not looking at me. I wasn't at all self-conscious, since they were most intent on hearing what I was saying with my feet.

At the time, I thought I was looking for a partner, but in retrospect, tap had become my significant other. My search for romance in dance was taking a backseat to the sound of taps slapping polished wood. Tap dancing was my Mister and we were tight. I became a tapping fool, practicing in elevators, or while waiting for the subway.

In a publicity shot for my all women's show, *Sole Sisters*, I was photographed surrounded by the other women, cradling a tap shoe as if it were my baby. The sole sisters looked on, smiling, proudly holding their own fake baby dolls while my younger colleague, Sarah Safford, held her real six-month-old Molly. In my number, "Career Versus Family," I chose career. I was married to tap.

Looking back, it was a fairly unbalanced life. I didn't realize I was subconsciously postponing my childbearing years, though I'd never really thought or talked that much about having children of my own. I wasn't a huge planner.

As the tapping reporter, I began to investigate the tap world, and began to notice there were alliances and rivalries to be negotiated. I wanted to know everyone on

Opposite page: As you can see, I had my photo taken wherever there was a sign for "tap" or "feet."

VERNEY FARM
STANFORDVILLE, NEW YORK

August 21, 1976

Dear Ms. Goldberg:

Thank you for writing me. However, I have had to
turn down requests for interviews for the past couple of
years because of the great number. Many of them came from
old friends and old colleagues, and I felt that if I did
one, I would have to do them all, in fairness. This could
lead to a lot of hurt feelings.

I'm sure I couldn't contribute anything to what Mr. Draper
or the others had to say. Draper's contention that he
danced because he had to just about covers it.

With all good wishes.

Sincerely,

James Cagney

JC:kmd

and off the mainstream in those heady early revival days. If I were to navigate the field, I needed to understand it. I wanted to know who exactly the Original Hoofers were, who belonged to the Copasetics fraternity. Why were only a few dancers allowed to move amicably between the two groups? Who was the real "King of the Paddle & Roll?" Was it Carnell Lyons who had defected to the jazz life in Europe after World War II or was it Lon Chaney, who had stayed right here in The Bronx?

Why were certain steps considered to be too masculine for women? Why was there a squabble over calling the Nicholas Brothers "flash" dancers instead of "class" dancers? And how could you do a delicate, slow *soft* shoe if you were wearing clunky aluminum taps on your feet?

I'd learn there was Broadway Tap vs. Jazz tap and Show Tap vs. "the real thing." "Jazz tap" became "rhythm tap" in some quarters, and I read somewhere that tap was just called "dancing" in an earlier time, because it was the type of dancing everyone in show business knew. Clark Gable tapped. Joan Crawford tapped. Burns and Allen tapped. Early modern dance pioneer Ted Shawn had called tap "the scourge of the devil, bequeathed to us by St. Vitus." To him, it was just low-life entertainment, not art at all.

———

Besides searching for hoofers, I was meeting club owners, record producers, film collectors, old jazz buffs, entertainment lawyers, celebrated musicians like Count Basie and Charles Mingus, assorted Ellington alumni, all of whom had worked with tap dancers at one time. I begged Joe Papp of The Public Theater and Max Gordon of the Village Vanguard to showcase tap dancers. I asked the old musicians who'd worked with hoofers "back then" and who were working now, if they'd include us in their gigs.

My apartment on East 4th St. became legendary drummer Philly Joe Jones' crash pad, since it was right around the corner from The Tin Palace, a jazz club where he frequently performed. I used to stay up all night long, watching him write music, begging him to tell me stories about his tap/drum connection.

I always had my tape recorder with me in case there was someone to record on my quest for the Holy Hoof. One drummer spent a whole night explaining to me how his "dropping bombs," the bebop expression for a loud crashing of the cymbals at the end of a phrase, killed tap. He told me the complex rhythms of bebop were often too loud and full of too many notes for the space needed by most dancers. (Some like Baby Laurence and Jimmy Slyde kept up with the new music, but most preferred the swing groove.) This sweet drummer's "Dropping Bombs Theory" was worth the price of finding his teeth by the side of my bed the next morning. After all, this was primary research.

I wanted to interview every tap great still alive, including one of my favorites—James Cagney. He wrote me back!

I soon became obsessed with learning about Baby Laurence, a dancer I never met, never even saw dance, but whom all the drummers and musicians, and fellow tap dancers referred to, even deferred to, as "the greatest." Baby had moved the art form forward, keeping the sounds even closer to the ground to stay with the "bombs" that the bebop drummers were dropping. Baby was one of the few able to keep working, a very hip thing to do in a culture that was rapidly changing not only musically, but in many other areas.

I was finally able to see Baby Laurence in a documentary called *Jazz Hoofer*, which made me understand his influence on tap. Even on a crummy outdoor, uneven, unmiked floor, you could see Baby's greatness, his smoothness, his musicality. I admired one part of the movie where he was giving a lecture to an audience at the old Jazz Museum in the West 40's. I felt like I knew Baby Laurence by the time I'd seen his cinematic self and had spoken to many musicians and dancers about him.

———

Like many of my colleagues at the time, I was following in Baby's footsteps. We wanted to educate the public to what tap dancing really was. People talk about Muhammad Ali unable to work in his prime fighting years; the same thing happened to the entire profession of tap dancers, all in involuntary retirement due to changing styles and times in pop culture.

In 1974, long before I had even heard his name, I was sent a Baby Laurence obituary written by the jazz critic of the *San Francisco Chronicle*. Whoever sent that article to me must have known that one day I'd be curious, no, *fanatical*, about learning everything tap. I tried imagining what it was like to be back in Baby's day.

In 1977, I tracked down a record label man, Herb Abrams, at a flophouse of a hotel on the Upper West Side when I got word that he had a copy of the album Baby Laurence had recorded in the early '60s. I found Abrams in his shady setting with thousands of sheet music pages pouring off of his shelves.

He gave me a whole pack of articles about Baby Laurence. I'd eventually look up all the authors myself. One of the most exceptional writers, Melinda Mousouris, turned out to be living in the West Village. I also spoke extensively with dancer Dee Bradley, an elusive Brit, who'd lived with Baby at one time, as well as with choreographer/tapper Buddy Bradley and Chuck Green. I wasn't the only tap addict.

———

I looked up the jazz film collector Ernie Smith, then living a secluded life upstate on Lake George. I told him I'd heard about his tap films, and when I mentioned the names Honi Coles, Cholly Atkins, and John Bubbles, he invited me up to his home, where I was privileged to screen his rare footage of a host of incredible hoofers. A cool cat from Pittsburgh, Ernie loved to jitterbug, and would also go the distance himself,

Those are dancer Traci Mann's "Young Hoofers" on the top left, me at Eleanor's Hollywood "Star," and of course, tapping on top of bars, a favorite pastime!

obsessing over his particular jones—footage of jazz dancing scenes. Though some of the old movies were in the public domain, Ernie went about paying for, trading, and surreptitiously swapping footage. He was one of Marshall Stearns' colleagues, all of whom belonged to the Institute for Jazz Studies. They listened to and riffed about jazz incessantly. Unlike many of these jazz fanatics, however, Ernie and Stearns caught the tap and jazz dance bug as well. That turned out to be a lucky thing for us tap fanatics.

I tracked down Irv Kratka of the early labels, Music Minus One and Classic Jazz. He had actually produced the Baby Laurence album. Irv was planning to melt down the five hundred remaindered albums that hadn't sold.

"Are you nuts!" I responded, when he told me of his plan. These were collectors' items! I ended up purchasing the lot. I didn't know what I was going to do with five hundred albums, but I had to save them from becoming wax. The five kids from the family who lived above me helped carry them up the five flights of stairs to my apartment. As of this writing, I still am hanging on to twenty-five of those albums. I also wrote an article about the album published in the defunct *Soho Weekly News*. An editor there actually published an article about a mostly defunct album on tap; that was très cool! That editor was hip! It was always hard placing stories on tap, even at the height of the revival!

By the '80s, I had built my tap hall of fame. All four rooms of my railroad apartment were crammed with tap videos, tap films, tap articles, tap photos, tap paintings, tap posters and postcards, tap jewelry, tap recordings, and the sheet music of deceased tap dancers. I even had audiotapes of my psychotherapy sessions, which almost always touched on issues related to my tap life. I had shoes in silver, green, yellow, purple, red, black, white, custom-made shoes, too—two-tone, three-tone, your basic black patent leather pumps. I had a roll-up tap mat that went with me when I did my tap-a-grams™, my patented tapping telegram service. My imagination ran wild as I dreamed of hoofers onstage again, great steps being passed down like secret recipes.

John Bubbles liked to call tap an "idea." In 1980, when he participated in *By Word of Foot*, the first festival my company produced, it felt like Rip Van Winkle waking up in Sleepy Hollow after twenty years asleep. Coincidentally, that was almost exactly the same length of time as the Great Tap Drought of the '50s and '60s. Surveying the goings-on at the Village Gate, Bubbles expressed astonishment that so many students were attending the event for "this idea."

The old masters were available to teach if people showed an interest in learning. We would have to create our own jobs if we were going to put tap on the map again. After all, tap at its highest form was about improvisation and we were improvisers.

In my growing desire to learn everything tap, I had to meet its Rising Star, Gregory Hines. Making my rounds in the mid '70s, I observed him closely whenever the chance

At one time I was known as "The Marxist Hoofer." Photos and flyers from Changing Times Tap shows.

arose. Once when I had insomnia at 2 a.m., I turned on the television and there was Gregory with his goatee and ubiquitous earring hanging from his left ear, tap dancing in loose, white, karate pants on a talk show.

I'll never forget how completely out of breath he was after he had improvised on Johnny Carson's *Tonight Show* in front of millions of television viewers. Carson had to run a commercial because he was not expecting Hines to be so winded after his neat improvisation. If every plumber, mailman, or investment banker saw what just happened on TV, with Gregory improvising and Johnny calling for a commercial unexpectedly, the world would be a better place, more spontaneous, full of risks, good risks.

Gregory also carried his shoes onto David Letterman's desktop and, in fact, got a leading role in Francis Ford Coppola's *The Cotton Club* by spontaneously tapping on producer Bob Evans' coffee table. Hines was what the legendary Bunny Briggs called "a hustler of the feet." James Cross, of the act Stump and Stumpy, once told me you couldn't push it. Tap wasn't like oranges and apples. But you *could* and I *did*. And Gregory was tap's most visible pusher.

One summer weekend in 1985, after *The Cotton Club* had been released, Gregory and his wife Pam Koslow flew to Martha's Vineyard for a weekend escape. I was already vacationing there. They called me up to hang out. I rented a car and took them all around the island, but my hidden agenda was to show Gregory what a tap fanatic I was.

I had discovered the greatest floor on earth—The Oak Bluffs Firehouse floor —and I couldn't wait for him to try it out. He was duly impressed, as he listened to me tap on the floor above the huge hollow space filled with fire engines. I did all the steps I'd learned from Leon, Honi, Cookie, and Sandman. I quizzed Gregory on the drummers who tapped, the boxers who tapped, and the comedians who tapped. I was especially impressed that he knew who Maurice Bishop was. The slain Revolutionary leader of Grenada, West Indies, was someone dear to my heart, as I had made a couple of pilgrimages to that island.

Over the years, Gregory and I talked tap all over the country. Even at his daughter's huge wedding, right in the middle of the antipasto course, with hundreds of people coming up to congratulate him, I planted myself in the seat right next to him. I whipped out my tape recorder and we talked about the relationship of Irish step dancing to tap. He was totally game.

"Jane, I can't believe you brought your tape recorder to Daria's wedding!" Pam admonished me.

But that's what being a tap addict is all about. ■

That's Gregory dancing with daughter Daria at her wedding and him laughing on Francis Ford Coppola's lap on The Cotton Club *set. The rest of the shots are of—what else?—feet.*

Sole Sisters—Les Grandes Dames and Prima Tapperinas

The curtain is about to go up at La Mama, Experimental Theater Company. Well, there's no curtain, actually, but the Sole Sisters, my first all women's tap troupe, are steadfastly going over routines backstage, and I'm nervous.

Only women in this show?

This is a culmination of my years tracking down the hoofers and finally coming up with some grandes dames. There are no flashy feet among us save for Brenda Bufalino, who, like the guys, can bring down the house.

She's the sole sister who mentored me early in the game, giving me the basic understanding that tap dancing was jazz. Only ten years my senior, Brenda straddled both generations, and during the Drought had worked in nightclubs doing a lot of jazz and Afro-Cuban dancing before moving to the country to raise two sons in upstate New Paltz, New York. She couldn't stop dancing up there, although, for a while, like most hoofers, she hung up her shoes, too. In her youth, she not only had studied with Stanley Brown, but had become the student protégé and then dancing partner to Honi Coles.

Pre-tap, I had listened to rock and roll mostly and danced free form to music like The Grateful Dead's "Sugar Magnolia" in Cambridge. When I listened to Brenda preach the gospel of jazz tap to a bunch of workshop students gathered around a campfire every night in the Catskills, I realized she was one of the people I had sat with at my first Copasetics Ball. We hadn't connected at that scene.

But in the Catskills, I was glued to her every word, and even began a weekly two-hour bus trek up to New Paltz to study with her. I'd stay overnight at her house, right across the road from a horse farm. My eyes bulged as I watched her cook spaghetti, using tons of olive oil. Goodbye to Weight Watchers, again, I'd tell myself, even if it was *extra virgin* olive oil. Under her tutelage, I got better feet, more technique, but I didn't really want to join

"Career vs. Family"—I opted for tap. Sole Sisters nursing the art (clockwise from lower left) Beverly Rolfsmeir, Sarah Safford (with sleeping [real] Molika), Marion Coles, Mable Lee, Harriet Browne, Jo McNamara.

Brenda Bufalino

any company. Brenda was one of the first women I had talked to about the dearth of tapping women.

She had mentioned then that women were always trained to look pretty and that the prejudices went back a long way, that women weren't supposed to express their drives. Well, we were certainly expressing some of ours in *Sole Sisters*. Brenda was a soloist in both seasons of the show. What *Sole Sisters* was ultimately about was community and collaboration.

As we are going over Marion Coles' intricate flowing moves to Sy Oliver's big band number, "For Dancers Only," I'm also trying to concentrate on my opening lines. "I love to talk, ya-ta-da, ya-ta-da . . . I love to tap, bop-be-da, bop-be-da . . . I love to tap while I talk, ya be-bop, boo-dah . . . I love to talk about tap." I repeat my lines a few times. I have lines! I'm in my own Off-Broadway production, billed as theater, not just dance.

I'm so proud to be here, watching all the women, my "grandes dames and prima tapperinas" warming up, testing their feet on this crummy old floor that looks like cardboard and sounds like it, too. Ellen Stewart, La Mama herself, didn't want us tapping on her old, dirty wood floor, so she had us cover it with this sorry sheet of Masonite.

Sole Sisters '85. Left to right: Sarah Safford, holding baby Molly, Harriet Browne, Mable Lee, Jane, Beverly Rolfsmeir, Marion Coles, Jo McNamara.

Oh, well, I lost that battle, but I still won the war.

In 1985 and 1986, Sole Sisters is a happening thing in New York City. At first it was a hard sell. But when TV's "Good Morning America" came to film us, I was riding high. Sole Sisters was a novelty! Sole Sisters was a great concept! Sole Sisters was an idea whose time had come. Tap had been male-dominated for so long. The idea for an all-women's show came from Sarah Safford and Beverly Rolfsmeir, two of the sisters I'd worked with a lot at the time, who, like most of us, found themselves eclipsed by the heavy black male tap tradition that they had chosen to study, absorb, and embrace. So we decided to establish the Sole Sisters Social Club. No guys telling us what to do. No one trying to one-up another sister. We had no prima donnas among us.

Issue-oriented tap. That's what we're doing, we ladies of the '80s. One of my number's tonight is "Career vs. Family," a collaboration with my writer friend Susan Woolhandler about feeling like I have to choose between having a family or dancing. *Newsweek Magazine* has just come out with its big cover story about women in my age group having a better chance of being the victims of a terrorist attack than of getting married. In the dance, I use a whisk and pot to stir up some percussion while I'm tapping and talking, running commentary over the feet. ("Every time there was a hijacking, I used to think my chances were improving."). Ironically, I would become a victim of a terrorist attack, vacating my apartment, mere blocks from the World Trade Center, on 9/11.

My friend and colleague, Sarah Safford gave birth to her first baby, Molly, in December of 1984. Sarah choreographed a number called, "Post Partum Blues," in which she croons with her six-month-old daughter riding on top of her shoulders. It's the big hit of the show, an original, a novelty for sure.

"Post Partum, Post Partum Blues, da–da–da–da–da . . . We got 'em, Post Partum Blues, da–da– da– da . . . Every mother gets 'em, Post Partum Blues—da–da . . . Then she soon forgets them . . . Post Partum Blues . . . If you wanna be a mama, you gotta sing those Post Partum Blues."

Almost all the Sole Sisters are in this number. What a thrill it was watching Sarah teach the older women brand new steps. The ladies were game, too. And everyone fell in love with baby

Sarah Safford

Dorothy Wasserman

Molly, taking turns holding her while they learned the dance. Sarah was the brain behind a lot of my earlier shows, too, including *Tapping and Talking Dirty*, where both of us realized one day in the loft where we rehearsed, that we both enjoyed talking about sex. *While we tap-danced.*

We would trade time steps while taking turns discussing what turned us on, what turned us off! Sarah made up the words for a piece about condoms. We never really talked "dirty," à la Lenny Bruce, but it was always fun performing that act with Sarah on the occasions we got bookings. Some of our friends even wanted to sell the act to the Playboy Channel with real Bunnies doing our bits, but we didn't go for it. Sarah's irony and humor proved liberating for both audiences and for me. She moved me into a form that I realized suited me best—talking and tapping.

At events like the *Sex and Dance Festival* at P.S. 122, a progressive performing space, there were even Q&A sessions. Well-versed in women's health issues—Sarah once used a Frisbee to demonstrate the virtues of the diaphragm. She also possessed an incredible memory and ability to steal steps. Things really took off, when, joined by our pal Dorothy Wasserman, we began taking our performance piece, *The Rhythm Method*, to a variety of cutting-edge venues from Manhattan to Chattanooga, Tennessee.

Finding the female veterans was trickier than finding the men. Marion Coles never told me she was a dancer when I called her home looking for her husband, Honi. Harriet Brown, known for her sand dancing, remained in the shadow of Sandman Sims. Whenever I asked the old male hoofers where the women were, they would usually all fall back into some strange ingrained habit of referring to long-gone women like Louise Madison, Juanita Pitts, or The Whitman Sisters. Or pipe up about the more renowned ones like Eleanor Powell or Ann Miller.

Maybe the male hoofers I knew didn't feel that their female counterparts should be unearthed. Maybe they just didn't know where they were, or what happened to them. But one thing was clear. The old male hoofers were romanticized, while the women were most definitely not. Just like in all professions, I thought. Especially with dancers, it was also a lot cooler to be a young woman.

As I peek behind the scrim to check out the audience buzz, I see Tommy Tune talking to Gregory Hines. I'm looking for Gloria Steinem, who I'm told is here tonight; I heard she was a closet hoofer herself. I also spot Bess Myerson, former Miss America, and now in Mayor Koch's administration. There's one of my writers, Murray Horwitz, listening to the World Series on his walkman. This is 1986, and The Mets and Red Sox are battling it out. My show is competing with this most important World Series!

I turn around and see Josephine McNamara, our veteran Irish step dancer, struggle with her tap routines. Jazz isn't her base, but she's a true trouper and learns how to syncopate. Marion is buttoning Jo Mac's orange costume. Jo had looked so authentic in her green get-up, but that was before we discovered that Ellen Stewart was superstitious about any performer wearing green in her theater. So, at the last minute, Jo had to find herself another costume.

Miriam Greaves-Ali is fixing the bells she's given everyone to wear for her South African boot dance. Dorothy is showing Frances Nealy the third step of her version of the Shim Sham. Constance Valis Hill, our director, is now giving us all last minute instructions, eyeing the costumes carefully. She's a tapper, too, with a great sense of structure and a deep understanding and love for the art.

New Sole Sisters '86. Brenda Bufalino, Jo McNamara, Miriam Greaves-Ali, Harriet Browne, Dorothy Wasserman, Frances Nealy, Sarah Safford, moi, in costume for "The Man I Love."

I am used to having trouble every time I put on a show, but these women are all supportive and really into the cause at hand—demonstrating the power of women in tap. Even when my piano player quits two days before opening night, good karma comes my way and I find Joyce Brown. Barry Saperstein (Gregory's best friend and drummer), has turned me on to her after I've made a million phone calls. Joyce can play both jazz and show tunes, just what we need. It was like looking for ten fingers in New York City, and coming up with Mary Lou Williams.

Marion and Sarah are sitting on chairs, now, going over "How Am I to Know?", the chair dance that Marion made up to accommodate Sarah's advanced pregnancy. "*Oh, how am I to know/is this really love/that's found its way, dear,*" Mable Lee croons a-capella nearby as the pair sit side by side, going over the gorgeous routine Marion has choreographed. Mable Lee, the soloist "tap mommy," has on this sexy top, showing lots of cleavage, her black skirt split up the sides. You'd never have guessed she was a grande dame in her late sixties. One of the chairs is losing a leg. This whole place feels rickety. But it's got an avant-garde cache, a good place for my all-women's tap show.

Frances Nealy looks very youthful, too, what with her gorgeous slim leggy frame, dark complexion, and snazzy royal blue pantsuit. The pants somehow loosen during her performance and slide down her legs. The audience cracks up when she just pulls them off in a huff, reflecting some kind of joie de vivre and surrender instead of embarrassment.

I had been so glad to bring Frances in for her first trip to the East Coast. I could hear her hesitation on the phone all the time, but I really wanted her to be part of Sole Sisters. At sixty-eight years old, she deserved a trip to New York City. She was celebrating her birthday during the run, so we ended up getting her a great big chocolate cake, which we all ate after one of the rehearsals. Frances was able to stay as a guest up on the top floor of La Mama's building complex. At least Ellen Stewart gave us that—a guest room for out-of-town performers.

"The main advantage I've got over you young people is my experience," I overhear Frances telling Sarah. "I was *THERE!*"

Harriet Brown has now moved over to her sandbox. This is going to be a hassle: all that sand on the stage. I love the silver glitter shoes she is wearing. She gives me a pair of them, which I still treasure; they make a huge statement, like Dorothy's red slippers in *The Wizard of Oz*. I also love my own red and purple-heeled pumps. They have a ring to them. It's great when taps ring. There's nothing that can beat a good Morgan tap. My shoes sing.

New Sole Sisters Social Club: From bottom left: Harriet Brown, in left box, Miriam Greaves-Ali center, Frances Nealy, right bottom box.

"Tapping and Talking Dirty," an act Sarah Safford and I created, dealing with sexuality and what else: tap dancing!

I also have on this neat green dress with different colored feathers streaming from the waist, a costume I've borrowed from New York's fabulous Costume Center. That's where I procured the tuxedos and top hats for the first number, "The Man I Love." The audience is going to crack up when they see all the sole sisters dressed as men and dancing to that song, while I'm eternally looking for my partner.

This show is as close as I get to making my fantasy of finding a dance partner a reality. I don't find the prince. But I get the reality that it's the ball that's the answer, for the moment anyway, not the guy.

Even though Marion Coles had told us it was a compliment in her day to be told you danced like a man, isn't this better—tap dancing like a woman in the 1980s? I can't wait to get out there and do my thing.

I hear the overture. I'm no longer Cookie's sidekick. I have to open the show by myself in the dark. Just me and my feet. I'm out there alone, the Star looking for a partner and, instead, finding romance in Sisterhood. It's not the partner; it's the ball itself—la dance—that is the perfectly swell romance. ∎

Always looking for The Partner: (Hint: It's the ball, not the guy).

Hollywood and Trading Eights

"Real Life, R-E-A-L, is very different from Reel Life, R-E-E-L, my dear."
—From my interview with Ginger Rogers, 1976, The Waldorf-Astoria

S uddenly, Hollywood was calling.

I first heard about the movie *TAP* from Gregory, who showed me an early version of the script. By 1988, it was all coming together—a Hollywood musical starring Hines, Sammy Davis, Jr., and featuring a teenaged Savion Glover and some of the old hoofers. My people! A movie that didn't just use tap to further the plot, but used the plot to further tap dancing. My kind of movie!

I was to make my Hollywood debut as one of the four Shim Sham dancers featured in a nightclub scene. Dorothy Wasserman, Dianne Walker, Frances Nealy, and I were to be the students of the leading lady (Suzzanne Douglass), who perform at a Times Square club on Tuesday nights, hoofer's night. Each of us easily had fifteen years over Suzzanne in the tap department and Frances Nealy had, at seventy-one, a lot more. Nonetheless, Suzzanne, with her charisma, could pull off looking like our leader.

In *TAP*, director/writer Nick Castle, Jr. has Sammy Davis, Jr. cast as "Little Mo," a visionary sage, who can see tap dancing's future in Max Washington (Gregory), a dancer whose career has been derailed by his criminal pursuits. Hobbled by age, wearing one of those do-rags like the ones I'd seen Cookie and Bubba and other hoofers wear to mat their hair down before a show, Little Mo (Sammy) hears Max practicing in his old studio and knows the prodigal son has returned to take up his role as present-day champ.

The movie opens with Max, behind prison bars, tapping to the rhythm of dripping water while his cellmates are screaming at him to quiet down. His hair is dyed an angry red and he is all bulked up from bodybuilding. He is returning to tap roots, merging the old tap sound with a new concept—*volume.*

The night shoot on the backlot of Universal Studios, 1988. Gregory (to the right of the hard hat) watching intently as Frances and I rehearse one cold April evening. Dianne Walker and Dorothy Wasserman are on the sides waiting their turn.

Gregory liked his taps turned up, *LOUD*. He once told me he wanted his contribution to tap to be in terms of volume. Nick Castle and Gregory use tap dancer Al Desio's invention combining tap and electronics, Tap-Tronics™ to bring Gregory's penchant for volume to reel life.

Max reunites with Mo's daughter, his old flame Amy, a single mom, who runs the dance studio where the old legends hang out and play cards most of the time. Amy gets Max to audition for a Broadway choreographer, the villain in the movie, so Max can get a "real" job dancing. Making a living at tap dancing had always been one of Gregory's big concerns. *TAP* also touches on a huge debate among tap dancers of the '80s: Which was the real thing: Broadway (or show) tap or the more acoustical John Bubbles kind of rhythm tap?

Castle Jr., whose father Nick Sr. directed and choreographed for such dancers as Fred Astaire, Gene Kelly, The Nicholas Brothers, Eleanor Powell, and Bill Bojangles Robinson, got the "go" from Tri-Star Pictures to pay tribute to his dad's and tap's glory days. Through the tap-vine, word spread quickly that there was finally going to be a big-deal movie musical that would put tap back on the map.

I wrote Nick Castle, Jr. my impressions of the early script, and soon his casting director was calling me to ask how she might contact the old hoofers. I was also

©CHANGING TIMES TAP ARCHIVE

Jane with director/writer Nick Castle, Jr., on TAP *set, 1988.*

Ralph Brown, of hot pink tap shoes, 1978, at Village Vanguard.

asked to sit in on the New York auditions. Screen Actors Guild (SAG) casting directors—even if they know the performers they want—are required to hold open auditions. I was rooting for all my tap daddies.

A particularly sad moment was watching veteran headliner, Ralph Brown, audition. He could barely stand up that afternoon. Ralphy, as I called him, had worn hot pink tap shoes when we worked together at the Village Vanguard ten years earlier. I can still see him sitting in his skivvies as he held court in the Vanguard kitchen, telling stories in his sweet southern drawl.

Ralph had been known for his specialty, "Heel-ology," in which he'd lean back on his heels, click his pink-shod toes across a long diagonal, all the while balancing along the narrow straight line. On that audition day, however, Ralphy looked like a worn-out boxer trying to get back into the ring. He fell, got up, started to dance a little, and then moved to another part of the floor as if a new spot might cut him some slack.

Fourteen-year-old Savion Glover livened up the afternoon by peppering his marvelously fast routines with flips and splits. I'd seen other youngsters audition too that day, but Savion was peerless when it came to the dancing. He zoomed in and out of the room in a flash; the casting director kept his mother for a while, repeatedly asking Savion's birthday and schooling, knowing he could easily outgrow the part.

In the early version of the script, Max's father, the fictional Sonny Washington, whom we never meet in the

The teenaged Savion Glover on the set of TAP, *1988.*

movie, is purported to have been one of the greats, but died broke and of a broken heart as well, a down-and-out hoofer trying to eke out a living doing tap-a-grams, the hoofer equivalent of singing telegrams.

In 1987, the year before I read the script, I was trying to make a living that way. I had even run down to City Hall to trademark the name, expecting every other tap dancer to pick up on it. (They didn't). It was a cool way to earn a hundred dollars a pop.

I tap-a-grammed for an Argentinean corned beef princess and on comedian Robert Klein's new cable TV show. (Klein scolded me for not being listed as Tap-a-Gram™ in the phone book). My new little business was profiled (humorously, but a little pathetically,) on the front page of *The New York Times'* popular Metro section. I "grammed" for one of Twyla Tharp's board members, singing "Twy-la-la-la-la" to "Deck the Halls." I met guys tap-a-gramming.

The "gram" business was thriving in New York in the 1980s. People were hired to do gorilla-grams, strip-a-grams, belly-grams, all kinds of gimmicky things. I ran small ads in *New York Magazine*. I was no desperate tap-a-grammer. I liked writing the jingles and carrying my little three-by-three foot roll-up mat all over the city.

Gregory wanted my tap associate Dorothy's Shim Sham in *TAP*. He had first seen her take on the Shim Sham, tap's national anthem, in my all-woman show, *Sole Sisters* in 1985 and thought it was something new for tap. The Shim Sham is a kind of throwaway dance, something all tap dancers know; audience members and other hoofers often come up onstage and perform it as a way of bringing people together for a grand finale. It's a relaxed dance, although the Dorothy Shim Sham is anything but. You have to be right on top of it to stay on it.

The regular Shim Sham is danced to a thirty-two-bar chorus with the rhythm changing every eight bars. Dorothy's Shim Sham is much more syncopated. She got her inspiration from the original chorus by Leonard Reed, who made it up from social dance steps, right on the spot, to a live audience. (I was in a cab once with him, and his story sounded true; as tapping reporter, you had to learn to decipher some tales).

Dorothy's Shim Sham, I thought, was our tight-knit quartet's ticket to success. In the early morning of our first day out West, we were whisked from our Hollywood Holiday Inn, deposited in a limousine, and driven through black neighborhoods to East Los Angeles, where one of the local clubs had been reconfigured for the film as "Charlie's," a night spot in Times Square. Sitting in my black sexy cleavagy dress near the stage, swaying to blues singer Etta James, I was in heaven. Everyone on the set was busy busy busy, bright lights and cameras all over the place. It was easy to get into Etta's groove.

It was thrilling to see how excited everyone got about the project. Grips, stagehands, first and second directors, the director of photography, even some of the producers were trying out steps on the set. "Hurry up and wait," the famous movie axiom, provided to be true, but all that waiting time was good for working out new combinations. My obsession over the years had become everyone's, everyone's on the movie set, anyway.

⁓

In a field where schadenfreude is rampant, it was hardly surprising when the mumbling and grumbling began, soon after the first rehearsals in a Venice Beach studio. I started to feel competitive with my sole sisters, Dianne and Dorothy. Some catty extras wanted to know how *I* got in the movie without auditioning.

With her lanky frame and long blonde hair, my pal Dorothy proved an attraction to all the guys on the set. Even in rollers and without makeup, she was a knock out. Plus, she was the choreographer for our big number and this gave her special status. But I didn't want to rehearse her Shim Sham for the millionth time. I'd learned it three years before, in *Sole Sisters*, my show, and she made me practice it with her before we even got to Hollywood. I wanted to be on the beach. After all, this was warm, mellow, laid back, sunny Los Angeles in April! I know I should have been more into the Hollywood thing, but days to me were a beach day or not a beach day. The weather pulled me. Every day was a beach day out there.

Frances got her kvetching in too, complaining that there wasn't sufficient time for rehearsals to learn this new syncopated version of the dance for a big splashy movie like *TAP*. Still, Frances lived in Hollywood. She could leave at the end of the day and go home, away from the increasingly unhealthy vibe.

My other girlfriend on the set, Dianne "Lady Di" Walker, who had great chops and a real sense of elegance, saw what serious feet there were hunkering down on us. This was no high-heeled dainty affair, and Dianne recognized that fact immediately. Gregory's consistent presence at rehearsals raised the bar high. He was a purist. Dianne went, "Ooooooooohhhh,

©PHOTO BY TOM NIEMAN

Dianne Walker aka "Lady Di": She got to wear her own costume in the movie.

I see what's going on," and replaced her high heels with well-broken-in men's shoes right in front of the main choreographer Henry LeTang, whom she'd worked with before in the show, *Black & Blue*, and who preferred high heels to the flats on women.

To dance like a man had always been perceived as a compliment. Dianne could not only lay down the irons, and beat the boards; she was the only one of us Shimmering Shimmettes (as we were called on the set) who could come close to hitting hard when she had to. The old veterans were paying attention to her—men like Bunny Briggs, Sandman Sims, Jimmy Slyde, Gregory's father, Maurice, Sr. This was hard core shoe/show business now, and I began to feel threatened.

In addition, I was unhappy with my costume, a pink horizontal striped skirt and sleeveless pink blouse. Here we were, all of us convinced we were on the edge of fame, and I was stuck in this *schmatta* for a month. I had squeaked through my first scene with Etta James in that black sexy-cleavage number I brought from home, but the costume designer saw the rushes and told me that black didn't work. I hid the pink outfit in my trailer for a while, but weighing the few other options given, succumbed to the pink.

Horizontal stripes! My mother had told me never to wear horizontal stripes. They made you look wider. Dianne and Frances got to wear their own clothes. Dianne was in her signature black pants and white jacket, Frances in some blue shirt over black pants. Dorothy was in boring beige but she looked good in anything. So did Suzzanne, the lead, although her pink prom-like dress was as corny as could be.

"The Shimmering Shimmettes" at "Charlie's." Left to right: Me, Frances Nealy, Dorothy Wasserman, and Dianne Walker (hidden) behind Suzzanne Douglass, "Amy," our teacher.

Did she have any say in the matter? I wondered. I felt like Hester Prynne condemned to her Scarlet Letter when my pink outfit arrived, freshly pressed in my trailer each day. Even Gregory, passing me on the set, cooed sympathetically, "Next time, Jane." What a jerk! What next time?

I had starved myself for that flick. One of my close friends in New York had warned me I should be concerned about what I would look like on celluloid a hundred years from now in "That's Entertainment 3000." I soon began to worry if the camera loved me. Nonetheless, as I scurried off to the makeup trailer, I acted blasé, and pretended getting my hair done and face painted at 7 a.m. was part of my normal routine.

During a final rehearsal before the shoot, Frances was still having a rough time getting Dorothy's third step—a long slide to the front, with a lot of syncopation. Somebody, maybe Nick or Gregory or Henry LeTang, spotted us all clustered around her, coaching her in a circle. Even in that competitive atmosphere, we all still wanted everyone to look good. They decided our being in a circle was the way to shoot the dance.

While the "go" of the script was unchangeable and built around the men, the women's dancing was decorative and improvised from the get go. After the Dorothy Shim Sham chorus, Gregory came up with a step to finish the dance in a line, presumably to get us off stage. Then, to top it off, he came up with a plan to have us trade eights, eight four-bar phrases of music, which each of us had to make our own.

CHALLENGE! The big challenge scene had already happened a week earlier, amongst the old guys, all staged to show off each man's specialty. We weren't shown that consideration. Trading eights, to me, was a euphemism for the Challenge, a true set-up for competition and one-upsmanship. I totally hated that part of tap's tradition and found it to be arcane. I take that back. I don't mind watching the Challenge, but I don't want to be a part of one. Gregory loved every bit of it, every minute of watching people compete. He loved a good challenge, any kind of competition. To me, his plan reeked of machismo, competition for the sake of competition.

Frances had a good eight because she came out of the old school of tap; she *was* the old school of tap! Dianne had an eight. Her main mentor, Leon Collins, loved being in the ring and taught his protégées—his angels—as he called them—all about survival tactics. He made sure his dancers knew plenty of pocket steps, too, those steps you could pull out of your pocket in a pinch, if you had to. Dianne was as ready as anyone could be.

Dorothy and I didn't have any eights. Cookie never gave killer eights. Sure, we were dancing in thirty-two-bar choruses, but so many of them were soft, melodic, not braggadocio Muhammad Ali turns.

Dorothy and I had to spend time in our own depressing carpeted hotel rooms working out our eights. I rebelled. I was going to wing it, that's what I'd do. So there! In my anxiety over this new development, I went to a telephone booth during a long break, right on the beach, and called a guy I was dating back in New York. I wasn't even very close to Steven, but he was sympathetic to my plight. He told me to try and calm down, that eights weren't *my thing*, anyway. I was a comedy dancer, Rhythm & Schmooze, remember?

Tell that to Gregory Hines, I wanted to say to Steven, but I tried to take in his soothing words.

At dawn, on "the day of the eights," Gregory asked me to show him mine. I told him I was going to wing it, of course, the way you do in a real Challenge, and his look said, "No Way." Gregory surprised me by leading me to a small area in the shadow of the nightclub stage. He made me meticulously go over every bar of music I could come up with to create my eight. Legs straddled over the chair, he watched me repeat each phrase until I had my eight down. It was just like studying with my tap daddies. I loved being spoon fed like that. What a baby! I treasured that moment with Gregory, though.

I needed this kind of close attention in Hollywood and especially from him. I was used to riding my bike right into his loft at home and hanging out, talking tap. But this was Hollywood and this movie was his *baby*. Now, I had to knock formally at his trailer door when I wanted to see him. Once, I walked in when he and his father were watching a fight on television and he asked me why I was crying. I told him it was because I was so happy to be involved in a movie about tap dancing.

That was a big fat lie, though. I was feeling increasingly alienated, disconnected from reality. It now made total sense to me why, during a previous film, he was constantly calling his wife from *The Cotton Club* set. That was a local call! Then he was only a borough away from home in Astoria, Queens, and he still needed a reality check.

I was in California, and knew hardly anyone. Being on a movie set full of gigantic egos can set you back some. I was crying because that talk with Steven, even a guy I wasn't that tight with, had been my first reality check with the outside world. After two weeks, it had become all too easy to mistake "reel life" for "real life."

In the end, our eights were edited out, plus most of the only dance number performed exclusively by women. The Shim Sham girls were barely talking to each other after that first scene, except for Frances. We all talked to her. Sandman got more screen time *during* our dance than any of us, either solo or collectively, shouting something to me—yes, moi—"Hey, Jane! You're stealing my step!" The editor went haywire

Mickey Mouse paraphernalia at Martha Urann's.

with Sandman shouting rather than us dancing. If you drop your remote, you'll miss our entire scene!

Lying in bed each night in my hotel room, I thought I was beginning to go nuts. I was losing it, descending into a full-fledged clinical depression. I wasn't being paranoid either, when during the filming of my eight, I heard the actor playing the Broadway choreographer villain tell the leading lady in a loud voice-over, "I see you're dancing with older women."

Older women? During *my* eight? Was that line written into the script? Hallucination time!

Between the Dorothy Shim Sham and the night shoot, I stayed with another protégée of modern dancer Claire Mallardi, comedian Martha Urann. She tried to show me some of the Hollywood ropes. Sitting in her kitchen filled wall-to-wall, floor-to-ceiling with Mickey Mouse paraphernalia, Martha told me how everyone drops in on people on the set, even if they're not in the movie, just to schmooze, to see and be seen. She tried to convince me to milk my friendship with Gregory and ask for a close-up or "special moment" on film.

She advised me to try some past life therapy. We were, after all, in the land of southern California's New Age. I almost did it, too, but then became practically paralyzed with fear, panic attacks setting in left and right.

Even off the set, I still wondered if the camera loved me. I kept waking up at 4 a.m. battling my insomnia by reading excerpts from a book called, "You Can Heal Your Life."

A week later, we were all back at our Holiday Inn hotel rooms in Hollywood, in the midst of a night shoot. Lunch was served at midnight, and we worked from 6 p.m. until dawn on a sequence called "Sounds of the City." It was unusually cold for April now at night, in Los Angeles, which made it a shivery week in heated trailers. Sometimes we had to be covered up in blankets between takes.

Each group of dancers had its own mini-set, and hoofers were always breaking out all over the Universal back lot, tapping on their specified turf.

I developed a little crush on the actor who played vibes, the character who tries to show Max how tap can be amplified to suit contemporary tastes. He

appeared to be a leftover hippie bouncing out chords like some Jerry Lee Lewis in a tie-dyed t-shirt. He looked like they'd just picked him up off of Venice Beach. Maybe they had! He was always in some enlightened groove as they shot us speeding out of "Charlie's" following Max, to witness all the rhythms the machinery in the streets made, "The Sounds of the City."

You could see Savion cuddled with his mother, or shooting imaginary hoops, lapping it all up. Tap dancing would just be breaking out everywhere, like sudden bursts of gunfire in a guerrilla war, but in this case, lovely bursts of rhythm. There would be sudden eruptions, like brush fires, everybody ignited, keeping the set warm, full of energy and life.

Except for me. I couldn't get into the spirit of it all. I loved the music, too, but I hated the hours. My arthritic right knee couldn't tolerate the damp cold. I wanted to feel part of the elation, but I was like some kind of party pooper. I even got insanely jealous when Sammy went over to a fellow tapper one night to tell her he liked the way she handled her feet. I wanted him to like my feet, too!

The Shim Sham girls operated on a mini-set that had a forklift modality. Jumping up and down on this crummy piece of plywood and concrete wasn't my idea of Hollywood stardom. We were in an emporium of cold. Did Ginger Rogers have to suffer through this kind of stuff on her night shoots when she jumped those tiger lilies to meet Fred's arms in *Carefree*? Maybe, but I bet she had her own heated trailer and say on what costumes she wore.

Why had this strange feeling of powerlessness swept over me? Used to asserting myself, running my own shows, I totally succumbed to the Hollywood system. Feeling lost and ineffective, worried about losing Gregory's respect, I couldn't heal my life!

"Reel" life and "real" life had merged for me. It was an uncomfortable fit. ■

Cast/class photo (left to right back row): Frances Nealy, Arthur Duncan, Dorothy Wasserman, Harold Nicholas, Suzzanne Douglass, Henry LeTang, me, Gregory, Bunny Briggs, (seated in front l–r): Ruddy L. Garner, Sandman Sims, Dianne Walker, Pat Rico, Sammy Davis, Jr. Bottom photo: Jane and Bunny with line of "New York" taxis on the Universal back lot.

Sammy Groupie

When Sammy Davis, Jr. arrived on the set of *TAP*, he didn't walk; he strutted. And he looked right at home in the world of hoofers, the "hustlers of the feet." That's what tap vet Bunny Briggs called the vintage black tap dancers from the old school.

Sammy stood out, though. Barely five feet tall, he looked so tiny and thin except for that gigantic smile and shiny glass eye. He gave new meaning to the words "larger than life." He was Vegas, Rat Pack, Mr. Showbiz, but still reeked of hoofer authenticity as he traded stories about Buck and Bubbles, the big band era, and everything else "back then." Sammy was always surrounded by his entourage of managers, agents, family, hangers-on.

I had never really been a Sammy fan, vaguely recalling that notorious incident when he hugged President Nixon, but little else. I had seen him perform live two years earlier at a benefit in Newark for the American Lung Association. I hollered approval when he pulled out his tap shoes from under the piano and started dancing. I wanted him to know there was a member of the tribe in the audience. My main focus had been with the guys underground, the underdog tappers. Sammy was no underdog.

We Shim Sham dancers and extras were eagerly anticipating Sammy's first scene with us. As we gabbed, waiting for him to arrive, the man himself appeared as if out of nowhere, jumped onstage, and said:

"You kids want to know where we got our material? Well, we *stol'd* it!"

Lots of laughter.

"But no one knew how Sonny Washington got his," Sammy confided. "He was an original."

Sammy Davis, Jr.: He didn't walk; he strutted.

Sammy and Savion: on the set.

Everything around me slowly became a blur, the way it looked in the *West Side Story* dance at the gym scene when the Jets and Sharks fade into the background, leaving the lovestruck Tony and Maria isolated in their own little world. Except this time it was Sammy and me.

Sonny Washington, Sonny Washington . . . The name sounded so familiar. Had I met him at a nightclub on Chicago's south side when I was performing at the Goodman Theater? I couldn't believe Sammy knew this dancer, too.

"I know where Sonny got his steps!" I yelled. "He got them from Al and Toody."

"Cut!"

The first assistant director rudely interrupted my train of thought and my ad hoc shout. The line producer barked something at me. My friend, Dianne Walker, sitting next to me, whispered urgently, "Jane! Stop watching the movie. You're *IN* the movie!" I'd ruined the first take of the day. It turned out Sammy was delivering his lines, not talking to me.

From that moment on, I became a full-fledged Sammy groupie. I was mesmerized by his acting and tried to watch all of his scenes. I wanted to find out what made him tick, what made him tap. I followed his every move. My memory of him hugging Nixon vanished.

I discreetly eavesdropped as he laughed in between takes with the other elders and told stories about the mob, the nightclubs, how great Buddy Rich was. Even though his devoted entourage always surrounded him, I managed to be there, too. I wanted to connect with him in some deep way, and to have him come to know me in my true incarnation—*The Tap Goddess of the Lower East Side.*

⸺⁙⸺

I had plenty of opportunity to keep watch over my new idol. Naturally, I encountered obstacles. Nearly everybody on the set was on a first-name basis, but that didn't mean that everybody was friendly. I managed to alienate Sammy's ever-present manager, Shirley, by landing hard on one of her high heels. I had been trying to get Sammy's attention and she was in my way. Murphy, his other loyal sidekick, was friendlier, but plainly didn't want strangers around.

Desperate, I pulled on my invisible reporter hat and convinced the Tri-Star people that, as an insider, I could scoop the story and generate press. Through much pestering and hanging out, even remaining in Los Angeles during the Shim Sham dancers' one-week break, I convinced Tri-Star to let me interview Sammy.

So, on the appointed afternoon, accompanied by three Tri-Star escorts, I entered Sammy's trailer thinking, *alone at last*! To my surprise and disappointment, his whole entourage was there, sitting at a table, playing poker. It was like being in a busy diner, squished in between booths.

I tripped over my first lines. This seemed so silly, so formal. I began again: Had Sammy ever stopped tap dancing?

"I didn't stop per se," he said, in that clear, clipped, precise, affected British voice. He paused for a moment. "It just didn't become an end-all or be-all of my act. Just like impersonations at one time—impersonations became the most important part of my act. Then singing became so."

"Was that because you thought tap was dying out?" I asked.

To me, the showbiz old guard always sounded so much in control of their lives, at least in the retelling. There was never indecision, never any self-doubt. They always knew in advance what their next career move would be.

Sammy was always surrounded by his entourage of manager, agent, hangers-on..

"It had nothing to do with fashion," he replied, a bit impatiently. "Nothing to do with anything artistic. At a certain time, you have to make a move for theatrical reasons and tap dancing was not the style I wanted; it wasn't superstar enough. Tap was a good appendage."

I began coughing. The card game was still going strong right beside us; cigarette smoke was swirling in my face.

"Still, I always kept my shoes in the piano," he continued. "Subsequently, by not tap dancing for a couple of years, I started to re-tap dance eight or nine years ago. It was a rediscovery. And it was FUN!"

I'd never met a hoofer who talked in such formal sentences, or a veteran who just hung up his shoes when he was good and ready. Most of the guys I knew went into involuntary retirement when tap died out.

Like La Ray, Selva taps disappeared, too.

"Have you always had the same shoes?" I asked, admiring his funny loafers. I wondered how he kept a pair of loafers on his feet while hopping around in a time step.

"Yes, and La Ray taps," he answered.

"They don't make La Ray anymore," I said, trying to impress him.

"I know they don't," he shot back. We continued talking floors, shoes, and taps for a while. What with all the shoptalk, maybe he'd start calling me by my first name soon. And, we'd be sharing a few steps.

I asked him about his favorite musicians and when he got done reminiscing about Count Basie, Duke Ellington, and the Dorsey Brothers, I still wanted to know why Sammy thought tap had fallen on hard times.

"See, the tap dances didn't live like the music," I said, quoting an article I'd published years before.

"Tap never made the leap the music made," I continued. "It didn't get recorded or documented. The music got recorded, but the same tap dances performed to that music didn't. You can disagree, of course."

The groupie was nervous.

"You know tap's an art form that belongs to the people," he said. "Everybody thinks he can tap dance. Not everybody thinks he can do ballet. I know a lot of people who tell me 'I just want to be able to tap dance.'

"All that stuff we talk about in the script—it was not just folklore then—it was actually happening. Sessions on streets, newcomers, guys saying: 'Did you see that step, man?' I remember anyone that was worth his salt had to go and learn that punky little flap, heel, toe, and shuffle slap. It's our culture."

I told Sammy about the resurgence of interest in tap in cities like New York, Washington, D.C., Philadelphia, Boston, Los Angeles, and how most of us reviving the art were Gregory's age—baby boomers at the forefront of the tap revival. I almost said, "women" Gregory Hines' age. It was, after all, women who continued to carry the torch when tap went underground. I wanted to talk about feminist feet, the barefooted hippies, Japanese scholars, astrologers, radiologists, modern dancers, and social workers who had stopped what they were doing to begin the long road back to tap and reshape the future.

"Women brought tap back. Did you know that?" I finally blurted.

"To see Gregory live onstage is such a thrill," Sammy crooned, ignoring my last sentence. "He's one of the few guys around that really thrills me for more than two minutes."

"Yeah, he's excited a lot of dancers," I agreed, wondering if Sammy's remark was a compliment. Two minutes didn't seem like a long time to me.

"So, was it always 'guys'?" I asked.

"Yes," he replied quickly.

The Smiling Threesome: Jane, Sammy, Dorothy: We were always on the set taking pictures and getting pictures taken with our "colleagues."

"Yeah, I heard it was considered a man's dance," I murmured.

"Well, there were a few good women around and I'm not being a chauvinistic pig by saying I wasn't exposed to them," Sammy said. "Eleanor Powell was probably the best tap dancer that graced the screen. She had thick heels and could cut anybody she danced with," he laughed. "She made Astaire dance his butt off in 'Begin the Beguine.'"

He hummed a few bars of the Cole Porter tune, as though the music was necessary to conjure the memory. "Because Astaire was always into syncopation, which was basically a black dancer's sound . . . that syncopated sound."

Sammy had finally brought up race. Maybe it wasn't such a big deal for him at that time of his life, but as far as tap was concerned, I had race on my mind most of the time. The 1970s and 1980s were all about race and affirmative action in all things, from college admission to tap dancing.

Race was often *the* unspoken subject between black and white dancers when I was learning about tap. You really had to be trusted to get the truth out of these guys. Riding in a van on our way back from a tap festival, Steve Condos, who was white, once told a story about how Count Basie didn't want to use him, maybe because he was white. Steve seemed embarrassed to tell that story, a negative tale he wished to forget.

Race was like a fault line. It could have been Count Basie's personal taste in dance styles that lost Steve the job. After all, Steve's "transcendental tap" rudiments didn't even fit the Basie groove, but Steve thinking it was racial made it "true." In oral history, if *you* think it's true, it's true. The reality is less important than the perception.

When Sammy's character in *TAP* talked about "the real thing," I knew he was referring to black dancers' contributions. He talked about the "real thing" being on the "third floor." "We don't count five, six, seven, eight," Little Mo hums. "We go, 'uh, uh . . . da dum, uh uh' . . . " He *gets down*, bending low, swinging his knees and "uh-uhing" with extreme coolness. In that smoke-filled trailer, however, I decided not to pursue the issue of race. Sammy's entire entourage was black and I didn't feel safe enough for that discussion with all of them listening in.

"Well, I guess that's it." I squirmed, feeling time was up.

"OK," Sammy agreed, but in no particular hurry.

"You know," he said, as I was getting up, "tap's demise was a combination of things. It wasn't like anybody was out to kill tap dancing. The chorus girls stopped, nightclubs closed. How can you have tap dancing if there are no nightclubs? You can't do it in the comedy stores."

"Right," I lied. I was actually trying to break into stand-up rooms myself, at that time with my act, *Rhythm & Schmooze*. Still, I never pictured myself as a chorus girl hoofing in Vegas.

———

The last time I saw Sammy on the set was during that delirious week of the night-shoot on the renowned Universal Studios back lot. *Good Morning America* came to tape segments of the movie and Sammy was all decked out for the occasion in his full-length leopard skin coat and gold jewelry. He really could act the star.

I had stopped trying to follow him around after the interview in the trailer. But one night during a break, I spotted him completely alone.

I had to make contact one more time. I had to let this original hipster—this man who wore bell-bottoms before anybody else, who married Mae Britt when intermarriage was taboo—know I was hip, too. I darted into his path for my last hurrah.

"Sammy, do you know any *other* Jewish tap dancers besides you and me?" He stared at me as if I was a ghost and, without so much as a word, kept walking.

———

Two years later, I had a conversation with Sammy's mother, Baby Sanchez, at the funeral of one of the legends. I introduced myself to her, giving my full name and telling her that I had had the pleasure of working with her son in the movie *TAP*. She looked up at me and snapped, "Are you the girl in all that publicity, making money off of Charles Cook?"

I stopped in my tracks. I hadn't worked with Cookie in years. At the time, however, another promoter, Susan Goldbetter, also one of Cook's protégées, with a Jewish last name similar to mine, was getting a lot of press for a photo exhibit she had put together called "Cookie's Harlem."

I suggested to Sammy's mother that she might be mistaking me for Susan. I also said pointedly that I didn't think Susan was making a lot of money off of Cookie or the exhibit. Susan was trying to let people know who Charles Cookie Cook was.

Sammy had converted to Judaism because a Jewish doctor saved his life after a motorcycle accident. He always wore the Star of David around his neck. Perhaps his mother had never accepted his conversion.

———

I watched a big television special right before Sammy died, with a lot of entertainers saluting him for his contributions to show business. A teary-eyed Goldie Hawn told the audience how Sammy gave her her first real showbiz break, noticing her go-go dancing in a club.

Gregory shone in that special, too, as he and Sammy traded fours. First Gregory danced to his Apollo theme song. As if he couldn't stop himself, Sammy leaped up on the stage after Gregory finished, no doubt against the doctor's orders. It reminded me of his scene in *TAP* when, as Little Mo, he threw down his cane and began to dance as his daughter, horrified, looked on. In true old school form, Sammy was reclaiming his rightful title; Gregory let the audience know who the authentic champ was as he bent down to kiss both of Sammy's feet. ■

"Hurry up and Wait!" Sammy resting on the set of Sonny's family studio. I had become a full-fledged groupie following his every move.

A Cutting Session
with Gregory Hines

Cutting Session: Jam session where people (men)
try to outdo and out-impress one another.

Floors are everything in tap dancing—how they feel, how they sound, whether they're so fast you slip and slide, or so slow you can barely lift a foot. Some tap dancers are into shoes. My friend Gregory was really into floors.

When I asked him one freezing January morning to meet me at New York University's School of Education building on West 4th Street—where I was teaching at the time—I rationalized, "Gregory Hines will add a moment of history to this floor." The NYU students were out on winter recess, and it was very quiet throughout the urban campus.

I was searching for a tap fix and when Gregory said yes, he felt like dancing, I knew I was in floor trouble immediately.

We were to meet on the top floor of the building, in a studio with an amazing floor. It was made of that blondish-whitish-pinkish hard maple you see sometimes in fancy art galleries. It was vast, gorgeous, easily the centerpiece of the studio. It would be the perfect sounding floor. I had gotten a key from the secretary of the department; otherwise that studio was always locked. And Gregory wasn't just going to add a moment of history to this floor—he was going to clobber it, brutalize it. He tapped so hard and so loud. In 1992, Gregory Hines had ferocious feet.

I adored Gregory and felt free to call him, write letters to him, eat dinner with him, even get into a studio with him, all for the sole purpose of talking tap. I felt special about how he loved talking tap with me. There was something wonderful, intimate, and intense about talking tap with Gregory, discussing the past, present, and future of the art we were both involved in at the same passionate level. As our friendship grew, however, it became increasingly clear that we had fundamental philosophical differences regarding certain issues.

Gregory Hines starring on Broadway in Jelly's Last Jam, *1992.*

Gregory, in afro, with another "Challenger" John Bubbles, at By Word of Foot, 1980.

He, for example, felt The Challenge was the essence of tap tradition and I personally hated it. Gregory liked to talk about champions, about being the best. "Who will be the next king?" he'd wonder, as if tap were a sport like boxing. I felt you couldn't compare artists on those grounds, and had no patience for that kind of thinking.

Gregory was totally into great feet, where I felt tap was a "sensibility". If the dancer had the right attitude, salesmanship, humor, I could just as soon watch closet hoofers and beginners as virtuosos.

Yet whenever we got to the subject of women in tap—women and wardrobe, for example—I saw red! We really locked horns about what constituted feminist or even female feet. We argued a lot, idolized our favorites, debated everything tap.

I used to write him letters from home, artist colonies, on the road. When e-mail entered the picture, Gregory was one of the first to embrace it. He was possibly the Original Mac Fanatic *and* he had never even learned to type. He was downloading, photographing, you name it, with the first Apple computer by Steve Jobs. Some red-hot e's flew between us in the five years before he died.

I lived in New York. Gregory, a native New Yorker, had moved back to Venice Beach, California. Venice Beach was where he'd gone after he'd broken away from his family act, come of age, joined a single father consciousness-raising group, led a rock band, and met two of his three life partners.

I loved absorbing all that Gregory had to say about tap. He was a purist, and true heir to whatever throne there was to be inherited. He had survived The Great Tap Drought. He appreciated my shoot-from-the-hip qualities, and I appreciated that he was a visionary, always intent on moving tap forward.

———

I was feeling a little under the weather on this day, though. My right knee was hurting and I was out of shape. I still wanted a "fix," however, so I decided to set up a warm, sunny, journalistic environment, one in which we could relax.

I brought pictures of tap greats to the studio for him to look at and comment on. I brought sandwiches and fruit. The only thing I forgot was that when Gregory sees a good floor, he turns into a terrorist. When he puts his shoes on, it is all out war. My relaxing atmosphere disintegrated as soon as he walked through the door.

"So, did you get any flak for the Kennedy Center Honors?" I inquired, after our usual big bear hug.

"What happened at Kennedy Center?" he asked, putting down his bag.

"You know, *no women*."

"Turn me on, Jane. Turn me on."

Several weeks before, The Nicholas Brothers had been awarded a Kennedy Center Honors for their contribution to the arts, and Gregory had produced the fifteen-minute sequence honoring the duo. He had hired some of the most talented young lions to dance with him and showcase their own material. At the end of this segment, Gregory jumped up and landed in one of those famous Nicholas Brothers splits—*almost*. When he couldn't get up from his hilariously failed attempt, his cohorts surrounded him to hoist him up. Still, I found it incredible that his lineup included men only.

"I assume you're in the forefront, the vanguard of tapping women," he said. "You have to turn me on to a woman who belongs. Give me names of five women who can challenge each other and hold their own in a show. And it can't look like we had to put a woman in there. Write down five names. You don't have to do it now. Our time is too valuable."

I stared at him in disbelief.

"I'm not your talent scout. You're more tuned in to who's out there than I am. You went around the country auditioning zillions of women for the movie *TAP*.

"But that was a long time ago."

"OK, I'll rise to the occasion," I told him. "But you told me once that you didn't want to hire a token woman, and you said that a woman would either steal the show or drown in it."

"I never said a woman would steal the show." Greg bent down to lace up his shoes.

"You said she might."

"Did I say that?" He looked surprised as he started to warm up, hitting the floor hard from his first sound. "That would be great, and everyone would come right out at the end of the show and she's there to challenge them." He sputtered into a long stream of sound, brushing his right foot back and forth as he zoomed across the width of the studio.

"Does a woman have to challenge in a competitive style?" I asked.

"Well, I like the kind of Challenge, too, where someone is out there and then another person will get out there and go into a completely different rhythm." He proceeded to illustrate a bunch of the old masters' steps while looking intently in the mirrors covering one wall of the studio.

I flashed back to an inspiring, woman-centered speech that Gregory had made at the Mile High Tap Festival in Boulder, Colorado, some six years before. Here we all were at our first Tap Summit, male elders like Eddie Brown, Honi Coles, Steve Condos, Jimmy Slyde, and Bunny Briggs, savvy organizers and scholars like Marda Kirn and Sali-Ann Kriegsman, consciousness-raised women including yours truly, all active in the tap revival and renaissance. Gregory had certainly seemed to be on the side of women back then.

"I've noticed that tap is thought of by people in power situations as a black, male-dominated art. Tap has always had that paternal quality about it since Uncle Bo and Shirley Temple. How people perceive it makes a difference in what happens. We men need to point our fingers at ourselves and get this happening. Ladies do more for tap dancing now. White women have brought the thing back. Something new might come out of it. Equilibrium of the races—it's all there in the tap."

⁓⁓⁓

I came out of my Mile High Boulder reverie. I asked Gregory if his style was changing.

"I'm doing much less pounding," he finally said, after doing about 20,000 spins and landing in an almost-split. "I was trying to force it out before. I wanted it loud. Now, I just hear things differently, lately. And you know, now, because of the floor I had built, I have gotten to the point where I have great stage sound. My stage is consistent. It's got the volume I like. I've been in halls with 2,000 people and I can be really delicate. I still feel driven, but as I'm creating steps I enjoy, I'm perfecting them and I have different steps I've already perfected, and now I'm trying to explore different syncopations.

"You know what I do in my classes?" he continued. "OK, here, I'll do four bars, and you do four bars. I'll do it. Then you do it."

©COURTESY BARRY SAPERSTEIN COLLECTION

"I'm doing much less pounding."

"I'm going to do my own steps!" I barked. "I haven't studied tap in such a long time."

"This will only help your tap dancing," he coaxed. "So, I'm going to do it, and then you're going to do it."

I knew other tappers who would kill for this moment. But though the discussion was hot, my feet didn't feel warm at all.

"Most of the things I've done tap dance-wise have been up tempo. But I remember how thrilling it was—and rarely do I use the word 'thrilling'—when Tommy Tune and Honi Coles did that very slow soft-shoe and we recognized Honi's step. Here, do it with me," he said, taking my hand.

I was giggling by now, my nervous giggle. Gregory always noticed when I giggled. He even referred to it in a speech he gave in my honor years later, saying "Jane may giggle, but when you talk tap with her, you better bring your lunch."

Gregory changed the way tap dancing was performed. He was the granddaddy of funk.

I was getting anxious. Some people, like Gregory, love this kind of pressure and perform well under it. I don't. Gregory was my muse, but *not* my teacher. I had broken out in a cold sweat and I hadn't even moved yet. Fortunately, I remembered Honi's steps: Yap, bop, ba-da ba ba—be de ba—dah, be de ba da bah-bah-bah da . . . repeat . . . yop bop, de bah dada ba, dad a da . . . dad a dada dah dah dah dah . . . smooth like Honi.

"You know the Challenge is such an archaic form, it's a relic," I said, as we sailed through Honi's step. "*You've* even used the word 'arcane' to describe the Challenge," I reminded him. "Right after the movie, *TAP*, I thought for sure you were going to let it go. But there it was again at the Kennedy Center Honors."

"No, no." Gregory corrected, stopping in his tracks. "I'm saying the real Challenge is—somebody gets out there and goes. And then another person has to get out there in that same feel, and then another person and another person. Where guys take you into their backyard and you have to find something of yours that fits into that backyard."

"Why is it always guys?"

"It could be women," he paused. "That's why I'm asking you."

"Considering it's mostly women tap dancing now," I added.

"I don't see a lot of women who are tap dancers," he said. "I see a lot of women who can tap, tap a little bit, but I don't see a lot of women who can really jump into a Challenge with these guys, with these ferocious guys . . . That's right."

"Who wants to play that game, though?" I asked.

"This is *not a game*, Jane. This is tap! It's what tap has been ever since it started right out on the street corner. Tap is competitive. It ain't ballet. Nureyev never came out onstage with Misha and did fours. Twyla never challenged Cunningham. No, tap has always had the Challenge at its red-hot core."

As he talked, he was once again gaining momentum, leaving me in the dust, coming up with new steps a mile a minute. Hard steps. He told me the young Savion Glover was keeping him in shape and challenged as they rehearsed for *Jelly's Last Jam*, the next Broadway show Gregory would appear in.

To me, it was like watching a dog sniffing for bones, digging into the dirt, and eagerly coming up with another bone, a different bone, a new bone.

"*That is* so status quo!" I could feel my voice rising.

"No, NO, *that* is HISTORY." His voice was rising, too. "There's a whole new breed coming up and there's plenty who can tap. That's how history works."

"I know history more than you know history." I pouted. But I also knew that he was a big part of the lineage, *the history*, and the connection between *old school* and *right now*.

Him: "I didn't say, 'Oh no you don't!'"

Me: "You wouldn't stoop to that level."

Him: "True. Even if I thought it, I wouldn't say it and I would never think it and not say it, you know." He danced off once again, thundering across the floor.

———

This wasn't what I had planned. A cutting session with Gregory Hines?

"Listen, Jane." said Gregory. "Jimmy Slyde is still dancing, Buster Brown is still dancing. These guys are still dancing and as long as they're still dancing, they're affecting young people coming up."

COURTESY PAM KOSLOW COLLECTION

He loved to call himself the pupil, even while teaching a master class. He aimed for audiences to hear silence as well as complicated rhythms.

"But the Challenge is such a heavy standard," I said. "Marion Coles and all those other women at the Apollo never had to challenge each other unless they built it into their own performances. No guy was telling them to *sic* each other."

"Yes, they did beautiful things," Gregory admitted. "But we're talking about the Challenge and your ability to be able to tap with me, to tap with the men, because it's been such a closed door, such a male-dominated thing. And the toughest critics are these men."

When Gregory had his shoes on, it was never just to fool around. Somehow I'd forgotten that, having recently joined him in an impromptu, relaxed improvisation to Jelly Roll Morton on his living room floor. I was wearing this long, straight, purple Norma Kamali dress that was totally inappropriate for tapping. But it didn't matter, because, as always, I'd brought my shoes.

At NYU, however, the atmosphere was anything but laid back.

"OK, whose step is this?" I summoned up all my energy and launched into as fierce a riff as I could muster.

Gregory dancing on crummy floor at the Top of the Gate nightclub, 1983, right before he started carrying his own custom-built floors.

©CHANGING TIMES TAP ARCHIVE

Me tapping on good wood in Vienna nightclub, 1983.

"That last part is *me*," he said, executing the step himself. "I'd love to put something together for four women." He did something with a wiggle in it and I giggled and winced at the same time.

"Check this out," I challenged.

Gregory was suddenly taking hold of my left thigh—holding my thigh!—and putting my whole leg down to get the heel sound.

"Don't rush the heel," he instructed. "Don't rush the heel."

I followed with my hardest step, replete with zillions of complicated sounds and lots of Stanley Brown turns. I've known this step for twenty years. Ever since I began to tap, I've pulled it out from deep within my bag of tricks when I needed it. Which was right now!

"That's a pretty step," he commented. "But you came out of those spins looking just as surprised as you could that you came out of them at all. You can use that step without doing a whole routine. Yes, that's the kind of step that has to be attacked. Brush that left, yes HIT IT!" he screamed.

I repeated the spinning step five times, each at a different tempo.

"Right, right!" Greg yelled. "Dig it in! Don't rush the heel," he repeated. "Don't rush the heel."

I can't believe he's holding my thigh!

"That's what you've got to do. I'm telling you, people will applaud and they will appreciate your humor, and you'll come across as someone who can be funny and do straight up tap, too."

My knee was killing me. I rubbed some Tiger Balm on it.

"You know, Jane, there are guys in basketball who have great outside shots, but they can't drive to the hoop. But when a guy has a move to the hoop, they don't get right up to his face. If a guy has a great outside shot, they're concerned, but they're also concerned that if they come up to try and stop him, he'll just whiz right by, because he can go to the hoop, too.

"The fact that you've started to talk and you're funny, people are going to laugh. But then you drop a good one," he said, dropping a fast spin on me. "Then you dig it in and they're going to realize you can also take it to the hoop. It's a whole different game. It's there and people will say 'she can really tap and talk.' You've got to make your presentation as powerful as you can!" he concluded.

Even though I don't know anything about sports, I always liked hearing his sports analogies to tap.

—ᴡᴡ—

I began to do a bunch of flaps (a step like skipping stones). I knew how Gregory was on an anti-flap kick because flaps were so basic. He thought tap dancers were

Gregory left and above: Leaving an indelible mark through his mentoring and master classes.

Gregory won a Tony for creating the title role in Jelly's Last Jam.

too willing to show their "basics" to audiences, partially attributing the decline of tap in our culture to the fact that people thought tap dancing *looked too easy*.

While no one would ever ask Baryshnikov to do a plié, Gregory was always being asked—by strangers on the streets of New York—to demonstrate his time step. He even got on Fred Astaire's and Gene Kelly's cases for showing tap basics on screen.

Gregory began flapping, too, and suddenly I was dancing as fast as I could, flapping with him across the studio floor. I was a little delirious and ready to get out the Tiger Balm again.

I was out of breath when I stopped flapping. I was going to eat lunch. He could keep going if he wanted to. I needed some fuel.

———

"Have feet always been your prime concern?" I asked, as we lunched on tuna sandwiches.

"Uh, as a tap dancer?" he said. "Yes. But initially I was a calf man, and then I moved up to the breasts, then the thighs. Then I noticed a tendency for a complete package.

"I'm a 'feet' man, baby," he said, seriously this time. "Oh, I'm appreciating the arms and the presentation and the humor and the experimentation, but for me the feet have always been the thrill.

"I ain't talking about speed, Jane," he continued. "I'm talking about the feet. I thought the feet Coles and Atkins displayed during their slow soft shoe was fantastic, their whole presentation was fantastic, but I really got into their feet. I saw a tap dancer at the Apollo in the '50s, name of Bobby Ephram, whose act basically consisted of his skill at jumping high, straight up in the air and clicking his heels together. His peak moment was clicking 'em together eight times. But baby, when he was on the ground, I loved his feet."

©COURTESY PAM KOSLOW COLLECTION

"I'm a 'feet' man, baby."

Gregory Hines (left), Jimmy Slyde (center), Savion Glover (right): They all stepped up to the plate when they had to (and they loved it).

I chimed in. "You might not like people showing their basics, but I loved Fred and Ginger; they had this certain sensibility that got me into tap dancing. It wasn't about the feet for me."

"Tap has changed from Astaire's day," Greg said. "I believe it has changed from the Copasetics to Funk University. It doesn't make sense to fight against this new expression that is taking hold now. Yes, it's very different from the old way, and for me the feet are more amazing now than ever before."

———

I still defended the "tap sensibility," telling Gregory more about the avant-garde, about a woman named Jill Kroesen who was doing performance art long before it was fashionable. She used tap dancing farmers in her work, and contextualized tap. The steps she taught those farmers were simple, but it was the perfect statement of tap for me, how tap *could* be.

Stewart Alter, my writer friend, also had that tap sensibility even though he didn't have great feet. He had studied abstract art, knew rhythm, but also knew how to put tap in different contexts, as in his tap-infused poems like "The Neighbor" (a parody of Edgar Allan Poe's "The Raven," and "The Frog Prince." Stewart, who wrote for Cookie and the guys, but also for me, knew that the key ingredient to the tap *sensibility* was "fun.").

Yes, I had wanted Chuck Green's feet at one time. But now I knew that tap is so many *different* things. To me, *that is* its primary appeal.

"Have any women influenced you?" I asked Gregory.

"I loved Eleanor Powell's feet. But I've never needed a woman to have feet like a man to appreciate her feet. Nor have I wanted women to dress like a man either. No . . . I can respect any woman who has some feet, feet that get to me, her own feet, a woman's feet, but feet. Ultimately it's all a question of taste, Jane. Mine gravitate towards the feet."

"Boy, am I *not* a fan of Eleanor Powell's," I retorted. "Maybe her feet were great and she was a great dancer, but I didn't like that goody-goody girl phony smile. I couldn't even keep my eyes on her feet."

We finished our lunch and got back onto the white maple once more, but I wasn't looking down at all now.

"You know, Jane, if I were a woman, a woman who could dance as I do now, women would be listening to me, and taking my advice about how important the issue of dressing up is. I'm telling you, Jane, I'd be making a living tap dancing, and I would stand out among that bland crowd of women tappers who aren't aware or who've been too intimidated by those who came before, to take the risk of standing out and being different. And before you knew it, there'd be a growing number of women tappers trying to get the most out of how they looked onstage," he concluded.

46th and 8th Ave: Even Gregory agreed the best-sounding (and grungiest) floors in New York were at Fazil's Times Square Studios. Once known as Mike's, then, Jerry LeRoy's, the rates were the best, and everyone from Fred Astaire and Eleanor Powell, The Copasetics, all people tap, Flamenco, Middle-Eastern (belly) dancing rehearsed there. Alas, in February, 2008, this rehearsal hall Mecca closed its doors for good after seventy-three years in business.

"Hey, you're talking to the tap dancer with cleavage here," I reminded him.

"No matter, what you say, I still feel you have a problem with women tappers looking sexy."

"Now *that* is real BS, Greg!" I screamed. "I have my problems, but it's not about women looking sexy. You raised two daughters. I'd think you'd know a little more about this topic than you let on. Our next 'studio visit' is going to be at a magazine store, and we are going to read all the sexist ads together. Sure, I'd like to see women making a living tapping, but I wince at the thought of a tapper coming out in a unitard. It's so very unhip. It's, it's . . ."

"I don't want to have to be redundant about it," he broke in, "because you know how strongly I feel about the subject of women and wardrobe."

"Yes, I do know!" I shot back. "And I also know you are *not* a woman in this society. If you think a woman can be in charge of producing and directing a woman's tap show, why don't you just let us women decide what we want to wear?"

By now, we were each in our own corners, yelling across the room.

"I'd like to see you in a unitard!" I shouted. Ever since he'd worked with Mikhail Baryshnikov in *White Nights*, Gregory seemed to have a thing for tights.

Panama Greg in rare repose.

Him and me

"I've worn 'em," he said. "It ain't too hard to go to the bathroom when the time comes. It's so easy for you to dismiss me as sexist, and to use 'women in unitards' as all I'm about. I know you know my stuff is way deeper than that. What other man in tap do you know who gives two shits about a conversation focused on the issue of getting more work for women tappers? Call me pro-work. Call me confrontational. But sexist? That's a cheap shot, Jane!"

Gregory headed toward the door, musing dreamily: "Women tappers, five or six of them, dancing their asses off, looking great, looking different than we've come to expect them to look. No more loose and comfortable. Hittin' it hard and surprising us 'cause like women who can do anything really great, we're surprised at just how great they really are . . . a woman up on the stage with tap shoes on . . . turning us on . . . Women tap dancers are great dancers *and hot, too.* This show is gonna run forever. Women's tap dancing sure has changed up from what I've gotten used to!"

I giggled again. This was one woman who didn't want to join in on his fantasy. As I followed him out of the studio, head held high, I imagined the lovely white wood floor beneath me pocked with scratches and dents.

Gregory sure had added a moment of history to that floor, I thought. I was relieved, but also sad, that our session was over. ■

Comparaholics Anonymous

How had I hurled myself into an art form that screamed competition, being the best, being the champ? I used to like to watch the hoofers battle it out, but I didn't want to jump in there myself. Not all tap was competitive, but my kind of tap was. It may have looked like they were just "having fun," "trading eights," or "fouring" one another, but they were cutting sessions and the best feet won. I'd heard stories from my mentors of how tap dancers would drive miles to do battle.

You didn't *know* what competitive was until you saw those men in the ring. And out of it.

Honi Coles used to tell the story of how the original Stumpy from Stump and Stumpy stole all of Honi's material—his entire act—and performed it right before Honi went on. That had to have cost Honi some work, because he often told that story, still outraged, when asked about his early days working.

Most of the hoofers of his generation began scrambling for work again during my era, but work was still so scarce. Would they be able to make a living in tap again? Would they have to keep their new sources to themselves? It seemed to be every man for himself when it came to work, even if they hung out at bars together. None of them were spring chickens, either. Often, their onstage tap-happy cliché belied an almost cutthroat impulse, not the one big happy family Stanley Brown used to talk about.

A desperation for work, mixed with ego and a yearning for some sort of security they never had, made some of them take any gig. When asked whether the floor mattered at one of our venues, Cookie Cook replied, "We'll work on rugs."

When tap dropped off, the hoofers had had to find other means of employment. Some of them had families to raise. Henry "Phace" Roberts of the "The Rockets" was a manager at Woolworth's. Ralph Brown drove a gypsy cab up in Harlem. Honi Coles stage-managed The Apollo Theatre. Leon Collins had become a car mechanic. LaVaughn Robinson operated a Zamboni machine.

Savion Glover and Gregory Hines in a Challenge during the Broadway run of Jelly's Last Jam.

Ernest "Brownie" Brown was a security guard at a Wall Street Bank. His partner and then mine, Charles Cookie Cook, claimed to be a "kept man" during those lean years.

The older guys were pitting us younger dancers against each other, too. When I started working, eking out a living in tap, I didn't realize how dependent I was going to become on grants and single gigs to get me by. There were few steady jobs.

I know about jobs, honest. When I was hired to do a tap-a-gram™ for my lawyer's mother's seventy-fifth birthday in Forest Hills, N.Y., she burst out crying when I sang a line about her deceased husband. (It was supposed to be a good memory, not a downer.) I bombed in front of a huge convention of Orthodox Jewish jewelers at the Waldorf-Astoria when I performed my Hebrew soft shoe. It was considered a sacrilegious act at their gala. *My people!*

I taught high school kids in Miami where tap was a required course. They'd straggle into the classroom, tap shoeless, and start making out as soon as I turned off the lights to show videos. I taught courses in dance history to college kids who didn't want to read, and even shot spitballs at each other during class. *College kids!*

How are the other hoofers hoofing it?

That's my bête noir—I'm forever comparing, competing, not competing, but feeling competitive, disliking feeling competitive, but competing anyway. Each day I'd seize on someone to size up in light of my own struggles and accomplishments. I've calmed down some, now that I'm tapping less, less on the scene.

In second grade, I made up a dance to a song from Walt Disney's animated version of *Peter Pan* and performed it on my elementary school auditorium stage. I can still see the bright yellow "unbreakable" 33⅓-rpm I played on our

Hula Jane: "I work alone."

turntable that I practiced so diligently to. I loved making up *The Pirate's Life* in my parents' basement. I didn't realize I was in a contest until the end of the night when the emcee lifted me on his shoulders as if I had won. But I hadn't. The contestant after me got the louder applause. That was my first conscious attack of comparaholism. There was a winner and a second place. Worst of all, I was beginning to feel there was a winner and a loser.

In junior high I was a competitive diver. I beat tall, lanky Candy Strange who was the usual frontrunner. The headline in the sports section of *The Washington Post* read "Little Janie Goldberg Upsets Champ." But I didn't enjoy beating her. I didn't want to beat anyone. I remember how my team, The Pepsi Diving Team, had a lot of fun training at American University. We'd each do our dives, waiting for coach Bob Frailey to comment on them, and I'd never feel competitive. That changed when we'd dive against each other at the meets because there weren't that many divers when I was twelve in the Jr. Olympics. That part of diving felt awful to me.

After playing a large role in the tap revival, I developed a *Ferdinand the Bull* complex. Ferdinand was the big bull who loved to sit in the grass and smell the flowers, rather than compete in the ring. One day, just as a bee stung him, a group of matadors drove by and saw the ferocious side of Ferdinand. They immediately packed him into their truck and drove him to Madrid for the bullfights.

Once there, Ferdinand refused to perform, no matter how many times the matador swung his red flag at Ferdinand, egging him on to fight. Instead, Ferdinand lay down as he always did, right in the middle of the ring, languishing in the Spanish sun, smelling all the flowers that the señoras and señoritas poured down on him from the grand stands. Ferdinand was finally packed up and driven back to his aromatic pastures, where he lay contentedly forever after smelling the flowers.

———

I didn't enjoy the tap ring. I wanted to go back to my hippie days, although communal life never lasted long for me. I do believe there is enough to go around, enough room for everybody. I hate war and have become more anti-war as the years have passed. I may seem like I like to fight, to argue, to provoke, but in truth, my desire is: "Can't we all have a good time and get along?"

From early on, even if I acted like I enjoyed the battle sometimes, I really didn't. My idea of winning was if everybody won. The best experience came when each individual felt good about participating and contributing for the good of the whole. That's what I remember feeling when I performed my first tap dance in Cambridge under Claire Mallardi's direction. Each of us choreographed our own dance and performed for ten minutes.

And, as I recall, we all got along. We were all so very different. That's what it felt like in *Sole Sisters*, too; although, I have to face the fact that I was "the star"

My broom and me: Sweep, don't compete.

pretty much calling the shots. Still, the women I chose to be in the cast all seemed to want to keep the show going for the cause of women in tap. None of my regulars were complaining. Since there was no money to be made in my productions (alas), money was never an issue with anyone.

This is not to say that all hoofing is fierce and competitive. There have been situations where everyone feels good about a show, where no one is comparing herself to anybody else, where the leader is respected, not envied. But those situations seemed to be rare, indeed, back in the 1980s. People "knew their place." With the development of ensembles based more or less on the modern dance role model of a choreographer and his/her company, the competition became less one-on-one, less "vaudevillian."

The tap tradition, set up from vaudeville on, maybe even a lot earlier than that, was based on a hierarchical structure. In vaudeville, a variety of acts—animal acts, children's acts, comedy, class, flash, ballroom, and Russian dancing—competed for their spots in the lineup. In his autobiography *Steps in Time*, the great song and dance man, Fred Astaire, wrote about he and his sister Adele's first important New York theater booking at Proctor's Fifth Avenue, on the corner of Broadway and 28th St. They were "surprised and disappointed" to find out they were the opening act. He wrote that after a short overture . . . "the curtain went up and there was—to use the old vaudeville jargon—'nobody in the house.'"

In that system "next to closing" was the best spot, the most important place for the headliner. By "closing," the last spot on the bill, people were already leaving for their dinner and for home.

My first show, *It's About Time: An Evening of Jazz Tap Dancing*, was a revue of sorts, structured similarly to vaudeville, but exclusively focused on tap dancing. I didn't know about the importance of the lineup until I started working with the old hoofers. The lineup still holds true at tap festivals, the only "steady" venues for some tap dancers where there is little time to rehearse, and the dancers come, practically ready to go.

The producers, usually tap dancers themselves, either do the lineup or select one or more of the experienced dancers to help out. This is an ideal situation for breeding a competitive/comparaholic atmosphere.

In 1984, I did a show with my company called *The Tapping Talk Show*, with Sarah Safford and me acting as talk show hosts at New York's Village Gate nightclub. We were getting ready to go to Europe and needed to be ready. Gregory Hines was my featured guest star. I remember sitting in his loft while his young daughter Daria brought me some whiteout to cross out his brother's name on the flyer my brother designed. At the time they weren't talking to each other. Arthur mistakenly thought Maurice Jr. was a guest. Pam Koslow, Gregory's wife, was co-producing with me for the 1983 show.

©ILLUSTRATION OF "SMOKING SHOE"
FOR "THE TAPPING TALK SHOW" BY ARTHUR GOLDBERG

A Renaissance for Tap, New and Old Style

Martha Swope (Battle), Kenn Duncan (Coles, Gregory Hines, Tune, Ribeiro), Lois Greenfield (Maurice Hines) and Pam Duffy (Goldberg)

By LESLIE BENNETTS

WHEN Hinton Battle, who had trained as a ballet dancer since the age of 10, auditioned for the Broadway production of "Sophisticated Ladies," he managed to fudge a soft-shoe routine even though he didn't know how to tap dance at all. But then he learned he had been cast to understudy Gregory Hines, the virtuoso tap dancer whose dazzling numbers stopped every show.

"I panicked," Mr. Battle says. "It used to be you didn't need to know how to tap. Tap was out for so long, and there wasn't much of it around to see."

He plunged into intensive instruction with Henry LeTang, who has been teaching tap for more than 40 years and whose students have included both Gregory Hines and his brother, Maurice.

That was three years ago, and these days Mr. Battle — a very quick learner — is himself starring on Broadway in "The Tap Dance Kid." Nor is he the only young dancer to embark upon such a crash course. "At Henry's school, you can hardly get in the room, there are so many people rushing in to learn how to tap," Mr. Battle reports.

For an art form long in eclipse and considered by many to be irretrievably moribund, tap dancing is enjoying quite a revival. Even as its eager new practitioners learn their steps, older dancers have emerged from longtime obscurity to join the resurgence of tap. This weekend both the old and the new will be on view as the Changing Times Tap Dancing Company presents "The Tapping Talk Show" at the Top of the Gate, Bleecker and Thompson Streets. The program will be given tonight at 10:30 and tomorrow at 8 and 10:30 P.M. Tickets are $10 and may be reserved by calling 475-5120.

The company includes such old-timers as Charles (Cookie) Cook, Harold Cromer, Buster Brown and Marion Coles along with younger dancers like its founder, Jane Goldberg. The program will present a wide array of tap styles, ranging from old-fashioned "sand" dancing, slapstick and soft-shoe to a number set to reggae music.

Joining the Changing Times ensemble will be several well-known special guests: Gregory Hines and Gregg Burge, another "Sophisticated Ladies" alumnus; and at the late shows, Mr. Battle and Charles (Honi) Coles, the veteran tap dancer who won a Tony Award last year for his performance in "My One and Only."

When he was named best featured actor in a musical at the Tony Awards ceremony last June, the 72-year-old Mr. Coles called it "the greatest thrill of my life."

Younger dancers were having similar experiences. "When I first got to New York in the 1960's, I brought my tap shoes, but I just had to put them away in the bottom drawer because there was no use for them," says Tommy Tune, who stars in "My One and Only." "Modern jazz was what we were asked to do."

Today Mr. Coles laughs when he considers how times have changed for tap. "I should have had the sense to know it would come back," he says. "All things work in circles. The wheel turns."

Many dancers credit the 1971 revival of "No, No, Nanette" with giving the wheel a push. Ruby Keeler's tap dancing won raves, but it was several years before tap began to crop up with any regularity on Broadway. Mr. Tune won a Tony with his exuberant tap dancing in "Seesaw" in 1973, but was then unable to find work on Broadway as a dancer

On Their Taps

Some of today's tap dancers, from left, Hinton Battle of "The Tap Dance Kid" on Broadway, Charles (Honi) Coles and Gregory Hines, who can be seen at Top of the Gate in "Tapping Talk Show"; Tommy Tune of "My One and Only," Alfonso Ribeiro of "Tap Dance Kid," Maurice Hines and Jane Goldberg.

shows featuring tap dancing has lengthened to include "42d Street," "Bubbling Brown Sugar," "Sugar Babies," "Sophisticated Ladies," "A Chorus Line," "My One and Only," "Cats" and "The Tap Dance Kid," among others.

Tap's growing popularity has spawned such companies as Changing Times, which will perform at the Vienna Dance Festival this month, and the latest entry, Ballet Tap U.S.A. Founded by Maurice Hines and Mercedes Ellington, Ballet Tap U.S.A. will make its debut next month at the Academy of Music in Philadelphia, where the company will be joined by Judith Jamison as a guest artist.

"Nobody's even seen us yet, and we're booked through most of 1984 and '85 on a concert level," Mr. Hines reports. "That indicates interest on a phenomenal level. I'm very optimistic. When we premiere it, it will be off and running."

Opening night, a huge spread came out on the front page of the weekend section of *The New York Times* trumpeting a tap dance Renaissance, complete with a splashy display of photographs of tap dancers in a lineup, many whom I didn't even know.

My show was highlighted in the article and a number of hoofers were interviewed. When the *Times* writer saw the "smoking tap shoe" my brother had drawn on the flyer, she asked Pam Koslow if there was a tap revival. In the 1980s media, for the most part, tap was always being "revived." It was never *here*.

That spread of photographs was phenomenal, and some dancers pictured must have felt they *had* to show up to get in on the bandwagon generated by the *Times'* publicity. The tendency to seize the spotlight with a Challenge situation came to the fore opening night with some of these celebrated hoofers sitting prominently in the front.

This was the first time I was going to witness a spontaneous unstaged group Challenge. I realized what the expression "Give it up to," meant. These guys were *totally* taking over. They couldn't help themselves. It was in their nature.

Once I figured out what was going on, I was horrified. I wanted to disappear from my own evening, but I couldn't leave the Gate. The news magazine *20/20* was there to film my show, and stayed to interview Gregory. I pretended as if it had been planned, but it wasn't my plan at all. I felt like The Invisible Woman.

At the top of his game in his early thirties, Gregory set the tone. After my company had taken its bows, he suddenly jumped up on the stage, and dramatically aimed the mikes down, almost touching the floor. His serious demeanor sent a warning to the boisterous crowd in the hyped up nightclub that he was going to *get down* and make the night serious. He was also getting more interested in volume and determined to be heard. A cutting session was about to begin.

Gregory performed a twenty-minute improvised soliloquy—with only a chair as a prop, which he seamlessly lifted, held, sat on, tap danced from, without missing a beat. When he finished, the audience rose up as one and cheered uproariously. Seemingly from nowhere, seventy-something Honi Coles, slowly climbed the three steps to the stage, and became the first contender. He called out to some of his colleagues to join him and I noticed not only old-timers joining in, but also a bunch of upstarts. This was going to be a real free-for-all, and I might have even enjoyed it if it weren't happening right on my stage, right after my show.

Buster Brown and Harold Cromer, still in the preacher and Japanese scholar costumes that they wore earlier, returned to the stage. Four-foot ten Ernest

This headline and article appeared in the front of the Arts section of The New York Times, *1984.*

Above: Harold Cromer in Japanese scholar costume; right: Buster Brown as preacher in "The Tapping Talk Show."

©CHANGING TIMES TAP ARCHIVE

Brownie Brown jumped aboard, too, as did two well-known Broadway show tappers, Greg Burge and Hinton Battle. Benny Clory, who had been in *The Cotton Club* movie, came up as did Dick Cavett, the "real" television talk show host. Harold Nicholas was the only one of the greats who remained seated, but he was acknowledged from the stage. (Maybe he didn't like The Challenge, either.)

There was only one tentative moment as the men all eyed each other. Full of their typical camaraderie, their fangs, or rather, feet were ready to go.

Honi began laying down his smooth "irons" close to the floor, moving back and forth with his spider web legs. He warned the audience he wasn't going to do "all that jumping around" they'd just had from Gregory.

Next in line, tiny Brownie, Cook's old partner, went into his signature shimmying routine, looking up at the roof, very eccentric, very weird. I didn't see a place for it at all in this ring. He was in the wrong circle, but Brownie carried that sense of entitlement always. My musicians, Jim Roberts and Montego Joe, remained on the stage for the action, and they played "Cute" when Buster took his round. Although it looked like he may have been falling back on something he knew, Buster let go of the time, and began to improvise riffs he'd never done before, none I'd ever seen anyway.

Benny Clory, another major contender, bulky and over six feet tall, fiery, handsome, a true stud, began with some simple flaps that spiraled into vertical percussion as he nearly hit the roof with his flips and turns. (Sadly, he died soon after, still in his prime, when he broke his neck rehearsing flips with his brother in his Queens backyard). I really dug Benny Clory because he always welcomed women to his stage when he hosted anywhere. He was a friendly gentleman who truly was interested in what other dancers had to say. You didn't have to prove yourself around him, even though he was gallant. People say he was in too much of a "hurry"; that's why he had that horrible accident. He wanted to "make it" too quickly. I don't know about that. He came out strong and left like a rocket to the moon.

Honi came back, moving like an inchworm, smooth as silk, taking the power out of Benny's high jumps. The two Broadway tappers were next and without the skill level of the feet before them, each took a turn with a lot of basics—flaps, kicks, turns. The pure joy in Greg Burge's expression lent him a big hand. Hinton Battle, also out of his league, did his specialty, a very high vertical Rockette kick, only much higher, and landed, toosh first in front of all the other hoofers. He saved himself by propping himself up on his hand and maneuvering his way back up to kick high again! He should have won the battle just for his sheer chutzpah. I'd never seen Harold Cromer really go for broke before, but he really went, delivering his punch—sequential time steps.

Excited by all this action, Gregory threw down the hat again, but gave Honi Coles the last word. This was proper etiquette to let the elder statesman win. Honi repeated the steps he had begun with his inchworm magnetism. Bowing down to the master, Gregory announced Honi, "winner and still champ." In 1984, while Gregory was perceived as the champ, he told me once he felt the title belonged to the lesser-recognized Jimmy Slyde.

This was a show after a show, not a show within a show and the spontaneity of it all was not lost on the *20/20* crew whose cameras were running a mile a minute. The audience itself looked out of breath at the end and very, very happy. We had all just seen the real thing, a *spontaneous* Challenge, unstaged and unlike most hoofer "battle of the taps" of my era.

With the audience cleared out, the *20/20* people came up to interview me, Gregory, anyone they could find to talk to about what they'd just witnessed. I was packed up, ready to lick my wounds, but I talked about how cool everything was, what a night it had been. Gregory was typically straightforward, saying The Challenge, the improvisation, all of it was just "to keep working." It

Gregory loved to compete: His first love was baseball, but his father urged him to, "Tap, son, tap."

wasn't until the last time I saw him when he was dying, that he explained how he embraced competition.

"As a mere boy, the concept, the need for, and the inevitability of competition was almost force-fed into me," he told me in our last interview. "Could it have been the first foot race in the schoolyard to see who was the fastest runner in the second grade? Or maybe it was the emphasis on the glory of winning and the sure pain of losing that every sports coach I ever had, that got to me."

"I remember how that TV sports show *The Wide World of Sports* opened every weekend with the announcer saying the phrase "the thrill of victory and the agony of defeat" while showing a runner beating the field and then a ski jumper crashing horribly. From as far back as I can remember I enjoyed competing. The more intense the competition, the better I liked it. Baseball, basketball, football, tap dancing. It was fun to develop my skills to the level that I was able to compete, and then get to the point where I could *possibly* win, and then actually win! I've always been attracted to men and women who enjoyed competing, and I've been beaten by both sexes many times in many ways. I love a heated NBA game or WNBA game. That's me, babe."

I know it sounds hubristic to compare myself to Gregory, but I felt the call to a Challenge, when I invited him to New York University to give my students a master class. I had also invited my friend, Herbin Van Cayseele, now Tamango, a wonderful dancer from French Guyana, who grew up in Paris and started tapping there. The minute he spotted Tamango, Gregory invited the younger dancer up and they immediately started "trading eights."

It took everything I had to get up and join them. I had to! What would my students think of me if I didn't get up to dance? I realized no one was *ever* going to invite me up for a "trade" the way I had invited Greg and Tamango to my class. I sometimes *had* to jump into Gregory's backyard. I didn't have ferocious feet, but I wanted to be heard, too. I embedded myself with my two friends in this age-old practice, and for once had no attack of comparaholism. This was my turf, too, and I added my own presence. ■

Tamango, the dancer formerly known as Herbin Van Cayseele. He is smooth and silky and has his own unique blend of tap with world music. He skims across the floor!

The Nicholas Brothers
Get a Salad Bowl

(Disclaimer: The Dance *Magazine* Awards ceremony has improved and changed since the one I describe in the following pages. The magazine is now published by Macfadden Performing Arts Media, LLC. The awardees *and* presenters wait backstage until their time in the sun. Now, there's even dancing live and/or on film to represent each award recipient).

Fiasco time: I was to present the *Dance Magazine* Award to Fayard and Harold Nicholas on April 17, 1995, a gorgeous spring day, and my worst scene scenario began early in the morning: I couldn't fit into my planned outfit; I had to resort to my trusty turquoise boob dress, the one in which my cleavage is right out there.

Later on that day, the totally uptight publisher of said magazine refused poor eighty-one-year-old Fayard a Coca-Cola. We were waiting for the ceremony to begin, and she was pushing her stupid Perrier and white wine on the poor man. I happened to be sitting next to him and was privy to that pathetic scene unfolding in its full glory. She even had the nerve to call The Nicholas Brothers "demanding" earlier in the afternoon when I called to request transportation money to get Fayard to the ceremony.

After I gave a kind of stilted, slightly scholarly speech telling the dance crowd of skinny-lovers what contributions the Niks had made, Gregory Hines jumped up on the stage, *literally out of nowhere*, totally unplanned and hilarious. He regaled the audience with stories about the Niks' slick hair, how it "moved" and how he coveted that hair, putting underpants on his head so his hair, too, would "move." He spontaneously, *completely upstaged me*. Cell phones weren't common in 1995, but did I ever wish I had one with me, onstage *right then*, so I could freak out to my friend, Dorothy, starting with, *"You're not going to believe this!"*

Fayard and Harold Nicholas with me at the Dance Magazine *Awards, 1995.*

Dorothy Wasserman was the vice president of the Gregory Hines Fan Club and I was the president. It was a pretty exclusive club, just the two of us, and for years we spent a lot of time on the phone talking about our idol, Gregory. As a friend of his, I had much more access than she, and kept her alert to his goings-on.

This time, I wanted to tell her how I was *stuck* on the stage, pretending to enjoy his humor, his good looks, his stardom. I wanted to tell her how I had to laugh phonily at all his remarks—which I have to admit *were* sensational—and how the Niks and the rest of the audience laughed uproariously, too.

(Gregory and I were able to hash the whole thing out fifteen years later on e-mail with him accusing me of not even knowing what a tap shoe was when *he* was idolizing The Nicholas Brothers as a kid and my shooting back that I did, too, and telling him about my year in tap with Miss Maxine. Plus, Greg told me he *had* apologized a million times for raining on my parade, and I was still holding a grudge [true!]. We were able to laugh about it—sort of—but back in '95, it wasn't so funny.)

The Nicholas Brothers are the ones everyone knows about when you mention black tap dancers of a certain age. You might not remember their names, but you remember their extraordinary talent. You remember Harold and Fayard's lickety split super precision classy, pyrotechnic, elegant, sophisticated, even heroic dancing.

You gasp, no matter whether you're in front of your TV or watching them on the big screen. Even after watching *Stormy Weather* a hundred times, I still laugh in astonishment when the Niks leapfrog over the heads of some of the Duke Ellington musicians, land in their splits, and slide effortlessly back up, not a drop of sweat on their faces. Even in Pullman porter or bellhop costumes, The Nicholas Brothers transcended the black stereotype of a Step 'N' Fetch it, or a shuffling hoofer.

Harold was the quieter and younger of the two, flirtatious and adorable as a kid and adult. He lived in France for a long time, during the Drought. In his last years, in New York, I'd see him sometimes heading into the Film Forum or the Thalia Cinema for some film noir, and other classics. He experimented artistically throughout his life, even working with a Flamenco dancer at Carnegie Hall. He rarely wore taps in his final years, but even in his regular leather tie shoes, he still had flair and a great sound. His singing voice was also terrific.

Fayard, the older and taller one, taught his little brother the ropes when they were The Nicholas Kids, starring at venues like the Cotton Club. Fayard learned a lot about the business end of things from their parents and did most of the talking for the pair.

On Easter Sunday, the day before the *Dance Magazine* Awards ceremony, I visited Fayard, who had just flown in that morning from his home in Los Angeles. We met at the old Mayflower Hotel right on Central Park and had a great time discussing Jews and blacks and showbiz and his unrequited acting ambitions. Race was the subtext of most of our conversation.

Fayard—what a great name—always spoke about The Nicholas Brothers in third person as a commodity.

"There were so many dancers who were working in the '30s and '40s, and a lot of competition," he told me in his bubbly falsetto voice. "But The Nicholas Brothers were the only ones that got a seven-year contract with 20th Century Fox. The others tried, but they just didn't have that little something that looked good on the big screen—the personality."

"And the business sense, too?" I asked.

"Right. The business mind," he replied. "Oh, it all goes together. A lot of guys wanted to do what The Nicholas Brothers did; they all thought they were better than The Nicholas Brothers. We didn't think we were better than anybody. We were just doing our thing, our dancing, doing The Nicholas Brothers thing, and we hoped they would do their thing."

He discussed his "stay ahead" philosophy, too: "I was always trying to stay ahead of the other dancers, be at the top. See, I'm *here* and I'm still going up. Now, they're *there*. So I'm saying, 'Come on, there's enough room here for everybody. Come on. Catch up with me . . .' So he catches up with us, but I slip away from him again . . . See? I keep going. But, still, 'Come on, come on. You know? But when you get there, try to stay with me, 'cause I'm gonna leave you again . . .' So, we just kept going and going, but we were never jealous. We were keeping up with the times. If you want to stay in the business, you've got to keep working."

———

At 4:30 p.m. the next afternoon, inside the elegant confines of the Asia Society, it was all brisk business as presenters and honorees were told where to sit, where to stand, where to speak. We were shown how to present each honoree with the award, which to me looked like a large aluminum salad bowl.

At the magic hour of 5 p.m., the doors opened and the audience began to trickle in.

All of us participants were already onstage sitting in a semi-circle. It began to feel awkward up there and after a few minutes, the presenters began talking to the honorees seated next to them. I wondered why we weren't backstage like in most awards ceremonies with some element of theater and surprise instead of with all of us here onstage like goldfish in a bowl.

I had time to mull over what my contribution would be to this spectacle. Two months earlier, the editor-in-chief of *Dance Magazine* asked me if I would be a presenter for the Niks. He called me up, knowing I was *MOT*, (member of the tribe—the tap tribe), and we had schmoozed pleasantly, for half an hour.

Harold and Fayard: No longer The Nicholas "Kids" but close brothers to their end.

The producers had decided to forgo any dance—live or on film—in keeping with the absurdly leaden feel of this event. Fayard had even requested that some of The Nicholas Brothers film footage be shown, but had been refused. Who were the Niks without their *footage*? I wondered who in the audience even knew much about who *The Nicholas Brothers* were. *Dance Magazine* had rarely recognized tap dancers for their achievements. *(Editorial note: Since 1954, when the awards began, only 9 tap dancers have received the salad bowl out of 173 awardees, and that includes the two-for-the price-of-one duos like the Niks).*

I also wondered how the Niks felt getting this award. They'd just received the Kennedy Center Honors the year before, so maybe they'd "earned" it now. Still, it's nice to get recognition when you're alive. Had either of them ever even *read Dance Magazine*?

I spotted a few of the old Copasetics scattered about the audience. Constance Valis Hill, who was writing a book about The Nicholas Brothers, was smiling at me from the audience. Dance critic Marcia Siegel was sitting beside her. They were laughing. Laughing, I discovered later, at my cleavage bursting out in the middle of such a stodgy affair.

True, I did feel like Gypsy Rose Lee about to do a striptease. My weight was a little "up" that evening, including my boobs. I had started out wearing my favorite black Parisian pumps, but they pinched my feet, so I'd replaced them with my green-heeled tap shoes. I had no intention of tapping in them, however. I didn't want to take away any of the Niks' thunder, *as if I could*.

———

I became so uncomfortable after twenty minutes of sitting on that stage, that I barged in on old Harold and Fayard's conversation.

"What are you guys talking about, anyway?" I demanded.

They both looked surprised. Fayard told me they were just shooting the bull. *My* brother and I never just shot the bull. If *we* were going to shoot, it would probably be at each other. For Fayard and Harold, it was like Old Home Week, as if they hadn't seen each other in ages. They had, in point of fact, just had Easter dinner together.

At the reception afterward, David White, the Dance Theater Workshop producer and power monger of dance, said to me, "Boy, you tappers always get onstage with each other and have such a good time, don't you?"

The editor-in-chief surprised me by asking why I hadn't tapped. So did many others. Why hadn't I?

I noticed Gregory out of the corner of my eye, so I walked up and briefly thanked him for his "added remarks." Then I went back into the theater and asked one of the custodians if I could take some of the beautiful flowers from the stage. He said I could.

Almost out the door, I felt a hand on my shoulder. The publisher began yelling at me, treating me like a stranger who had just walked in from off the street, looking for a handout. I was told the flowers cost $400 (the program, which I read later that night, said they were donated), and didn't I know they were *needed* all week and wasn't this just horrible? An old dance/classical music agent watched the scene unfold in disbelief. I might have burst into tears of humiliation had the editor not come over to apologize to me for his publisher's conduct.

Although it was still Passover, I took a cab down to my favorite Italian bakery in the Village on Bleecker Street, and downed some biscotti and cappuccino. I had no time for matzoth on that very *different* night. I had a hard time falling asleep later on, too, although images of Coca-Cola and artificial flowers kept surfacing in my dreams. ∎

Stop-Time:
New Tap, New Art Deco

My dance colleague, Sarah Safford, told me, in the early '90s, "Janie, I can see you in Miami—'New Tap, New Art Deco.'" She knew about my pioneering days in the tap revival. She also knew that I loved the beach and New York City was becoming glutted with tap revivalists. I decided to check out South Beach.

I knew nothing about Art Deco when I first walked along Ocean Drive, the main tourist drag of Miami Beach, in June 1992, even though there had been a lot of media attention already paid to the Art Deco district down there.

Initially, I used the excuse of a dance conference on multiculturalism, which was right up my alley anyway. In June, there was hardly another tourist in sight, so I felt like I, too, was discovering the Art Deco gold. Every morning I'd jump into the ocean, swim out a ways, and stare at all the Deco hotels dotting Ocean Drive. There weren't people smothering and crowding the road like there are now, summer, winter, fall, spring, all year-round. The hotels were just beautiful to me.

I hadn't even heard of Barbara Capitman then.

The following winter, however, I met Jeff Donnelly, an historian and activist in local Beach politics. He was part of the Miami Beach Preservation League and told me about Barbara Capitman's campaign to save The Senator, a Deco hotel. She also wanted to save the myriad of other gorgeous buildings defined as Art Deco.

Capitman sounded like a fanatic and she also sounded like me concerning tap. We were both women obsessed about '30s American art, art we deemed genuine. "The real thing."

It was eerie to read the introduction to her book, *Rediscovering Art Deco*, where she wrote, "Art Deco is my whole Life." I myself was married to tap dancing. I knew how she felt. We even both shared the same sad bedroom eyes.

<hr>

Like Capitman, I wasn't alone. There were a bunch of us tap revivalists finding, studying with, and "preserving" old-time hoofers at the same time Capitman was

It was a city where I could swim outside year-round. And all that Deco!

saving Art Deco. Capitman had her band of volunteers, too. "Barbara Capitman" is now the name of a street right at Ocean and 9th. She died in 1990. We were both doing time for "the cause" starting in the mid-'70s.

1978 was a standout year for all of us. In 1978 Capitman started The Miami Beach Preservation League, and that was the same year several tap revivalists and I came out with our first self-produced shows in New York. In 1978, Gregory was starring in his first Broadway show, *Eubie*.

Both revivals could be perceived, in a way, as archeological digs. We were digging up the 1930s. I organized my company, Changing Times Tap, in 1979 to preserve tap and create new work. Maybe it wasn't a coincidence at all! All of us wanted to save something "real," even though Art Deco didn't really start, like tap did, right here in America.

When Capitman and her cohort in design, Leonard Horowitz, made their historic Art Deco tour in 1981, I was on tour with the tap veterans, Cookie, Bubba, Leon, Buster, in Boston, Washington, Philadelphia, and other American cities, "bringing tap back."

―⁓―

Like Capitman, I had a background in journalism. In fact, reading about Capitman's promotional skills, I wish I'd have had more of her Madison Avenue approach when I was promoting tap. Although it might have turned some purists off, tap could have used every bit of hype it could get. Our problem in the media was that we were always coming back. We were never here. Buildings were more concrete, pun intended.

Where a lot of money was riding on Capitman's fight with the real estate developers, our tap crusade didn't have that cache. There wasn't any obvious "Goliath" to our "Davids." Nonetheless, I loved coming up with ways to promote tap. When I met Dennis Wilhelm, one of the Miami Design League's preservationists, he speculated it was "benign neglect" that killed tap, not some "enemy" developer.

I surmised that if tap at its highest form of development was improvisational, it defied institutionalization, by definition. Tap dancers can be housed in that bastion of Art Deco, Radio City Music Hall, but they aren't, after all, set in stone.

Though there was CETA (Comprehensive Employment Training Act), that put a few of us in service to the art and audiences, there has never been any real institutional support for tap. We don't even have a "Jazz at Lincoln Center" which is trumpeter Wynton Marsalis' baby, and as institutionalized as jazz can get.

The Miami Art Deco District stretching from 5th St. to Lincoln Road, with a smattering of hangers-on in other neighborhoods outside the preserved area,

Art Deco flourishes in Miami Beach and other parts of the world.

"Definitely Deco."

has often been referred to as beautiful in the sum of its parts. It wasn't just one building, but the whole district that got recognition. It is viewed "holistically." On one of my bicycle tours of the Deco district, I began to see a resemblance of the black tap acts I knew to the buildings on the beach streets.

Like the Three Chocolateers, The Nicholas Brothers, Moke and Poke, Buck and Bubbles, Chuck and Chuckles, Tip, Tap, and Toe, all the dancers were lumped into the same genre: black hoofers. They spoke the same "language," but each act was known for its specialty such as soft-shoe, flash, class, and comedy.

Similarly, in the Miami Deco revival, Henry Hohauser, L. Murray Dixon, and other key architects with last names like Skislewicz, Anis, France, Pancoast, and Nellenbogen, were great masters who contributed to the whole "effect," but created individual "specialties" with each of his buildings.

While all these Deco buildings had a common language, too—"eyebrows," over the windows for shade, the use of the number "three," in everything, smooth metal surfaces, and all were made with similar materials like glass, aluminum, Bakelite—each building, too, made its individual statement.

And is it any coincidence that aluminum was the material of choice for the metal taps as well as Deco fixtures? During the Depression, aluminum was economical, modern, and flashy.

When I first went down to Miami, I remember some of these Deco buildings still were covered up with aluminum, but it wasn't for the purpose of style. The aluminum was used to board up the buildings so that drug users wouldn't be able to get inside. There was a big transition going on during the Miami Art Deco revival not only because of Capitman, but because Fidel Castro had launched the Mariel Boatlift to Miami to get rid of people he considered non grata for The Revolution, and many landed on the beach.

Luckily for those few streets in Miami Beach, with much struggle and perseverance, Capitman and her gang of Deco-ites were able to obtain historic district recognition. President Jimmy Carter sent someone to the area and his representative recognized the entire district as "definitely Deco." Surrounding it now are incredibly (in many cases) awful high-rises that take away from the relaxed resort nature of what Miami Beach was developed to be.

Tap continues to be a neglected art, though many people study it, and perform it when they can. I can see the same thing happening today with Miami's Art Deco district and its surroundings. Another point of interest to me: Both revivals have conflicting elitist and populist forces. With the buildings the comparison is dime stores such as Woolworth's, once on Lincoln Road, to the exclusive 5th Ave shops.

With the dance, it was Fred and Ginger in their lavish escapes versus The Nicholas Brothers in their servants' attire. Tap itself is perceived as a lower class (black) art, although some of its roots also seem to be costumed with top hats, white ties, and tails in gorgeous Deco settings. Low art, high art.

Lastly, both Art Deco and tap have often been described as uplifting. I think a big part of why these revivals may have happened at the same time was that we were all looking not only for the genuine in art, but maybe even, some "fun" again. These revivals followed demoralizing times after wars (the World Wars and Vietnam). And who doesn't want some fun or to be uplifted?

Escape? Perhaps. The streamlined buildings with their winking eyebrows and those feet slapping wood both have the ability to make people feel good again. ■

Miami Danny Rose

I started to think about moving to Miami in 1992, after my first visit there. It was a city near an ocean where I could swim every day; I could enjoy the warm winters and the great Art Deco architecture. I could become a snowbird, too. Not an original idea, granted, but I could be the first Jewish feminist tap dancer to fly to Florida without a single relative to visit.

I fantasized that all those retired seniors loved entertainment. I'd heard about the "condo market" full of old Jews who at one time spent their vacations and money in the Borscht Belt—the Catskills. I began by setting up small gigs in artsy environments on South Beach and got very good response.

But I kept my eye on the mainstream condo market. It was far more organized, a genuine circuit with agents and captive audiences. My plan was to trot out *Rhythm & Schmooze*, my act, which would get them reminiscing about Sammy Davis, Jr. and Fred and Ginger while they ate up the jokes and the tap dancing.

True, my act was issue-oriented. But surely my Woody Allen-ish angst, my bits about Bathsheba Goldberg and her Wandering Shoes, my tap-rap about career vs. family would have them rolling in the aisles. And what about a singing tap-a-gram™ set to "Bei Mir Bist du Schoen?" That would definitely kill.

After a couple of years of hit-and-miss hustling down Florida way, sending my video and press kits to Miami, while still living in New York, I landed a call from a Bobby Breen. He informed me that he had been a famous child singer and now ran an agency in Florida. He talked fast, said he had seen my press kit, wanted an exclusive with me. Could I send him my videotape *NOW?*

Then I got a call from Breen's wife Audrey. Would I open for Eddie Fisher in November? *EDDIE FISHER?* Not exactly someone on my mind at the moment—or on anyone's mind for that matter—but I was thrilled to think I'd be part of the mainstream at last.

I went to the Museum of Broadcasting to do some research on Eddie Fisher. I'd remembered his big hit, "Oh, My Papa," but I wanted to know more about

"Doll, when I get the money, you get the money." I overheard one Miami agent using this line on the phone to a girl singer. I was hoping to get booked for the "Season" (November through March).

him. I watched his appearance on *The Colgate Comedy Hour* starring Milton Berle. You could tell this was really early television by the way they were pushing government bonds and had women sitting on cars in ads for Chesterfield cigarettes.

Milton Berle and his cronies greeted young Eddie, fresh out of the army, heralded as the new Sinatra. It was more exciting for me to watch the somersaulting Nicholas Brothers on that same segment, but I suspected that once I had spent some time working with Fisher, we'd end up hanging out and talking tap, comedy, and showbiz in general. Maybe we'd even get to "Debbie" and "Liz."

Much to my disappointment, Fisher ended up canceling. The Breens replaced him with impressionist/comedian Frank Gorshen. They decided that back-to-back comedy acts wouldn't work, so they canceled me. While flattered that they viewed me as a comedian, I wasn't going to give up without a fight. I begged them for the gig, assuring them that I would "just dance". But it was a no-go.

I heard from the Breens again the next year. They invited me to open for The Four Aces, a group whose big hit was "Three Coins in a Fountain." I revisited the Museum of Broadcasting. These singers were just plain corny; at least Fisher had had a certain hipness about him. Still, it was a booking.

Just prior to this Florida gig, I performed my show at Dixon Place, a downtown Manhattan space known for its cutting-edge acts. The audience was small but very enthusiastic, and my director gave me only a couple of notes—project more, talk slower. I was sure I'd fare well in Miami with this material.

I loved landing in South Florida in January, the warm humid breeze blowing in my face as soon as I got off the plane. A young, good-looking guy met me at the airport and my hormones began jumping. I was to stay in a little dive of a hotel in Coral Springs and do one gig a night. My limo driver told me I looked young for one of the Breens' acts. I persuaded him to have coffee with me at the hotel before taking off for his next pickup. This is going to be fun, I thought as we flirted with each other.

I asked him who else the Breens had on their roster.

"Oh, you know, old folksingers . . ." I imagined Allan Sherman, a favorite of mine growing up, who would be considered very kitsch now. He had specialized in hilarious, Jewish-infused parodies of folk and popular songs. But no, Sherman had died years ago.

Another driver, a well-worn and cranky guy, came early in the evening to pick me up for my one and only rehearsal just prior to show time. He told me some old jokes that I'd heard from my father. My father's delivery was better. I thought about my father a lot as we rode to King's Point, Del Ray Beach.

When I arrived at the large condo complex's theater, The Four Aces were rehearsing. This wasn't the nonprofit theater world of "spaces" and "venues." I was in a condo hall, and the next gig could be an "activity room." I'd be doing "dates," "making appearances," not just performing. I only had half an hour for my rehearsal. The thousand-seat hall was totally empty and there was a good wood floor as I'd been promised. I rehearsed my one musical number with the in-house band.

I got into my costume—glittery gold pants and top, kelly green tap shoes. My props were ready—matzoth for some matzoth dancing, a sauce pan and whisk to bang for percussion, a bag to hold everything.

Slowly people trickled in; eventually every seat was taken. It was almost completely quiet, with virtually no buzz of anticipation. It hadn't occurred to me that this senior citizen crowd would be hard of hearing.

I did my opening lines in eight bars of rhythm: "I love to talk, I love to tap, I love to tap while I talk, I love to talk about tap." Then: "See, a lot of people think tap dancers are happy people with happy feet . . . Well, I've been tapping for twenty-one years straight and I'm *still depressed*."

That punch line was always my indicator of whether I had the audience or not from the get go. This was the first time that I heard absolutely no response. Not even a sigh. Not one chuckle. Nada.

I knew I was in trouble. But I continued, "See, tap dancing is a healthy physical addiction. I go to my tap encounter group every week. It's called 'Codependent Feet.' We do 'The Twelve Steps.'"

Silence.

At this point I should have just started dancing to music, any music, and make my stay as brief as possible. But I was insistent. Plus, I was booked for 45 minutes.

I launched into the bit about Bathsheba Goldberg and her Wandering Shoes, an ironic take-off on the complex roots of tap.

"I used to think people really wanted to know about the roots of tap—the black roots, the white roots, the social forces that killed tap or at least made it go underground. Then I realized after awhile that all people really wanted to know was who does it the best, who does tap belong to, and who gets the credit. Well that used to upset me . . . but it doesn't anymore. I now just tell them the Jews started tap."

Thud.

"In fact, it was Jewish women who started tap. While all the men were on the top of the mountain getting the law, we were just standing around waiting." I assumed a position of impatience, my arms akimbo and my feet drumming against the floor.

Thud.

Leonard Reed, inventor of the Shim Sham, booked acts, too, and was as fast-talking as any agent.

"In fact, it was my ancestor Bathsheba Goldberg who started it. She threw down some matzoth (you know, this was a forerunner to sand dancing) . . . and Moses' brother, Aaron, heard her and was so impressed with her matzoth dancing, he opened up the Golden Calf Café and booked her. She started her own group and began an international tour: Bathsheba Goldberg and her Wandering Shoes."

Thud.

I began reading my father's jokes, meticulously crafted stories and one-liners that he'd sent me over the years. These jokes went over great in New York, where there was an ironic punch to every line I recited. But they weren't playing here, in a crowd that was thoroughly familiar with this sort of stuff. They were there to judge, not to be entertained.

Much later, an acquaintance of mine whose parents happened to live at Kings Point, laughed when I told her how little response I'd gotten. No, she acknowledged, her parents weren't into "irony."

Standing before these poker-faced people, half of me wanted to run offstage, while the other more self-destructive half stayed to finish the act.

I tried another angle, the singing tap-a-gram™ to the old Yiddish ditty "Bei Mir Bist Du Schöen" that Sarah Safford had rewritten to be delivered by none other than George Bush, Sr.:

> *Dear Mr. Hussein*
> *You're giving me a pain*
> *Dear Mr. Hussein*
> *You're making me mad.*

You took over Kuwait
You wouldn't negotiate
You made me sit and wait
You made me look bad . . .

I heard a few coughs. This was one of those halls where you couldn't see into the audience at all, not even the first row. The silence was like thunder. Suddenly, a voice over the loudspeaker intoned:

"JANE GOLDBERG, ladies and gentlemen. Let's give her a hand." I was still singing my theme song, "I Wanna Be Happy," as the piano player played me quickly offstage.

———

The old limo driver held back his tired jokes and treated me gently on the way back to the hotel. "Some audiences are more serious than others," he consoled me. But when we reached the hotel parking lot, he made an ominous cell phone call to the Breens. Even before I entered my room, the phone was ringing condemnatorialy.

"WHAT WERE YOU DOING OUT THERE—A DANCE HISTORY LECTURE?" screamed Bobby Breen, as Audrey sobbed audibly in the background. "My son told me you were the worst opening act we ever booked into King's Point!!!!" I'd have liked to have had a few words with their son.

"I didn't change a word of my act!" I finally screamed back after letting him rant for a few more minutes. "You looked at my tape. Why did you book me in front of that deadbeat crowd if you knew what I did?" I was tired of defending myself, especially with Audrey Breen crying her crocodile tears.

When he told me I had to be out of the hotel room and onto the earliest plane in the morning, I threatened to call my lawyer. The trouble was, I didn't have one.

———

I still want to be a snowbird. In true showbiz style, when I get back to Miami, I'll do what everyone else does: reinvent myself. Next time I'll go as "Goldie Berg" and meet up with agents who have names like Jerry Rainbow, Candy Casino, Honey Lamb, all names I got when I was aiming for the condo market.

Better yet, I'll be one of those agents or own my own nightclub, like comedian Belle Barth. That was Sarah's idea from the beginning—to open up a nightclub.

"I can see you in Miami," she had said. I can still see myself in Miami, too, but with my New York pad intact. A real snowbird. Arriving there after Hanukkah, staying until Passover, flying back to New York or some other cool place for the summer.

The good life. It'll be expensive, but not impossible. I wonder how hard it will be to get a liquor license. I truly love the gorgeous Miami clouds, ocean, and winters. ∎

Carry Your Shoes— Tap Dancing in India

Tap dancing in India! Hoofing at the Taj Mahal! Spinning in Madras! Bombing in Bombay! I was going to India on a Fulbright Scholarship to research the relationship between jazz tap and Indian classical dance, primarily kathakali. There was none. I had made it all up. I had meant to write "kathak," where at least the feet move rhythmically. I wrote that I was fascinated with the "foot cultures of the world."

Naturally, I went into a major panic attack when my acceptance letter came a year and a half after I began applying. I kept filling out the forms, thinking nothing would happen. This was my girlfriend Betty's idea, anyway. Betty was a feminist-theater professor who fell in love with India— its theater, dance, and culture. I wasn't at *all* attracted to Indian theater, dance *or* culture.

One night on her way back to California, where she headed the theater department at Pomona College, Betty stayed over in my apartment in New York and projected slides of elephants, textiles, and Indian dance onto my bedroom wall. She enthused, "Jane, you've got to go to India."

Thus, a year and a half later, I was on a Delta flight. I was the first one to arrive at freezing Kennedy Airport *four* hours early, the day after Christmas. I felt like I was leaving on a dare, and broke out into hives right before departure.

My nerves were already frayed way before I left. I thought I had made one breakthrough when I heard Badal Roy, an Indian tabla player, who I had invited over to accompany me after getting his number from Jonathan Hollander, another Fulbright scholar. Badal Roy's drumming sounded just like tap. In fact, he had previously played with Miles Davis and had a jazz "feel" himself. He came to my apartment, sat on my floor with his tabla set, and we did some "tabla tap." Drinking tea afterwards, he told me to travel with my boyfriend, that it would be hard traveling alone as a woman in India. I went into more panic.

Kathak meets tap in front of the gorgeous "sex temples" of Khajuraho.

In my panic attack modality, I started putting the word out that I needed contacts, and I needed them bad! My anxiety was allayed somewhat when I met Bombay's jazz impresario, Niranjan Jhaveri in NYC. Niranjan saw a videotape of my dancing and got me my first solid booking. I would be tap dancing at the five-star Oberoi Towers on New Year's Eve. He warned me to wear lots of glitter.

The month before I left, I attended an artist residency in Virginia where I saw a lot of cows on its grounds. This was a true omen of the sacred cows I would soon be seeing all over the Indian city streets, roaming like dogs on their way home. Luckily I didn't have that much time to fret over the trip at the writer's colony. Working on my book proposal, I burned lots of incense and nearly set my studio on fire when it burned through the empty toilet paper roll I was using for a holder.

———

I finally left for the subcontinent with a "hit list" prepared by Betty and her guru, Kailash. I packed two pairs of tap shoes, skirts, t-shirts, audiotapes, a bag full of every medical supply you could think of, and a ton of glitter. I also had my boob dress, the turquoise and black rayon one Dorothy had made me. Kumudini Lakhia, a renowned kathak choreographer/dancer/innovator was the first person I contacted by phone (this was pre e-mail for me, even pre-fax; I'm a bit of dinosaur in the techno department). When Kumudini heard my garbled voice on delay, she shouted back, "Sounds interesting. Come." I looked up where she lived, Ahmedebad, and discovered that *Lonely Planet* called Ahmedebad "the city of dust."

Needless to say, I didn't *want* to bomb in the Oberoi Regal Room in Bombay. I wasn't prepared for the seven hundred drinking businessmen who, after midnight, were all too happy to ignore a tap dancer. "Georgy," the emcee had to beg the audience to be quiet. I warned the management that dancing after midnight wasn't the best time for my act, but they were insistent.

Experiencing the omen of the sacred cows, in this case, bull, firsthand. Above, doing yoga in Pune.

©CHANGING TIMES TAP ARCHIVE

The kathak masters and me in Jaipur. I loved tapping to the tablas, 1994.

Oddly, it didn't feel like a bomb, because the drunken laughter made up for the sound of "dying out there." The Regal Room was only one of three venues I was to perform on New Year's Eve. Rushing around in an Oberoi Towers bathrobe to cover up my sequins, I danced in two other spots in the Disney-like complex. One young jerk tried to imitate my tapping by rattling some spoons at his table in the fancy steakhouse room (an oxymoron for veggie-populated Bombay). The third room, however, gave me hope that tapping might work out in India, after all. I played with three jazz musicians—a group called "Take Five"—and the crowd was more my kind of scene.

Although the floor in the lounge was slippery marble, I fulfilled my weeklong gig, tapping for my supper—room and board. I caught jetlag, however. That's right. Caught it! I was soon making crazy decisions like the night, well, morning really, 5 a.m., when I was wandering around the hotel sleepless. In the all-night restaurant, more like a diner, I met an Indian man who promised to take me to a "Zen Room" for one nostril yoga.

That night, after my gig, he and his friends took me to the streets of Bombay where we stepped over a lot of sleeping Indians to score some bong, the Bombay way to get high. Then the "Zen Room" turned out to be this Indian's parents' apartment and I had to talk my way out of the apartment by listening to him read his 1971 account in *Seventeen Magazine* of British Colonialism at his high school.

I swore myself off men for the rest of the trip.

I did meet a great father figure in Bombay. Through my Oberoi bomb, a lighting designer had told me about Colonel Rege at the National Center for Performing Arts, right across the street from my hotel. Although the name "Colonel Rege" didn't scream out to me "man of the arts," he was, and one huge articulate fan of kathak, the dance form I was in India to research.

Colonel Rege told me about the temples and courts and Mogul empire where the kathaks danced and were married to God. Kathak means "storyteller" and when the dancers aren't telling their stories with their "abhinaya" or expressions, they slap their bare feet on hard marble floors creating magical, unimaginable rhythms. Ankle bells are tied on each pair of feet to enhance the sound.

As Colonel Rege and I drank tea, he reminisced about the Astaire-Rogers movies that came to India in the 1930s and his own ballroom years during the British rule. I didn't have my tap shoes, but Colonel Rege wanted to hear me dance so he pulled off his loafers and I tapped in them. Even though they were three sizes too big, he snapped his fingers to the beat of my feet. It was through Colonel Rege I got the biggest lesson of all on my journey: Carry your shoes *always*. I never knew when or where I was going to tap.

Colonel Rege helped me chart my itinerary, and told me the difference between tourist and regular taxis. He also gave me lessons in etiquette making sure I brought a single rose to Bombay's kathak maven, Sutari Devi. Meeting this grande dame reminded me of how I chased after the old black hoofers of vaudeville, getting their stories and steps.

Sutari Devi wore lots of makeup and her bright red lipstick complimented her large red bindi or "dot" painted on her forehead. As she held her puppy, she sang rhythms to her student one on one in her apartment. I tapped for her in my silver glitter shoes. She told me she loved the old Nicholas Brothers movies

The auto-rickshaw, a common form of transportation in Mother India.

I preferred riding on the back of moter scooters. Here I am in Goa, trying to learn how to drive one.

and Eleanor Powell. Thirties Hollywood had certainly hit "Bollywood," Bombay's movie industry.

———

Shaktiji, an American kathak dancer who lived in Jaipur, "the Pink City," invited me to visit her after we met at a major kathak conference in New Delhi full of the old remaining masters. I was amazed by the three-wheel bicyclist who drove me straight to her home on one of the busiest, most chaotic streets in Jaipur. Things had become very freewheeling at this point of my journey and nothing held me back from seeing what I could, and dancing where I could. Shaktiji had married some abusive guy but remained in contact with his family, who were major kathakers. She took me to meet them and naturally I tapped for the whole clan. They smoked cigarettes and listened and smiled knowingly at my "foot culture of the world."

Shaktiji also took me to the great Krishna temple and I spun with her and all the other Krishnas. It wasn't like your average Hare Krishna saffron and incense-bell-wielding spaced-out crowd. These were middle class, older people and it was very physical and fun, nothing religious or even phonily "spiritual." Shaktiji also hired some Eunuchs to dance for me in her living quarters, and paid them afterwards.

What impressed me the most about this American kathak dancer, living in Jaipur, was how *proud* she was of her home, one large room, even though there was no bathroom or running water. She swept her floor a lot, though it wasn't dirty. If you had to go out of her living quarters for those conveniences, you never felt she was in the

Sharon Lowen, an American dancer living in New Delhi.

least ashamed or embarrassed, given that both her parents were professors who taught at The New School in New York City.

You could easily mistake her for being Indian because of her fluent Hindi. People often talk about the poverty in India, but I was sometimes more startled by the opulence there. Shaktiji didn't act impoverished. She was proud of her life.

The same goes for another American I stayed with, Cubby, who I met as a contact from my hairdresser in NYC. Indian friends of mine in Bombay told me it was hard to tell she was American because of her fluency in the language as well and how she'd adopted the conservative dress of the shalwar kamezes. No cleavage for Cubby! She'd get on my case, too, when I left her apartment to buy fruit or run errands with anything low-cut. Just not a cool way to be in Khar, a suburb of Bombay, she told me.

Another American who has lived in India to dance and whose daughter married an Indian, is Sharon Lowen. No dancer's trip to India is complete without a visit to Sharon. A Detroit Jew, she's our ambassador, who fell in love with Indian classical dance, went over there on a Jr. Fulbright, and is considered a renowned Odissi dancer, accepted by Indians as one of their own.

———

In Pune, I stayed with the jazz impresario's daughter Neesha, in a *real* Indian setting, eating *real* Indian food, which I saw prepared every night, as opposed to five-star Americanized hotel food. Neesha was a modern dancer and we talked shop for two weeks. I phoned my two kathak contacts in Pune, Rhohini Bhate and Prabha Mharate and began teaching tap to their students. Although the kids

Rhohini Bhate instructing one of her kathak pupils in Pune.

were barefooted, they could easily learn how to tap. They had "feet" already, though the jazz rhythms were hard for many.

I also met a caterer Dilip Borowake, who insisted I see his gardens. I didn't realize he was one of Pune's czars. When I admired his gorgeous green mosaic floor and did a little soft shoe on it, four nights later Dilip Borowake presented me with a microphone, sound system, and one hundred of his friends, Pune's finest.

I guessed this was how Isadora Duncan started out, dancing for the well-heeled in European salons. I tapped to the renowned tabla of Ustad Zakir Hussein and though I didn't get all (any) of his counts, the Indian audience appreciated my stab at their music. They even "got" my humor and one man said he remembered the famous picture of Kent State when I did my "anti-war" tap. I was really touched by that. He had lived in New York in 1970.

Renowned psychiatrist/actor Mohan Agashie, possibly awaiting another haircut.

An expat acquaintance had urged me to look up the renowned psychiatrist/actor, Mohan Agashie, so I did, leaving him a message on his phone machine when I first arrived in Pune. He picked me up in a large car and took me to his hairdresser Joshi (pronounced Yoshi) for our tête-à-tête.

Me and my camel: No one knew of St. John's Wort at the spice and herb markets on the ground, but I bought Prozac over the counter cheap, cheap, cheap!

We talked while Joshi cut Mohan's hair. I kidded him about our meeting over a haircut and not the usual milk tea, and he retorted that, at least, he returned my call. In New York, he told me, no one returned any of his calls, or they took a few weeks if they got around to it, and by then he was already gone.

Indians were often spontaneous about making plans, seeing people, setting up performances. Mohan was a household name in Pune and a renowned classical actor who had also appeared in the film *Mississippi Masala*, which only showed him as a goofy drinker, not the great actor he was. I couldn't quite figure out the psychiatrist angle.

Once I visited him at work, where he was running an honored film institute, and I was mulling over whether he was gay or not; he lived with his mother or was taking care of her, in any case. He sat at a big desk with this gorgeous colorful crown-like hat on his head, the kind you see on Arab men. He told me people come to India either to learn about the culture or to be salesmen for their own country's goods and which was I, pray tell? Was I a seeker or a salesman?

I emphatically replied, "Salesman!" Even though I was there to research kathak, I was there more enthusiastically to export tap dancing.

Thanks to Mohan, the shrink part of Mohan, I went to see a colleague of his for medication when my clinical depression hit hard during my Fulbright. I was sorry I'd gone off the St. John's Wort pills, the then new popular herb for depression in New York. I figured for sure I'd find it in India, since I read that cows love to eat the flower St. John's Wort. Often curious for trying New Age anti-Western remedies, or anything to help get through my depression episodes, I was sure there'd be no problem securing some St. John's Wort, with all those cows roaming around.

No one, however, had ever even heard of the stuff. Instead I bought fluoxetine, that is, Prozac, over the counter, cheap cheap cheap. I also discovered a cream called "Sensur," which was stronger than Tiger Balm and felt hot and wonderful on the muscles.

Also in Pune through Prabha Mharate, I was able to finally see the kathak master, Bhirju Mahraj dance with the appealing tabla master, Zakir Hussein, in a live concert where I sat on the ground with other Punites and watched, listened, clapped. It was impressive how the audience was so educated; people knew when each phrase was going to begin and end. They would shout out at the last syllable with the players, and clap to punctuate the end of the ragas. Everyone went wild when an old revered female singer was brought to the stage for an encore. Indian performances are long, but their audiences are into them.

—〰〰—

I went to the famous Osho Ashram out of curiosity. An old Pune Indian couple I sat next to at the Zakir/Bhirju concert told me that you can't leave Pune without spending a few days at the Ashram, packed with mostly Europeans. I

My Ayurvedic doc in a field of flowers in Kerala, South India.

©CHANGING TIMES TAP ARCHIVE

wondered if it really was the sex commune of its rumors when upon entrance, the first thing I had to have was a test for HIV.

It reminded me more of a Beverly Hills spa than a spiritual environment. Osho himself was long gone, but his spirit lives on. The ashram was named after him and is run like clockwork, clean and efficient. Even a packet of soy sauce is priced at one rupee! Osho was known in the States as the "sex guru." He was reviled for his obsessions with Rolls Royces and the controversial incorporated community he founded in Oregon.

I discovered how I felt about authority in those few days at Osho's. There were rules galore. I could certainly put up with wearing the saffron and maroon robes, twirling dervishes, and changing into white at seven p.m. Osho would then himself appear on a gigantic video screen to deliver his famous evening lectures. He came across like a Borscht Belt comic, telling his stories with set-ups and punch lines. I shouted in unison with the room full of devotees, "OSHO!! OSHO!!" to the video screen.

I had to draw the line, though, when the lifeguard at the swanky outdoor pool insisted that I conform to the maroon color code as far as bathing suits were concerned. I just couldn't submit to buying one more maroon colored garment in their well-stocked store or from any of the many vendors surrounding the cashram (sic).

I tried to get away with wearing some hot pink underpants and a red bra to no avail. It was the lifeguard's will over mine and his won out. I left the pool, humiliated and relieved that my stay in Pune was drawing to a close.

Hours before I left Pune on a two-day train ride to South India, I got a phone call at Neesha's and learned that the feminist collective of Madras had booked me into another five star, the vintage Connemara Hotel. Again, I was to stay a week in exchange for my "feet." Despite a nice young man meeting me at the train, I was so lonely when I arrived at the old hotel, I started to cry in my bed the minute I laid down. Fortunately, *White Nights*, starring Gregory Hines and Mikhail Baryshnikov, was on television. Suddenly, it seemed like an old friend had come to visit me.

The next morning I dutifully began calling all the dance contacts from Betty's and Kailash's "hit list." I had to be careful whose names I mentioned, I was to learn, because there was competition amongst the dancer/players. Just like everywhere!

The further south I went, the less jazzy the music became, but I adapted. In Madras, I played with a group led by a guy who called himself "Elvis." A dance lover named VR Devika organized a lot of performances for me in schools, colleges, the IIT—an equivalent of our MIT—and even her brother's Rotary Club. I have

©CHANGING TIMES TAP ARCHIVE

Get your Cultcha kids! Hundreds of Indian children sat watching tap live for the first time. They were so polite and respectful, it was eerie. Who knows what they were thinking?

great pictures of me with thousands of awestruck children, experiencing tap dancing for the first time.

I started to bomb with the history of tap lecture/dem for the Feminist Collective of Madras and luckily switched to tapping and talking about my personal life midstream. *That* interested them more. The collective, run by grandmothers, began to enjoy my performance at the Connemara, especially my tale of the "Zen Room." I read out loud some of the "matrimonial" personal ads about arranged marriages in the newspapers. One of the women's husbands owned a brand new television station called "Asianet" and when he heard I was going to Trivandrum, he offered me a place to stay at the TV station's guesthouse there.

An actor who caught my act offered me a place in Ahmedebad with his grandfather Popatlal Shah (I love those Indian names!), should I ever get to the "city of dust." I was experiencing the renowned Indian hospitality.

On the overnight train ride from Madras to Cochin on the Malabar coast, I lost a huge tooth, froze in the first class open window berth, which I shared with three old Indian men, got my period, and got off at the wrong stop the next morning.

A reporter from *The Indian Express*, eagerly awaiting my arrival, asked me to show her my "rapid fire feet" and I burst into tears. The next day, my birthday, the headline appeared, "Tip Top Tap of a Lonely Heart." The article brought me lots of interesting people, including a student dying to study tap and a freelance writer who moonlighted in dental products, and who took me to a dentist who glued my tooth

I love the one cracking up the best.

back in. My mother had told me to meet Jews in India and Cochin would have been the spot, but there weren't even enough left to make a minyan! (Ten guys usually.)

Babu Varghese, *the* man of Kerala at the time, who owned a tourist agency, ran quaint boats up and down the river, and had a passion for artists. He met me at the train. I'd seen his name on Betty's hit list and thought "Babu Varghese" was an *address* until I read a book on the overnight train, *Chasing the Monsoon,* and realized Babu was a man.

He took me to a truncated version of a kathakali concert; sometimes those evenings last all night and into the day, like a Robert Wilson piece. The old men with the bright green painted faces seemed to improvise their stories, even though the movement was turtle-like slow.

I'd read the beautiful sad description in Arundhati Roy's *The God of Small Things,* and Babu confirmed the fact that like my old tap gurus, the old kathakali masters, had also turned to alcohol and gone to seed. They, too, were not treated with reverence or respect in their final years, as their country's national treasures. Instead they were treated like some old relics sent out to pasture. I wondered if it was true Japan really held its own national treasured artists in high esteem and treated them accordingly.

In Thiruvananthapuram (Trivandrum), progressive citizens were always on strike for something. In fact, when I arrived, the strike was about electricity and

Right: Babu Varghese built treehouses. I stayed in one of them to escape India's incredible May heat.

THE HINDUSTAN TIMES

Published from Delhi

Vol LXX No. 64   Late City   New Delhi Sunday March 6 1994   38 Pages

Arts & Culture

French poem reveals Prerna's talent

Dance/Shanta Serbjeet Singh

LIKE the bitter-sweet fragrance of spring, and as if these balmy evenings will never come back, a flurry of dance activity mounted the city stages from the conventional bilateral cultural exchange programmes like "Days of Mongolia" to the heady experimentation of the jugalbandi between tap dancing and Kathak, from the old-is-gold flavour of the all-veteran show of this year's Bindadin to the ...

extent that Prerna's Kathak vocabulary managed to freely and creatively mirror these images, holding the mind fast to other essence, not just the literal word, it was a tribute both to Kathak's hitherto untapped potential this young dan ...

search of that tablet) to the Sisterhood of the nineties. Goldberg's act was a delightful mix of rapid-fire dancing and racy commentary on all aspects of modern life, family and even politics. But when Shovna began, sensibly stressing the ni ... the feet in Kathak ... and "Phi ...

... e Goldberg and Shovna Narain in "Rhythm and Schmooz ...

Kerala

INDIAN EXPRESS KOCHI

Tip-top-tap of a lonely heart

KOCHI

IN New York they call her the lady with the rapid-fire feet, and that's an understatement as far as tap dancer Jane Goldberg is concerned. The dexterity with which her feet tap to the equally rhythmic rapid-fire movements of her verbal message is a sight worth watching.

Relaxing at Malabar Hotel in Willingdon Island, Goldberg spoke to *Indian Express* about her pet passion – her "tip-top-tap"

Jane Goldberg has been tapping for the last 20 years. And along with the tap-tap of her feet have come issues she has been espousing all her life. Of feminism, freedom and family.

"Topical tap – that's what Goldberg is perfecting today. She loves to talk and she loves to tap. She mixes words and steps to astonishing effect. Topical tap has autobiographical overtones. It gives Goldberg an opportunity to talk about her political affiliations, her romance, and even her loneliness.

"I've been tapping for the last 20 years. Yet I am depressed," she sings as she taps, thus opening up a vulnerable spot in the life of an artiste – a whole life of emptiness where there's no room for family or close relationships.

Like comedians and clowns who make others laugh even while living through moments of agony, dancers too delight audiences wilfully putting away their pain. Goldberg emphasises this point when she says that tap dancers need not always be the stereotyped "happy people with happy feet."

"Tap dancing is going through a renaissance and America is avidly seizing this medium of rhythm as a means of self expression," says Goldberg ... self is a pioneer of ... renaissance ...

Very m ... originate ... ghettoes ... represent ... free spi ... its effo ... of the ...

G ... "hoo ... some ... the s ... perf ... fus ... rhy ...

misses a beat. So perfectly has she mastered her style.

Ever since Goldberg perfected her own brand of tap dancing, she has gone all out to ferret out potential talent. She has organised shows and seminars and conducted workshops all over New York. She hopes to exploit the interest Europe is showing in tap dancing.

A Jewess, Goldberg takes pride in tracing the origins of tap to the ... wish women, while ... come ...

Jane Goldberg displays her special tap dancer's shoe

---

32 Pages Rs. 2.30

MADURAI, SATURDAY, FEBRUARY 12, 1994.

THE HINDU

India's National Newspaper

Printed at Madras, Coimbatore, Bangalore, Hyderabad, Madurai, Gurgaon and Visakhapatnam.

Of tap dancing and politics

From Our Staff Reporter

THIRUVANANTHAPURAM, F ... Ms. Jane Goldberg tap dances as about war, politics and social issues performance by her in front of the Secre ... Thursday took strollers by surprise.

Ms. Jane Goldberg from New York ... her talk as she performs to revive a d ... form. She also uses it as a vehicle of ex ... on wide-ranging issues.

But her larger mission in India is to st ... affinities between tap and Indian dance ... Tap and Kathak rhythm converge at ... points, she claims.

"Tap is essentially of racism and sexism ... Ms. Goldberg who is on a scholarship fro ... New York University. Back in the US ... "Keeping tap moving" campaign is spearhe ... a renaissance of the dance form which he ... ed from the limelight some 20 years back.

Onlookers watched in fascination as ... Goldberg tap danced to the couplets su ... anti-liquor activists who are on a dharna be ... the seat of power. Later, Ms Goldberg went ... her routine – swift steps, shuffles and swive ... and the occasional drumming on a dish.

പുസ്തകം 14   ലക്കം 79

മാതൃഭൂമി

THE NATIONAL DAILY IN MALAYALAM, PUBLISHED FROM KOZHIKODE, KOCHI, THIRUVANANTHAPURAM, THRISSUR AND KANNUR

Regd No.KL /TV (N)243 Thiruvananthapuram Friday February 11 1994   തിരുവനന്തപുരം 1994 ഫെബ്രുവരി 11 വെള്ളി

പേജ് 12

വിലരൂപ1.90

... n America ... found the ... uch issues

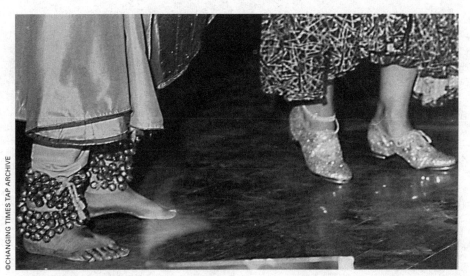

Kathak Meets Tap Again: A "Ka-tap" performance in New Delhi.

the driver that took me to the beach had to avoid all the marchers and picketers. Once upon a time, I'd probably have been in those marches!

My most dramatic demonstration of tap happened in the streets of Trivandrum, now known by its full-blast Indian name, Thiruvananthapuram. When Babu's good friend Soman, a powerful journalist of Kerala, discovered my tap was "topical," he and Babu plotted and staged a demonstration at *The Secretariat*, the seat of the government of Kerala. I would tap for the people.

I never did much street tapping in my day, but I did it as a favor to Babu's generosity in showing me around his city. I began spinning to the rhythm of a line of chanting men protesting alcohol. They were banging on cans and provided rhythm for my act. The next day I made the front pages of five of the Kerala newspapers, pictures and all. I became a household name for a week! People who'd read about me wanted to see the bottom of my shoes everywhere I went.

I couldn't understand the language, Malayalam, but it looked wonderful in print, round and curvy. It was the first time I could feel my politics in synch with my dancing. I was performing for people who couldn't understand English at all, but could relate to the percussion, even some of my banter, it seemed.

I remembered what a friend from New York had told me right before I left for the subcontinent.

"You'll love India, Jane," Stan told me. "Dance for the people. Carry Your Shoes." ■

The bottom clip (left) is the script of Malayalum in South Kerala.

End of an Era—
Buster Brown, A Real Class Act

News of Buster Brown's death on May 7, 2002, two weeks shy of his 89th birthday, spread through the tap-vine fast. Four days later, his funeral at St. Peter's Church—the "Jazz Church"—overflowed with adoring friends and fans. Buster was probably the most beloved of all the old school hoofers. With him gone, there were only a few vintage ones left. Buster, I'd venture to say, symbolized something very deep for anyone touched by him. He was a unifier—someone who could get people to lock arms and, in our little kingdom, unite.

In the last decade of his life, Buster was known best for hosting a jam session at Swing 46, a little nightclub in the West 40's, where young hoofers could practice their new chops under his supportive, nonjudgmental guidance. It didn't matter if the dancer didn't have good timing, or rhythm, or went on too long, or couldn't even dance at all. Buster created an atmosphere where everyone felt safe to perform anything—new material, old routines—on that little stage.

I'd seen tiny tots shuffling around on that floor for the first time who eventually morphed into experienced pros à la Savion Glover. Dancers were always dropping in on Buster's Jam. Singers, too. Some spent the whole night there. It was a totally international scene too: Japanese, German, Brazilian, Finnish, South American tappers—everyone knew about Buster's Jam.

Short and slim, Buster remained slight of frame until the end. He wore a pork pie hat on his head and his pants a little loose. He had a great laugh and great smile and was always humming something. He was often on the road working, because everyone wanted to have Buster on the team.

In a world rife with rivalries and allegiances, he managed to straddle The Original Hoofers and The Copasetics when dancing was involved, performing on rival turf. He was a guest artist on many a company tour. He wasn't one of those

James Buster Brown—I love this shot of Buster. It captures him!

extraordinary-looking hoofers like tall, handsome, suave Honi Coles, or even the most spectacular of dancers like Jimmy Slyde or Leon Collins, but he was all right with everyone.

At the tap breeding ground, the old American Tap Dance Orchestra space, Woodpecker's, in Soho, Buster would always join in, no matter who was dancing. He loved to dance too much to worry about whether he was getting paid, or how much older he was than the rest of us.

———⁓⁓⁓———

In 1984, I organized a tour to Vienna, and Buster came along. At Kennedy Airport, someone stole his tape deck and tapes. The rest of us—Leon Collins, Leon's main squeeze and pianist Joan Hill, our wonderful pianist Jim Roberts and conga player Montego Jo, Marion Coles of the famed Apollo chorus line, Harold Cromer of the comedy team Stump and Stumpy, and my two compatriots, Beverly Rolfsmeir and Sarah Safford—were all scurrying around, checking our luggage, so we didn't even see the theft. It was painful. The thing about the old jazzers is you have to know how much they love their music; they live *inside* their songs, live with them all the time, around the clock. We would have to figure out some way to get Buster music in his hotel room.

When we arrived in Vienna, some expat musician friends of Joan Hill's met us at the airport. One of them yelled out, "Who-eee, the cats are here!" Somehow, I knew instinctively I wasn't one of the "cats." That name was reserved for Leon, Buster, and Harold, maybe Montego and Jim, mainly the older jazz musicians and dancers, black or white, of the swing and bop eras. They were a different breed; they knew all the solos and players of the big band days, the way fans know players on a baseball or basketball team. Buster was the ultimate cat.

In Vienna, we were part of the New Dance Festival, appearing nightly in a stately old Viennese theater. By day, Buster slept. Each night, after our performance and a meal of Wiener Schnitzels he was ready for somewhere else to prowl. Around midnight, he'd end up at a jazz club that played canned music and was a fabulous place for dancing.

Buster was a smooth Lindy-hopper, a regular at *The Cat Club*, a swing dance venue in New York's East Village, always with live big bands. But I never saw him swing harder than he did that week in Vienna. Now, there was a guy who knew what a party was really supposed to be about.

———⁓⁓⁓———

Buster was never one of my tap daddies, the guys who taught me steps, but I would have him teach my NYU students a master class every semester over the twenty years I taught there. Over the phone, he'd say he didn't want to teach more than an hour, but he always went overtime. Like the other tap daddies, he'd sing the class, no tape deck needed. The students would automatically divide themselves into groups, the advanced and the beginners.

One of Buster's theme songs in performance was a tune called "Cute" by Neal Hefti, popularized by The Count Basie Orchestra. It was a true tap dancer's song because of the breaks and space left for the dancer to improvise. Even though he often stuck to one tune—"April In Paris," "Laura," or "Fascinating Rhythm," Buster could also let go of the time. He would always start out with a thirty-two-bar chorus, like the rest of the hoofers teaching, but then he'd go "outside" the time and be teaching phrases that had nothing to do with thirty-two bars, but somehow stayed related to the tune. This way of teaching was picked up—intentionally or not—by Savion Glover and his acolytes years later.

———

St. Peter's Church in midtown, on the East Side of Lexington Avenue, is as modern as any church can be. With its streamlined cushions and large stage, its design seemed to fit in with the corporate look of the Citicorp Building, the complex of offices and stores it resides in. You might have a hard time imagining spirituality coursing through the place.

Yvette Glover, Savion's mother, had obtained permission to hold the last minute service on the condition that we were all out by noon. People were crying, and laughing, and hugging, so it got off to a late start. There was a sense of

Buster in contemplative modality at my fiftieth birthday party.

©CHANGING TIMES TAP ARCHIVE

PHOTO BY AND COURTESY OF JAMIE LAROWITZ SHERMAN (MOTHER)

Buster loved babies and children. This is my little niecela, now eleven, August Sherman.

expectation in the air. Much to my surprise, my name was on the program as one of the speakers.

I had just visited Buster in the hospital a few days before he died and knew from looking at him that this was the last time we would be together. A bunch of us had been on "The Buster Watch" bringing him soufflés, duck, Chinese and Indian food, calling him up, getting him to places. Two of his closest New York protégés, Heather Cornell and Max Pollak, took care of some of the last details of his life, making sure he had health insurance, getting him to doctors. Jamie Larowitz Sherman bought him an air conditioner for his rambling apartment, and provided him with a home away from home in Massachusetts.

⸻

Max Pollak read *The New York Times* obituary at the opening of the service, and Yvette, a fabulous gospel singer, led us in "Amazing Grace." Little Hannah, Andrew Nemr, and Michela Marino Lerman, all Swing 46 protégés, danced, and I did one of Buster's rhythms from *Cute* that everyone would recognize for sure. Patience Higgins played his saxophone amidst the tears and laughter and silence. There was also a long rambling talk by a minister right out of the church of saints and sinners, swaying the crowd with a lot of racial rhetoric, ending with "as long as there are black people, there will be tap dancing." True, of course, but it wasn't really in the spirit of this particular service.

A highlight of the memorial was Gregory's talk to the community. Gregory had just flown in from Toronto—of course he would do that because of how important Buster was to him and the tap community, and how important Gregory himself was. He begged us, he pleaded, and cajoled us to unite in the name of Buster.

Gregory kidded us about our rivalries. He listed all the petty reasons why we built up animosities: "You might not like the way someone dances. You might not like their shoelaces. You might think you're better than they are." I squirmed in my seat, feeling a little guilty wondering to whom I should be making amends. I was thankful for Gregory's directness, his addressing us like the Capulets and Montagues. For once, we seemed like a unified, diversified family.

—⁓—

Buster's family from his hometown of Baltimore was sitting in the front row with Shawn, a stepson from Boston, who had lived with Buster during his last months. We all knew about the Baltimore family—Buster often went there on Christmas

©CHANGING TIMES TAP ARCHIVE

Bus at my New York University class.

—but because Buster was *our* family, on the scene all the time, it was still hard to figure them at the church. I flashed back to the funeral of his young son, Ricky, killed on his bicycle by a hit-and-run driver just before he was to have gone off to college. Buster had looked so grief-stricken that morning as he greeted me on the steps of the church. Now, Buster was to be buried next to Ricky, in his own old neighborhood on upper Riverside Drive.

There were a lot of tearful faces when the service was over. A whole lineup of regulars from Swing 46 tap danced the "Bill Robinson" routine as a final salute at the gravesite. The next day I got this e-mail from Gregory:

> *"What I wanted to do yesterday, in the name of our sweet Dr. Buster Brown (who lived it), was to provoke many in the assemblage (and believe me they knew who they were) to search deep into their hearts, their love of Buster, and indeed, Tap Dancing. I wanted to encourage 'em to "let go" of the negative criticisms, jealousies, and petty, divisive backbiting darkening their souls like tar and nicotine blackens the lungs, and truly enjoy our wonderful art and everyone who wears the shoes.*
>
> *This is what Buster did. This is the example he lived and set down for his contemporaries and all of those Swing 46 children to see. Over and over before, during and after the service you could hear it ring through St. Peter's: 'He never said anything bad about anyone and no one said anything bad about him . . .'*
>
> *Buster's passing, though a very sad one, had so much good to say about how deeply one human being reached and touched so many through his art and humanity. How, with his gentleness of heart and kindness of spirit, he influenced a whole new wave of tap dancers, not only as dancers, but as citizens of this world. How he gave 'em the 'Busterness' to hold onto and pass on to those who come under their influence in the future. No, I choose to see Buster's passing as a new and beautiful beginning, Jane. More fun to come."* ■

"He never said anything bad about anybody and no one said anything bad about him."

Savion Glover:
Tap is Young Again

2002

NOISE/FUNK REDUX

When *Dance Magazine* asked me to interview Savion Glover, it had already taken years for me to catch up and talk tap with him. I tried to set a time on National Tap Dance Day, May 2000, at Town Hall, when he got his Flo-Bert Award for Life Achievement. That was when hundreds of teenagers deluged him for autographs. I tried again when he invited me to watch a rehearsal of his dancing with some of the old Harlem Globetrotters, but the rehearsal ended abruptly and it wasn't the time to talk.

Then one evening he was outside on the street with his posse, hanging after one of Buster Brown's tap jams, and I suggested that the next morning maybe we could talk tap. "Morning?" he asked doubtfully.

I'd been watching Savion Glover since he was 12 years old, tap dancing his way to stardom in the Broadway shows *The Tap Dance Kid*, *Black and Blue* and *Jelly's Last Jam*. I followed his stint on *Sesame Street* through my friends' children. Then there were all the memorials for the tap greats throughout the eighties and nineties. I'd attended his birthday party at the 23rd St Y, where he played basketball all night as the theme of the get-together.

I had a huge file on Savion in my archives. I had even had many conversations about Savion with Gregory Hines and others in the tap world when his mercurial hit musical *Bring in 'da Noise/Bring in 'da Funk* first rocked the New York Shakespeare Festival's Public Theater. Telling me that working out with Savion was what kept him in shape, Gregory Hines confided: "Savion will keep the weight off." Would an interview with Savion Glover inspire weight loss?

When I got the call that he was about to go on the road again with a revival of *Noise/Funk*, I knew to lay low and let the publicist and manager discuss the terms of our interview. I was invited to a rehearsal, but the interview would have to wait. He'd be gone for at least a year.

Savion Glover in Classical Savion, *with Gregory's photo on the piano every night of the NYC run.*

Noise/Funk *billboard at the Public Theater before show moved to Broadway.*

Then, one late afternoon, the call came from Atlanta, where his tour had begun. I had received many emails and calls from his manager and tour publicists about "the call" that week, so I was ready.

"I'd like to speak to Jane Goldberg?" he said. Immediately followed by: "I can't talk now." And then he hung up the phone.

"Give me a couple minutes," he continued after calling back. "My cell phone's running out of juice." I had learned not to hold my breath about this guy. But about ten minutes later, he came back loud and clear.

"So what's different about doing *Noise/Funk* now?" I began.

"Nothing."

"Isn't it a lot harder on your body now that you're almost thirty—not twenty-two anymore? And you're dancing with younger people?" I trailed off. I'd read an entire *New York Times* article about the chronic pain plaguing the *Noise/Funk* dancers during the show's Broadway run. His cast for the tour included his twelve-year-old protégé, Cartier Williams.

Savion ignored my questions, in favor of his own agenda.

"I want to get the information out there again—you know, chunks, little pieces of history that the kids aren't getting, but that the adults have. I also sharpened up the choreography. Plus, Dormeshia is in it now. She's portrayed as a lady, like she should be, not just one of the regular dancers. We grew up together in *Black and Blue*. I call her 'Mutha.' She's clean, she's our generation. The next new generation of women tap dancers will see her. She's protecting the art."

Tapper Dormeshia Sumbry-Edwards is married to Omar Edwards, a cousin of Savion's and an excellent tapper himself, who performed in *Noise/Funk* on Broadway. Edwards had told me that Savion was a genius, that his famous relative was so gifted, he didn't have to practice the way most dancers do.

"I had to practice," Savion laughed. "Of course I had to practice. I didn't just roll out of bed and tap. I often go over material in my head, what I think I'm capable of doing. I'm always practicing in my head. I studied with the hoofers."

Savion also keeps tapes, what he calls his "footage," with him and carries a VCR on the road. One tape, in particular, from his "Aunt" Dianne Walker's collection, he calls his "orientation tape." It includes the work of Tip Tap and Toe, The Nicholas Brothers, Fred Astaire, Leon Collins and others.

"I used to think if you didn't have this tape, you weren't a tap dancer," Savion said. "These are our heroes. We all know who Baryshnikov is. Kids should know who Leon Collins is. When there's a stamp that has Bunny Briggs on it, I'll be satisfied."

He has immortalized four of his heroes in the show during a poignant solo called "Green, Chaney, Buster, Slyde" where he faces mirrors in the semi-darkness and "does" each master as he talks about their styles.

For Savion, his mentors were *not* entertainers, a word he actually repudiates in the show. His unrecognized teachers maintained "the real thing," as Sammy Davis once said. It is "the beat", he claims, that kept African-Americans going. If Savion Glover is on a mission with *Noise/Funk* this time around, it is to continue to get the "information"—his word for tap dancing and its roots, out there. "I just want everyone to know about the dance and the people behind the dance and their contributions—why we do it, who paved the way," he explained.

Savion is often compared to great jazz musicians like Miles Davis for his originality, genius, and long, inward, meditative improvisations. Some in his audience hate it when he looks down or turns his back on them as if to ignore them. But in *Noise/Funk* he tells the story through tap and creates crowd-pleasers as well. His work pleases the theater industry, too. He is the youngest dance-maker in theater history to win a Tony for choreography.

"I was always hearing about the use of my arms," the tapper mused. "With choreography, I paint a picture and see how the audience responds. I can calculate some of the response. I know when they'll applaud more. I know where to put the pocket steps—you know, pocket steps: what is gonna get 'em. Henry LeTang had a world of pocket steps. It looked like Chuck Green, Lon Chaney, Buster, Dianne were doing the same routines all those years, but they had these pocket steps and they were always flipping them, so you never knew which step they'd be doing.

You have to incorporate them during improvisation, too. My generation is forgetting about the pocket steps. They're falling back."

"But aren't these pocket steps entertainment?" I asked, knowing he usually rejected that term.

"I like the word 'edutainment,'" he answered neatly. "That's from *KRS-One. (Knowledge Rules Supreme)*."

I'd never heard of it.

"It's from an old album," Glover said. "I learned more from this album about what it's like to be an African-American of this world. We don't only entertain. We don't only educate. We edutain."

Lately, jazz saxophonist John Coltrane has inspired Savion and his tap colleague Chance Taylor. "Chance has inspired me to be a better human being," Glover said. "He disappeared for a year, and when he came back, he was *there* already. He's so focused. He turned me on to Coltrane's 'India'. Chance will go where 'Trane goes. My whole approach is like one of a horn player's at this time— I'm just blowing."

Savion dancing at one of the renowned "La Cave" sessions, a nightclub on Manhattan's East Side. While master Jimmy Slyde held court each Wednesday night, "La Cave" served as a breeding ground for some of the top (international) tappers today—That's Tamango and Roxane Butterfly standing in the back of photo.

Savion has been hailed in practically every review, book, TV show, and article I've read or seen as "the best tap dancer in the world," but he's not a great believer in being the best.

"Gregory [Hines] was the first person I heard where tap dancing sounded like a drum beat—percussive, not just dancing. Once I saw that, I could bring it out. It's not about being better than others. I try to keep my chops up, so I can just be," said Glover. "We need to be individuals first. We're strong. The public will see individualism and see how strong the dance is."

He's also weary of the experimentation going on in tap. At the New York City Tap Festival in July 2002, he was openly upset at some of the offerings.

"Where are we?" he asked an audience. "Tap is in a frantic place," he said to me. "A lot of people want to do it. Those who see that it's popular can take advantage of this. I hope it doesn't get too experimental."

Is Savion a tap conservative? He defends his position. "Not only do I have to watch this [experimentation], but now we have people who have never seen the dance. Say you might go get this guy from New Zealand and bring him to a festival," he hypothesized. "You see dragon heads, monster heads, nothing to do with the dance. They're just moving their feet, not even shuffling. I've seen classes called 'gymnastic tap' and 'hip-hop dance.' They're ruining us. Keep it with the dance. Experimentation is in the music, two entities coming together. I don't have to come out of my realm. Keep to the essence. It's like if I'm a chef and they're coming to my culinary school and they eat with nails when we use knives and forks. You don't mix bananas with macaroni cheese and yams."

Ah, food. This tap talk might actually take us into the realm of weight loss, after all.

"So, what kind of food do you eat? What do you wake up to?" I asked.

"Leftovers," he laughed. On that note, it was show time in Atlanta, and Savion Glover was off and tap dancing.

—◆—

I saw *Noise/Funk* four-and-a-half times. The first time was in its more intimate version at The Public Theater in 1996. It was clear that it wasn't only tap people flocking to see the show; it had broken through to non-aficionados. It was considered theatre, not only dance, and director George Wolfe had made sure there were plenty of production values. It was such a hit, that it had to move to Broadway. That's when I saw it for the second time with main squeeze, Owen Gray. I noticed how different the lighting was, just beautiful. The production values were even more intense. Jackie Raven had me see it the third time with her, close to the end of its Broadway run. We paid $75 each for crummy Orchestra seats where you couldn't see all that well, but it was great to see it with Jackie.

Savion had provided the raw material needed to create a show about "da beat" and how the black world passed that beat on, secretively through slavery, vaudeville, Hollywood, all kinds of venues to keep it going. Some people were angry that The Nicholas Brothers were satirized on stage as Grin and Flash, a pair of smiling Uncle Toms. I saw it as a more generic portrayal. So many of my mentors had been faced with the dilemma of having to accept demeaning roles, just so they could keep working. In any case, the dancers cast as these ersatz Nicholas Brothers didn't even come close to their genius style.

I "second-acted" the last show of the Broadway run, when Savion had an open "mike" or jam session at the show's closing for anyone brave enough to do some trading on the Broadway stage. I watched the whole thing from the balcony. Gregory flew in special for the last show. Like my pal Jackie Raven, he felt that this show made a victorious statement for tap dancing. I saw it a fourth time at Newark's NJPAC, and this time Dormeshia Sumbry-Edwards was in it, too. In high heels and "hitting" in high heels!

I was especially taken by the fact that a tap dancer was able to construct social commentary through dance. A lot of us tappers were trying to push tap forward, away from nostalgia. Savion, with the help of George Wolfe, had actually succeeded in a big way on Broadway. It wasn't the whole story of tap. It was a particular story, an important story, the black story.

—⁓—

2003
AUGUST

I saw Savion at Gregory's memorial service in Los Angeles. At the end of the service, Dule Hill, one of the original Noise/Funk tappers, who went on to become a TV star on "The West Wing" and "Psych", started the jam session at the end of the service. You heard some quiet tapping from the back of the church as Hill moved closer to the front, near the closed coffin.

I had taken Matia Karrell, my first New York roommate, who I was staying with in L.A., to the memorial. "Janie!" she whispered, "You can't *not* get up there!" So I did, and jammed with all the hoofers. Savion didn't get up at all. He remained in his pew, standing tall, stricken. I saw him afterwards outside on that sunny, early evening, in a circle with all the young lions, locking arms with each other after the service. It was a time to bond. He then took off alone in a limo.

A few months later, at the New York memorial that Gregory's brother, Maurice Jr., produced at the Apollo Theater, Savion danced. He moved back and forth and side-to-side in the shape of a cross. He quoted some of Gregory's steps, particularly a rapid-fire, gunshot-sounding pattern with the right foot zigzagging and the left swinging back and forth. Even though he was dancing fast, he seemed

The Young Savion teaching a class to a wide range of old, young, pro, impending pros. That's Olivia Rosencrantz in the front and Ira Bernstein, next to piano, both professionals.

suspended in time. Maybe he was remembering his nightly Challenges on Broadway as the young Jelly Roll Morton to Gregory's cantankerous adult Jelly.

Savion always upped the ante, but on this night, with splashy, dressed-to-kill stars like Baryshnikov and Isabella Rossellini in the first tier, Savion took no bow. He stunned all of us into a moody silence. For him, this was a dance of grief, not celebration, and it was obvious in every sound he made.

At my home/archive the next summer, I showed him a snapshot of Gregory "in transition," after Gregory had lost a lot of weight and was only one month away from death. It was a private picture of the two of us that Gregory's fiancée, Negrita Jayde, had taken and sent to me from Venice, California. Savion stared at the photo for over half an hour.

2004

IMPROVOGRAPHY

Savion named his show *Improvography* to pay homage to his fallen mentor/father figure/friend, Gregory Hines, who invented the term. Savion and Gregory appeared on a number of shows together over the course of their lives. Their most regular contact was jamming every night in *Jelly's Last Jam*. Gregory was Savion's most vocal booster. He never stopped kvelling.

His right foot: Faster than the speed of lightning!

The word "improvography" itself is a fairly obvious combination of improvisation and choreography. Gregory defined it as the repetition of certain rhythms, due to the frequency of takes in a movie or television show, as a way of "setting the step" for the directors of those shows. With "improvography" you never did the step the same way each time. It did mean the dancer would know what he wanted to say in *advance*.

People are generally afraid of the word "improvisation" because it implies "making it up as you go along." Improvisation is unpredictable, risky, and makes some people uncomfortable to do. Gregory told the "By Word of Foot" festival students that he loved the routine dancers, but it was the "improvisationalists" who turned him on. He also felt that tap, at its highest form, was about improvisation.

"I loved watching them get out of their mistakes right in front of you," he said. As children, Gregory and his brother sat through the four shows a day at the

Apollo and got to see a lot of mistakes.

I remember when I first taught Carnell Lyon's students in Germany, they were petrified of improvising. They had never done anything like that before. Their teachers had given them a step and taught them exactly how to do it, count for count, heel for heel, toe for toe.

When I ran the word "improvography" by another well-known dancer/ improvisationalist, Steve Paxton, who had a main hand in creating the duet form "Contact Improvisation," he thought it the perfect description for what it was he and others of his ilk were doing. "Improvography" definitely resolved the worrisome concept of "winging it".

Savion also paid homage to Gregory, the consummate song and dance man, by adding singing to his *Improvography* run at the beautiful Joyce Theatre in Chelsea. Rather than selling the song, he scatted, missed, and laughed through the tunes. He even notated the rhythms of his music out loud—"shuffle heel, shuffle toe, a flap, a flap,"—something all tap dancers do in their heads. He joked, and quoted old hoofers, dead and alive. He trance-danced, staring into some far off space, and took the audience through four decades of styles—swing, bop, cool, and hip hop. It was a 180-degree turn from the "anti-entertainment" stance of *Noise/Funk*.

In the middle of every set he would suddenly slow down the time and become a lounge lizard crooning and shim shamming along a diagonal to "I've got the routine . . . so put another nickel in the machine." It was fun watching him having fun, even as a veritable Niagara Falls of perspiration flowed from his beard, reminding us of the exertion it took to make everything look so easy.

Savion gained showmanship skills each night of the run. It was clear he was making up a new program structure, his first half a one-hour non-stop virtuosic solo with his live band, the second featuring Savion and his then company Ti Dii of six, doing "numbers." In addition, he led the band, his right foot serving as the conductor's wand. Fred Astaire may have sung about it in "I'd Rather Lead a Band," but Savion took it literally.

2005

"CLASSICAL SAVION™"

Armed with his conductor, ten classical and four jazz musicians, Savion Glover conquered new turf in *Classical Savion*. He wasn't the first tapper to hoof the classics, but he may be the most original in combining his improvised jazz with the European music of Vivaldi, Bach, and Mendelssohn.

Webster's Dictionary defines "classical" as "relating to a form of primary significance before modern times." Savion has always related to the past while moving the art forward, even in his hip-hop nation years of *Noise/Funk*. During a

Dianne Walker, Savion, and Jimmy Slyde often worked together.

Q&A session at the Joyce Theatre, Savion told the audience that the distinction between playing classical music and playing jazz was the difference between dressing up formally for your school principal versus hanging out with your best friend.

On opening night, just inches away from the violin section, Glover seemed to be coaxing and yanking notes out of the music that didn't exist as the young players furiously stuck to their written pages. By the end of the week, things had loosened up so much between the orchestra and Glover, that the same violinists were riffing off of "Carmen" with the jazz pianist, and the harpsichordist was trading eights with the violists. Savion had brought the musicians to him, and he to them, getting inside the music, copying it, riding it, flying underneath or beside it.

His own five-piece jazz band ended the show with Savion's work song, "Stars and Stripes Forever, For Now," a rendition of the Sousa classic. The curtain would dramatically fall and curve into the shape of the American flag. Stars lit up the floor. Savion marked out a soft-shoe, indicating the steps, and dropped a little sand on the floor, picking up his shoes from the piano, where a dramatically lit photograph of his late mentor Hines was displayed.

I enjoyed watching Savion "think" on stage, coming up with different ideas every night of the run. His eyes took on a kind of maniacal expression as he punched the air. There was the Savion walk, fast paced in a large circle, a fusillade of taps as he prepared for the next big statement. Most of all there was the wonder of watching and listening to a great percussionist of the feet interpret the classics.

―――

2006

HAPPY FEET—RESPECT, NEGLECT

"Respect is so worth fighting for," wrote Gregory Hines in his last email to me. I was about to interview him one more time, and he admonished me to stay home if I didn't get the respect—the money—I needed from the magazine I was writing for to fly out and interview him.

Savion Glover is our "champ" in today's tap world, but you rarely see Challenge sessions anymore, and Glover's acolytes don't particularly like the notion of "being the best." But their ears prick up when I talk tap lore and use the word, "respect."

On December 28, 2006, John Rockwell of *The New York Times* wrote a story with the headline: *"Penguin, Shmenguin! Those are Savion Glover's 'Happy Feet'!"* It focused on the surprising lack of attention garnered by Glover for the outstanding choreographic work he had done for the Academy Award-winning animated movie *Happy Feet*. Savion's credit is listed on page thirteen of fourteen in the imdb.com database, and shows up way down in the credits at the end of the film. And yet director George Miller claimed he couldn't have made the picture without Savion Glover committing to "playing" the central character of Mumble the penguin.

Tap dance itself is strangely dissed in the movie. Mumble is born without the ability to sing, which the film portrays as a requirement in penguin development. When Mumble taps, his parents, especially his dad, are embarrassed and his fellow penguins make fun of him for his weird rhythmic feet. The term "tap dancing" is never mentioned in the movie. An intelligent teenager who saw *Happy Feet* twice told me she wasn't even aware that the style of dancing that Mumble engaged in was tap!

"Maybe dance, even in a film whose entire plot hinges on dance, is so far from the concerns of most people, that Mr. Glover's credit escaped everyone's attention," writes Rockwell. "But that omission seems especially worrisome when the dance being slighted is deeply rooted in the black American tradition." Rockwell points out that this is a business where agents and lawyers haggle over words like "and" and "featuring" in the credits to enhance their clients' salaries and prestige, but Glover himself professed total satisfaction with his credit to Rockwell. I myself wonder what contractual agreement was made with Glover about such matters.

Rockwell concludes: ". . . if tap is to be respected, its greatest living exponent must be respected too. To win respect, you have to do more than be the best there is. You have to fight, meaning negotiate, for the recognition you deserve."

Of course, the other side of respect is neglect. Consider how tap has been ghettoized in the dance world. Jazz critics tend not to consider tap their turf. Neither, for that matter, do dance critics. It has been an uphill battle to get the form recognized and respected in the worlds of jazz and dance, let alone in pop culture.

⁓

I first heard about Savion playing a penguin when I saw a video clip of Little Mumble online. Mumble's feet were clearly dancing Savion's animated rhythms. Mumble was Savion Prime.

Savion Glover started out drumming and through Hines, could hear how tap was like drumming, using his feet to play the percussion. He found these bucket players on the streets and put them on Broadway!

NJPAC (New Jersey Performing Arts Center) floor of fame! Savion Glover is a proud Newark native.

Still, I wasn't prepared for the gigantic billboard of the movie in Times Square. I didn't see Savion's name up there. I tried not to think about Savion's missing credit. I rationalized it was just some gross error in marketing.

The title *Happy Feet* is certainly ironic, since Savion, the antithesis of the happy hoofer, made tap angry, full of edge and "hitting"—Savion's word for slamming the feet down on the floor, getting it right. A lot of kids began hitting after *Noise/Funk*. I once saw one young girl apologize to Savion after the show for not "hitting," just doing "regular" tap-dancing, whatever that was.

Starting in the late nineties, this wunderkind of tap was responsible for a major surge of interest in the form and made the art a very happening thing for young people to do.

"Tap is young again," he once declared to me.

Still, like everyone in the field, Savion has had to deal with a media that doesn't follow the art, and an art that has few regular venues.

It's a pity that Mumble/Savion is best showcased at the very end of the film, when most people are on their way out of the theater. As the interminable credits roll, the choreography is at its most inventive. Not only Mumble, but each of the major penguin characters is given an individual choreographic statement, hewing very closely to tap's tradition. ■

Stop-Time:
The Drum is a Tap Dancer

One of my greatest pleasures was tapping to the sound of drums. So staying up all night to watch Philly Joe Jones write music was always a revelation. He was totally obsessed with writing music, not just his own drumming.

For a time, my East 4th Street apartment became his crash pad. He'd finish his gig at the Tin Palace, a jazz club a block away, and then stay up the rest of the night with his music. I'd stay up with him, pestering him about what he knew of the drum/tap connection. I met lots of other drummers, and I always asked them what they knew about tap. But Philly Joe Jones had actually *started out* as a tap dancer in Philadelphia, the same time as some of my dancing mentors.

One steamy August night in 1977, right outside The Village Vanguard, I actually got to see him in a tap dance Challenge. It was already in full swing by the time I had arrived on Seventh Avenue in front of that most renowned of clubs where Cookie and I had tapped.

A Challenge, right out on the street, gave this particular performance authenticity. It could have been 1935, when tap actually did flourish on the streets. Philly Joe's Challenge was over in a flash, just like the Tyson/Spinks fight at Madison Square Garden the night before. Watching Philly Joe trade fours with other dancers and musicians made me wonder all the more about the rhythm relationship between tap and drums.

I knew Gregory Hines had stacked up comic books at different levels when he was a little boy to learn how to play drums, but how did Philly Joe Jones learn how to tap dance? I knew many tap dancers considered themselves drummers "playing their feet," but what about the drummers? Did they think of themselves as tap dancing with their sticks? What was tap's influence on drumming?

I myself had tapped to drums for a couple of years. I learned my earliest routines with Stanley Brown on traps to give our class *time*, but I never considered

Baby Laurence was the one dancer everyone *talked about when I was "growing up" in tap lore, including all the musicians.*

That's Louie Bellson, on traps, drumming behind Cookie Cook and Bubba Gaines.

the drum/tap connection until a few years later when I heard Dannie Richmond playing "steps" with the Mingus band. He sounded *just like a tap dancer!* When I went backstage after Richmond's last set and asked him if he knew tap, his face lit up. He told me he had studied the legendary Baby Laurence "night after night after night" for nine months when Mingus was in residence at *The Showplace,* a defunct Greenwich Village nightclub.

Baby Laurence died in 1974, just when I was learning how to tap. When someone sent me an obituary of him, I didn't realize how prominent a role he would play in my quest down the road.

⸻

Staring out my window in the wee hours of the morning waiting for Philly Joe Jones to get off my phone, I was impatient to get the story. It was just after I'd seen him dancing on the street, and I put on one of my five-hundred Baby Laurence albums for atmosphere.

Philly Joe told me he learned to tap when he was a little boy, and like all tappers of his era, he learned it by himself on the streets until the "good fairy or something" told him he should play drums instead. Dancing was his first love. Listening to his tales—how Sandman didn't hold a candle to the elder statesman Honi Coles, how Teddy Hale was polished, but Baby Laurence was *ultra polished*, how Sammy Davis, Jr. insisted on tapping last in his all-night marathon so as not to be upstaged by Baby or any of the other hoofers that night—I could see competition was also the name of Philly Joe's game.

"I've never seen a dancer out-dance a good drummer," he said. "When I played for Baby or Teddy, it would be a Challenge. Baby could keep up. I'd find all kinds of different things to do and I would do some of the hardest licks I could think of. I'd do what I wanted to do but close to him, to his rhythm. I'd add maybe four or five rudiments, but he couldn't do all that rolling."

Philly Joe switched to drumming not only because the "good fairy" told him to, but also because he could say more with sticks than he could with his feet. "It's a different kind of coordination," he said. "The drummer's moving arms, legs, and mind. With the dancer, it's just legs."

Being a dancer, I knew that wasn't true. We had minds, too; and we had to move across space. That was also a different kind of coordination.

I asked him if tap helped him as a drummer and he replied that the drummer who has been a dancer can play better than someone who has never danced. "See, the drummer catches the dancer, especially when a dancer's doing wings," he said, moving his arms, *kaboom*. "And the cymbals move at the same time to catch the dancer."

I asked Philly Joe if he thought tap was a lost art. "It's people like you saying it's *lost* that makes that kind of statement true. Look, dancers are a dime a dozen. A whole lot of them will come out of the woodwork if some Broadway show opens with tap. You don't see a lot of them 'cause there aren't a lot of shows."

Of his own transition to drums he said, "Anytime a dancer finds another love, something that he can also really do, he'll get involved with one more than the other—whichever way he leans, that's what he does the best."

—⁓—

Dannie Richmond, Charles Mingus' drummer, enhanced my own romantic notion of the drum/tap marriage. He even called the period of time he played with Baby Laurence a "light little love affair as musicians—as people admiring each other's talent."

I met with Dannie Richmond one blustery day outside The Village Gate, motorcycles revving up loudly in front of us. Talking tap to drummers always had a double purpose. I was looking for the answers to what killed tap, but I also wanted a gig. That hope kept me going.

Me with Max Gordon, proprietor of the Village Vanguard.

Back in 1961 when Richmond played with Baby Laurence, the Mingus musicians at The Showplace on West 3rd St. also included Booker Irwin, Jaki Byard, Eric Dolphy, and Yusef Lateef. Interestingly enough, it was from Baby Laurence that Richmond learned drumming technique at that time, rather than relying strictly on other musicians.

"The band would play the head on the theme and Baby Laurence played the breaks. Little by little we worked it where at first I was just doing stop time, fours, twos, so much, I'd memorized every lick of his. I learned that it wasn't just single strokes involved in the drums. My concept was that if you had the single strokes down, you could play anything.

"But it's not true," he continued. "It's almost true, but not totally. And the way Laurence would mix paradiddles along with single strokes. He could do all that with his *feet*. It got to where we're doing fours together. He'd dance four, then we played threes, twos, one bar apiece, but I was copying him. I'd more or less play what he danced. I was trying to keep it in the context of melody dance and, mind you, to me that was the same as a saxophone player trying to play like Charlie Parker. He was the only one who could dance to Charlie Parker tunes."

From what I could tell, Richmond was most impressed with Laurence's musicality. "It was a gas for me to duplicate what Laurence danced. When he switched up on me and changed the time, there was no way I could play that. To see Laurence change the time, even though I could sing one of his routines from start to finish and that's fifteen minutes, I couldn't keep up. Every tap I could *sing*, sing every note. I learned that Baby Laurence danced in a series of four bars." I wondered what Richmond thought of the Stearns' theory of bebop drumming getting too complex for tap. He seemed to agree.

"When time opened up, the drummer was no longer in the role of accompanying the soloist," he said. "The beat is now accented, not always on two and four or one and three. The accent could be on the upbeat or middle of the beat. I could see how this would throw a dancer. But I don't agree it stopped the jazz dance. When there's something new, many times it won't take the imagination of a lot of people. It takes sometimes years before it's really grasped by the masses. Baby was the epitome of getting out of the mold. He could play anything. He knew where the *one* was all the time."

Max Roach, one of the "bomb droppers" that the Stearns wrote about, clobbered any major romantic theories I might have come up with about the tap/drum affair. He agreed with the Stearns that he got a great deal from the dancers. The dancers, he claimed, were the premiere acts in theater from just before the 1930s through the early 1940s, when Roach entered the scene. "But when you played for a dance act, there was written music. You had stops and breaks and certain attitudes you had to do to play for that act," he told me.

We were sitting at Lady's Fort, a jazz loft run by singer Joe Lee Wilson on the Lower East Side. I still held out hope that one day one of these great drumming masters would ask me to dance. I didn't want tap dancing to be just something they *used* to play for. I wanted it to be *now*. But I did appreciate how Roach brought tap into the realm of politics when he talked about its demise.

"It was the twenty percent War Tax levied just after World War Two," Roach said indignantly. It was levied on all places where they had entertainment. It was levied in case they had public dancing, singing, storytelling, humor, or jokes onstage. This tax is the real story behind why dancing, not just tap dancing, but public dancing stopped."

I had heard about Max Roach's riffing with the legendary Groundhog, who once showed up at The Village Gate, then disappeared again. Groundhog was only known to dancers, since he didn't make New York his home. He wasn't interested in holding on to his title, "King of the Gate," though he was perceived as a legendary "Champ," winning a major NYC cutting contest.

"When we got to Cincinnati with Charlie Parker's small band, Groundhog was looking for me, because he heard the records," Roach said. "We sat outside a church and I played brushes just on a cardboard box so as never to intrude. He must have danced on that concrete, doing flips and turns all night long."

Max Roach also had a stint with Baby Laurence. "We usually did our act as an encore. I would play brushes on the snare and he would just dance and we'd exchange things, call and response. I would imitate him and then I would play time over it." Referring back to the Stearns dig, he remarked, "Drummers who started dropping bombs were just not sensitive to what they were playing for. Dance acts always had their music. It was all very well-prepared."

Roach rose up at this point and started doing Baby's famous circle dance, crawling around in a big circle. He talked about how dancers would show him steps. When I got up to show him my own paddling he theorized, "See, some people say South African boot dancers influenced tap and some say Irish clog dancers, but actually none of these folks resembles the thing you just did. I'm talking about the music that grew out of the American experience."

———

Buddy Rich was another drummer who tapped before he picked up the sticks. He began his career as a child hoofer in vaudeville.

When I caught up with him, Rich was in the middle of recording the tune "Birdland" in midtown with his big band. He told me he had just had his teeth redone—"a whole new face," he claimed.

I told him I was interested in how tap influenced him. He began to roll out the names of all the dancers he had worked with: Tip, Tap, and Toe, The Berry Brothers, Stump and Stumpy, Bill "Bojangles" Robinson, The Condos Brothers, Bill Bailey, Teddy Hale, Baby Laurence, and "the guy with the floppy bow tie, you know, he was a pigeon dancer." (that sounded like Bunny Briggs, but I didn't know what a "pigeon dancer" was.)

Buddy Rich was confrontational and in my face. He also destroyed my romantic notion that tap and drums were like a musical marriage.

"You know, for some reason or another," Rich began, tuning his drum set during a break in the recording. "People like to think that if you danced at one time, it's a great advantage to your playing drums. I don't know if that is really the truth or not, because then it should work that if you're a helluva drummer, you're a bitch of a dancer, and I don't know of any, do you?"

I had seen Rich dance with The Condos Brothers in an old movie and was about to compliment him when he cut me off.

"I don't think the two are really that compatible," he barked. "I don't think that tap dancing has anything to do with the actual ability to play. I think the only thing you can reckon is that they're both rhythmical and pulsing, but I don't think the two are remotely responsible for each other."

Since Baby Laurence seemed to be every drummer's favorite, I mentioned that Baby Laurence was said to have been inspired by drummers.

"Baby Laurence could hear things as a drummer. If he wanted to take drumming seriously, he probably would have been a badass drummer 'cause he was that great a dancer," Rich said.

I asked Rich how he learned to tap and, in true tapper fashion he replied, "Stealing. Stealing from everybody! Hanging out with everybody I knew who had talent. It's not exactly stealing, but if you hang with people enough, it'll rub off on you. I always had the good taste to be in the know, to know who was better than the next guy, because anything less than perfect didn't please me."

"Then why did you stop dancing?" I asked.

"I'm too involved in what I'm doing with my band, working excessively hard behind the drums, to come down front and screw around for sixteen bars," he replied.

"Is dancing screwing around?"

"If I were doing it today, it would be screwing around," he shot back quickly.

I wondered if drumming just turned him on more, as it had Philly Joe. I couldn't fathom anyone wanting to give up tap for drumming.

"Listen, I'd been up there when I was a kid," Rich said. "Where are you gonna go? You're gonna dance up four flights of stairs, dance down four flights of stairs, do a couple of splits, a couple of six tap wings, and then where are you going? You're going to be an opening act all your life. It wasn't that dancing was limited. There were no calls. When vaudeville died out and nightclubs started putting in *thirty girls thirty*, and Radio City put in sixty Rockettes, where was the tap dancer? It was a dying art."

His new teeth suddenly seemed to shine right in my face. I was persistent in sticking to the tap/drum connection. I wanted to know more about his playing for tap dancers.

"Look, I could think in terms of dancers when I worked with dancers," he said. "I could accompany a dancer and probably make it sound like I belonged in the act. I was brought up in vaudeville and pit drummers are the best drummers in the world.

"Now *that's* an art that has died," he continued. "They had to play for dance acts, adagio acts, and comics. They had to have the facility to play everything, to learn what it meant to accompany. That experience and working with every dancer helped me play what I do for dancers.

Buddy Rich: "And nightclubs started putting in thirty girls thirty . . ."

"See, most people consider art to be pop today. If you're used to eating at McDonald's, no matter how good the steak is at 21, you're still accustomed to McDonald's. And that's what happened to dancers. They were just too good for the average public. So it died out. Nobody wanted to be a dancer anymore."

"I do," I chimed.

"Well, I hope you bring it back. 'Cause if you're that good, I'll hire you."

Finally I was going to get my big break! I told him I had studied with some of the masters.

"It's not only the masters, my dear. It's what *you* bring to it. If you can't do *bop-bop-be-de-bop—da-bede-da-da* then doing a time step ain't gonna get you to the Rockies."

I brought up the Stearns' quote about drummers dropping bombs.

As usual, Rich was direct. "People who write about jazz know nothing about it. No band is out and out louder than the man who's dancing in front of the band. If you've sixteen bars to play, you can't make it loud. The reason jazz dancing cut out is because there were no more jazz dancers. Everybody wants to come down on the musicians. If it wasn't for the drummer, there would be no such thing as 'time,' no such thing as 'swing.' Don't bust the drummer's balls."

Was that what the Stearns were doing in their probe of what might have sent tap to the basement?

I apologized. "I was under the impression there was a kind of rhythmic equality in the heyday. The dancing and music grew up together, right? You know, trading eights, influence, evolution?" I began groping for words.

"Drummers played 'time' for everybody," Rich remained combative. "For the band, not for the dancer. Nobody gave a goddamn about the dancers. The dancers had an act. The drummer is top hat to your very sophisticated set of tails. If you go out without the hat, you're not totally dressed." ■

The Horse is Out of the Barn

EXERCISE, EXERCISE, EXERCISE!!!!
That word has such a knee jerk reaction for me.
Oh, my aching knee.

I can remember the exact moment I felt my first jolt of knee pain. It was twenty years ago, on the dance floor at the Village Gate, where I'd gone to hear my friend Ray Anderson play his trombone on Salsa Night. There I was doing my thing in a dark corner of that cavernous basement and suddenly—total agony! Uh-oh, I thought.

My right knee soon became my Achilles heel. Over the course of fifteen years, I tried every remedy I could think of to avoid a total knee replacement.

My brother Arthur asked me if it was "cartilage," short hand for osteoarthritis, which runs in our family. My mother, father, and Arthur turned out to have crummy knees, too. And in addition to my knee genes, I had broken my right tibia and fibula in a diving accident when I was twelve. I had had the leg set; then Dr. Backrack had to rebreak the bones the following week. That's right! He didn't get it right the first time. I bet he got it wrong the second time, too, because I developed hardcore osteoarthritis at thirty-five. They didn't routinely send you to a physical therapist in 1962. When my leg came out of the huge cast—all nervous, emaciated, wobbly—my muscles were gonzo. I never went back to diving.

By 2001, I was putting so much weight on my left leg that I hobbled around like a tortured pretzel. I liked using a cane—a female Moses—but I hated the walking. I finally bit the bullet and set about researching the big enchilada: total knee replacement (TKR to those in the biz).

I interviewed fifteen or so orthopedic surgeons around New York, and one in Miami. I had X-rays, MRIs. One of the first doctors I saw charged $325 for fifteen minutes and told me I had "knee disease" and that I was a little flabby.

Some of my canes. The bird beak one, from my brother, was my favorite. The two "short" ones were for Cookie and me in the duet, "Old Man Time." Jackie Raven gave me the one with the ball on the top; and modern dance mentor Beverly Blossom gave me the African wooden one on the left.

The doctor is in . . . a bamboo hut . . . in Bali, 1998. Hey, Doc. It's the right knee, not the left.

While in India, I saw an Ayurvedic guy but his areas of expertise turned out to be psoriasis and hitting on me. In Bali, I saw another practitioner. He offered me Eastern platitudes as I lay on a mat on his floor.

I was getting desperate, but everyone kept telling me that at fifty years of age, I was too young for a knee replacement, that I'd eventually have to have a *replacement* of the replacement. It was suggested that I lose weight, but I couldn't bear to order my cappuccino with skim milk. Skim milk looks blue! I know, I know. Weight loss would help ol' Kneesickle.

I did take off the weight in India. Got sick, the Delhi Belly. I even moved to Florida to commune with the ocean and give Kneesickle a break. Along the way, I tried everything. My knee was massaged, chiropracted, injected, acupunctured, Feldenkreised, Traegered, Alexandered, Kundalinied, crystallized. I hung upside down on ropes in India. I attended a workshop on dreams where I built a sculpture of my knee and adorned it with rhinestones.

I heard magnets were good for arthritis, so I got completely magnetized. I slept on a sheet of magnets, underneath a cover of magnets, on a magnetic pillow. I wore magnets in my shoes, on my back, and I even ate magnetic candy bars. Well, they're candy bars that the magnet company sent me as a bonus for waiting so long for my magnetic mattress to arrive.

———

OK, OK. So I didn't *always* do the exercises my massage therapists, physical therapists, and bodywork gurus gave me. I can remember doing the one my physical therapist friend Carla gave me to work on while at Yaddo, the artists' retreat. She had drawn me a diagram of all these little stick figures showing me how to do it. I was motivated until I got there and started my sedentary writing life. When I got home, Carla held my quads and admonished me, "You have no muscle tone, here!" She picked at the blabby skin above Kneesickle like it was dead meat.

"Build up the quads!" she hollered at me, in perfect personal-trainer speak.

I consulted with a host of dancers—dancers who had become Pilates trainers, dancers who talked only bones and muscles, dancers who were anti-quad building.

I got used to the pain.

Most of the orthopedic docs I'd seen over the years agreed that arthroscopy, the laser miracle operation, would not work for my bone-on-bone arthritis.

Upon reading my X-ray, one doctor told me, "Tap 'til you drop."

He didn't take into consideration that tap dancers DO tap 'til they drop—dead. Unlike other dancers, tappers get more determined with age. I discovered most of my tap daddies and mommies when they were well into their sixties—all enjoying renewed careers, many of them plagued with knee problems.

Dancers use medical doctors as a last resort. Why was there only one dance medicine department in all of New York City in 1997? There were zillions of sports medicine departments. I had even come across sports medicine departments in India, land of alternative medicine.

I went to the most famous knee doc of them all, the one who partially invented the total knee replacement, and the one whose medical miracles put basketball players back on the court after only a few weeks. He didn't even want to see me walk, as did most of the docs. Or tap. He looked at my X-ray and announced, "The good news is the horse is out of the barn."

A poet, I thought.

"I love to operate," he declared, practically salivating at the thought.

Another doctor told me I had an old lady's knee in a young lady's body. That was a nice compliment. One physical therapist told me to learn to tap dance horizontally. It wasn't funny at the time. Finally, another major orthopedic guy, the only one I really liked, told me I was now bone hitting bone on the knee, in too much pain to postpone the TKR.

Friend Jackie Raven and modern dance mentor Beverly Blossom reflected two different points of view concerning my knee pain. Beverly took one look at me at the Whitney Museum of Art and said, "Boy, are you in denial," as I limped around. She herself had had two hip replacements. Jackie, on the other hand, thought I was too depressed for such a major operation. I was depressed! Despite the depression, I finally bit the bullet in 2001.

I knew he was right. It was time to bite the bullet. I settled on an old-fashioned surgeon, one who took my health insurance. The operation went well, but my doctor didn't think I needed to have physical therapy. He said that since I was a dancer, I should be able to do it on my own. Oy.

The recovery took a good solid four months, during which time I cursed the day I had the TKR. My leg turned blue and black at one point. It was scary.

I eventually went down to Miami to see my friend Kerry's physical therapist, who told me he was going to tie a scarf around my mouth so I wouldn't scream when he bent my knee back. Burt was old school. I did scream, though, and he relented at least a bit. The water in Miami was great for ol' Kneesickle.

After those heinous months of recovery, something clicked. My pain vanished, and I was walking normally again. No limp anymore! The long and short of it: I have a great new knee (one leg is slightly longer).

Six years later, the only reminder that I once had a total bum knee comes every time I go through airport security and the titanium in my leg sets off the alarm. It's worth those women hitting my bra under wire, the top of my head, my stomach, up and down my legs, my entire body, as if I was a terrorist, for the price of my painless knee. ■

From Goddess to Emeritus

OK, I'm not crazy about the word "matriarch." Too old and stodgy. Jennifer Dunning, at *The New York Times* once called me "The Matriarch of Tap." I liked it better when she called me "the engaging free spirit of New York Tap Dance." But I did get older.

My friend in India, Sharon Lowen, told me the difference between grande dame and matriarch: The grande dame is more out in the world, with pearls and peons scattering at her command, a woman of some years, who has experience, and is listened to. The matriarch is a mother figure, familial. Those of her extended "family" defer to her in her position and attendant experience and wisdom.

They are both women who wield influence and respect. I don't think I'm either. I'm more like an icon without a job.

And then there's "emeritus," which is defined in the dictionary as: 1) to earn by service, 2) retired but retaining an honorary title, 3) corresponding to that held immediately before retirement. That sounds more like my job description right now.

In May 2002 I was getting a life achievement award in tap dancing, so I had to begin thinking about my past and present beyond the realm of psychotherapy.

The New York Committee to Celebrate National Tap Dance Day had selected me for the award in the autumn, and I was to be feted on May 25 at the National Tap Dance Day 2002 Tap Extravaganza™. May 25 happens to be Bill "Bojangles" Robinson's birthday. The event was to be held at Town Hall.

Each honoree gets a "Flo-Bert," a plaque for life achievement, named for Florence Mills and Bert Williams, two black veterans of vaudeville. This year I would share the limelight with Frank Owens, the fabulous piano accompanist for many tap shows, who was known as "the tap dancer's best friend."

Tap Extravaganza™ always feels raggedy on the edges and 2002's was no exception. The honorees usually sit in the audience and speechify, or dance, or

Drawing from a Wall Street Journal *clip about me. I'm dancing at a club, "Jazzmania."*

speechify and dance. The first of these events proved to be a funky free-for-all with anyone and everyone tapping. But over the years it became more formalized.

This year, my year, the evening ended with a bunch of young dancers stampeding the stage to memorialize Buster Buster's recent death, and committee members announcing the end of the show while some performers were still cutting the rug onstage! It went overtime and the Town Hall union guys were chomping at the bits to close down the place (not joint). New York's Town Hall is pretty classy.

In years gone by I had seen Bunny Briggs cry when he received his Flo-Bert, Bunny of the doe eyes. I missed the years when Ann Miller and Donald O'Connor received their awards, but I'll bet they were something.

When I found out I was to be honored, I was recovering from my total knee replacement and the World Trade Center tragedy. I'd been displaced from my apartment because I live so close to Ground Zero, six blocks away. Old friends from my life in tap tried to get me appropriately revved up for the occasion.

———

Of course there were the last-minute decisions to make. What to wear—that was a big one. Would it be the vintage Mexican wedding dress from the '60s I had hanging in my closet? Jackie Raven made a big pitch for that. "You don't have to shop for vintage clothes," she told me, looking through my wardrobe. "You were *THERE.*"

I opted for elegance instead. I was glad I still fit into the cleavagy black dress Dorothy had made for me years before. It was a version of the boob dress I toured all over India in. I needed something to wear over the dress and had six people in my living room deciding if I should go for my mother's grey mink stole that hadn't been worn since my brother's bar mitzvah, or a glittery white sweater.

I always seemed to pull out my mother's furs when Jackie was around because I always admired her clothes and sense of style. The three women in my apartment were in favor of the white sweater. Jackie's former partner, Neil Applebaum, told me I had to make up my mind. Finally I went with the mink stole. I liked the pockets—I could put my hands in them. The mink looked good with a hat that I managed to dig out at the last minute, from my ex-sister-in-law, Fruitcake. I dressed the part.

———

Tap aficionado and producer Laraine Goodman rounded up the remaining Sole Sisters from the '80s to pay tribute to me at the awards ceremony. Laraine herself opened the segment by riding a bike onstage in a curly-headed wig and lots of cleavage. She looked like me! It was a great sight gag, although I wondered how many in the crowd knew that I actually did ride a bike everywhere.

Top of the heap: flanked by Gregory and Savion, 2002.

Then came Sarah, my dance partner and friend, who invented so much of the tapping and talking we did together. She and Dorothy performed a great tap-a-gram™ to the tune of "You Gotta Have Heart." Brenda Bufalino sang and tapped "My Secret Love" and that touched me. Tap had once been so far underground that it had seemed like our secret, but now, Brenda sang and tapped, "My secret love's no secret anymore." It was the perfect tune for the occasion.

The veteran Irish tapper Josephine McNamara, my administrator Kathleen Isaac, Miriam Greaves-Ali of South African Boot Dance fame, and Beverly Rolfsmeir—who, together with Sarah, had come up with the concept of an all-women tap show—rounded out the cast. Constance Valis Hill gave a very enthusiastic and touching speech, paying homage to the late Frances Nealy and Harriet Brown.

Jackie Raven was there with her kids. Even in pain with her deadly cancer, she made the trip in from Long Island and compared me to Jason Kidd, that year's reigning basketball star, who was known for his assists on the court. She called me the "Jason Kidd of Tap Dance" because I assisted so many people in making connections for them, and like Kidd, knew at all times what was going on, on the court.

My student and surrogate daughter, Jodee Nimerichter, a big macher (co-producer of the American Dance Festival), spoke about what a great teacher I had been at

Gregory talking at the big event, Town Hall, 2002.

NYU. She gave a wonderful speech and everything was so warm and homey and fuzzy. I felt appreciated.

Then surprise, surprise! Gregory showed up! All the way from California! That really knocked me out. We had argued a lot the winter before because I wanted him to be the emcee; I was worried about nobody showing up, since I'd become an unintentional underground icon.

He looked great in his brown Armani getup. He told the audience how much he loved me and how intimidating I could be with my focus on tap. I laughed in surprise with the entire audience and Sole Sister gang when he talked about my taking him to a nude beach. He said that minutes after he met me, he knew we were going to be friends for life.

Dianne Walker did the actual presentation of the award and told some stories about my *schmatta* in the movie *TAP.*

Savion Glover was the emcee, and he escorted me across the stage to the podium, telling the audience he admired my "style of life."

That was real high praise coming from Savion, but I wondered just what he knew of my lifestyle; I thought immediately he meant my bike. Maybe he knew I was a leftover hippie or, like him, was addicted to tap dancing. Is that what he admired? My tap addiction?

On some level, the praise for my making *Sole Sisters* happen probably didn't register with some of the younger dancers, who didn't realize what a struggle it had been for women to be heard as soloists. That struggle had been waged in the '70s and '80s, so it was not until the '90s that a lot of women got "feet" like the old masters; the skill level of tap had risen rapidly in those decades of the revival/renaissance. I was glad I didn't have to do anything but sit there and appreciate it all.

—⁓—

I had written my acceptance speech that afternoon before the ceremony. Here it is:

> *"Thank you for that wonderful presentation. I would like to thank my parents, Jack and Molly Goldberg, who used to do a mean Charleston in our basement and who inspired me to dance. They both flipped out years later when I actually did take up dancing seriously and, in fact, rarely came to any of my performances.*
>
> *My father always liked to quote the great philosopher, Buddy Hackett, who said it was bad luck to have a close relative in the audience. I told him, "Daddy, we're not that close," but he still didn't want to jinx me. Nevertheless, he helped make it possible for me to tap dance my life away.*
>
> *I would also like to thank my brother, Arthur, who also isn't here tonight because he's at his daughter, my niece Amory's, graduation from college. But he did, in fact, come to most of my shows with his then-wife, Fruitcake. He did all the artwork and flyers and promotional materials for my tap happenings.*
>
> *I'm in humble gratitude to the New York Committee to Celebrate National Tap Dance Day for this honor, and to my dear Sole Sisters, many of whom are not just colleagues, but close friends, to my students with whom I could share the incredible story of tap, to my main squeeze of eleven and a half years, Owen Gray, to all the Hoofers and Copasetics and grandes dames and prima tapperinas who literally took me by the hands and showed me how to talk with my feet.*
>
> *I'd also like to thank my massage therapist, my former and present psychotherapists, my couples therapist, my past life therapist, my psychopharmacologist (yes, I'm on the right medications), my tap encounter group, Codependent Feet.*
>
> *I'd like to thank all my friends who are the best part of my life. It's been possible so far to tap dance my life away, and as all of us in tap know, tap dancing through life is a great way to go."* ■

The Brooklyn Food Co-op Dance

"It's very important to marry a good dancer."
—Molly Goldberg

I did finally meet my partner, dancing. It was the Saturday night before Thanksgiving, 1990, shortly after an improvisation class Gregory gave at Woodpecker's Studio in Soho. I always felt I had to prove myself to Gregory as a tapper, and that late afternoon was no exception. I wanted to feel special, but froze, paddled around, sputtered, then giggled and backed off when it was my turn to solo.

When the class was over, I walked Gregory home. That's when we were living across the street from each other. He was looking forward to taking his daughter out that night for her birthday.

I then remembered that Sarah Safford had told me about her annual food co-op dance in Brooklyn. I changed into a long purple skirt and top, not looking forward to schlepping over to Brooklyn on the subway. In 1990, Brooklyn to me was still foreign soil. It still is now, even though I know it's where a lot of great people live and great culture happens. Did I need my passport? Ha Ha. I'm such a Manhattan provincial.

You know how they say you never meet someone when you're looking? Well, I was *definitely* looking for Mr. Right. That was my sole purpose for heading out on the subway at 9 p.m. I wasn't feeling very open to it, but I had to give it the old college try.

In my deflated mood, I walked up the stairs of the synagogue turned dance hall. A group therapy member of mine was sitting at the little table taking the entrance fee. I was very surprised and happy to see him, but it was a bad omen. Steve was gay.

Even worse than thinking it would be a dance full of gay men, was the reality of standing alone, watching all those happily married couples (probably with babysitters and children at home), dancing with each other. I hardly saw any single people, men or women. That was Bummer Number One.

Owen Gray: I met my "main squeeze," dancing!

At Owen's art studio in Brooklyn, circa 1997.

Bummer Number Two was that I hadn't eaten dinner and the Brooklyn Food Co-op, famous for its incredible variety of ethnic delicacies, offered only pretzels, chips, and soft drinks. I was hungry!

I was ready to turn around and go home, but a guy finally did ask me to dance and he turned out to have halitosis. I learned quickly though, that he had a car and hadn't eaten dinner either. I wasn't attracted to him, but I was attracted to the thought of a good meal and a ride home. Despite his halitosis, I would have gone in a second.

As I was leaving, I briefly told my group therapy friend, still sitting at the door, that I really didn't want to go, but I didn't want to stay, either. He told me "Jane, you don't have to go."

As if I needed permission from some grown-up, I decided to tell Mr. Halitosis I was going to stay, after all. I was standing, a total wallflower on the side, lined up with other wallflowers, when the man next to me, who I hadn't noticed, asked if I wanted to dance.

I said, sure. We began to boogie, not the kind of dancing where you hold each other, not ballroom dancing. It was more free form, a little Motown, the kind of dancing where you can do anything, which is exactly what I was doing, not paying my partner any mind at first. I could see he was blondish, WASP-y, wearing jeans and a horizontal striped jersey and not looking me in the eyes either.

But then something funny happened, kind of miraculous really. As we kept dancing, into the next song and then the next, and then the next, without breaking at all, I noticed that this guy was playful. He was imitating my moves, shimmying a little, going up and down, making all kinds of arm circles.

I began to totally watch how he was moving, almost a-rhythmic, sideways as if he was boxing in space with his fists at times. Not aggressive or anything, but he had this sideways thing happening which looked interesting to me, very non-confrontational.

I soon began to "test" him to see if he was really paying attention, or if he, too, was in his own world. He wasn't. And I soon joined him in the playfulness. It was all kind of happening in slow motion, the whole rest of the night, as dance after dance, song after song, we kept going on the floor.

He gave me a lot of space to do my own thing and yet, it felt like we were connecting without ever even touching each other, just watching each other and playing.

This was the kind of feeling I so hoped I would have had in the Gregory improvisation class—feeling free because I was dancing. I didn't expect that experience that night. Even in the slow tunes, where we finally did touch, it didn't feel sticky or too romantic or like falling in love in that cinematic way I had pictured my whole life.

It was one long great groove and we danced all night. Well we danced, at least, until the Brooklyn Food Co-op people decided to end the dance. We were the last ones on the floor at 2 a.m.

When we left, we were both very sweaty and relaxed. This stranger walked me to the subway and told me he painted houses and apartments. I said I was doing a tap show at the New York Marxist School and felt stupid after I told him that, like I had to make sure right from the get go he knew my politics.

At the subway, I learned his name was Owen. Then he did something strange for him. Right as the train came, he asked awkwardly, "Aren't you going to give me a kiss?" I kissed him lightly on the cheek and gave him a flyer to my show. We also quickly exchanged phone numbers.

I didn't know Owen was a real painter, a focused painter, a terrific painter of animals, people, and nature. He probably thought right off the bat I'd want to know what he did for a living. He did come to see my performance at The Marxist School with its Stradivarius floor.

I must have passed "inspection" because after Thanksgiving we went out on our first real date and saw Robert Altman's *Vincent and Theo* and made out right during the movie! We've been together ever since around 1990 or '91 (there's still some confusion on the year). It's not exactly like I met Fred Astaire and I'm in some feathered evening gown on an Art Deco ocean liner. But it's nice that Owen can dance. ■

Acknowledgments and Thanks

I was very fortunate to have Pamela Sommers, a lover of tap herself, step in to shape and edit the final version of this book. With pen and paper in hand, she sat with me and, in old school style, was wonderfully ruthless. She understood that each word mattered, like a sound in tap

To Susan Woolhandler and Ann Bartholomew, who walked and talked me through a lot of the heart of the book with their huge hearts.

To my designer Kathi Georges, who was enthusiastic, talented and patient to the end. To Peter Carlaftes who was also there in spirit and design.

To the writers and editors who helped in different ways—there were several cooks in this gumbo, and I'm deeply indebted to each of their tastes: Kerry Gruson, David Hinckley, Jardine Libaire, Molly McQuade, Jackie Raven, Chris Segura. And to Jennifer Dunning, who always got me from the get go.

To my father, Jack Goldberg, who, in true Polonius form at ninety-seven, still wants me to see the light. He reminds me each time I visit, how Uncle Phil's book about the secrets of getting a job with the U.S. Government was almost halted from publication; how I have two copies (one, signed) somewhere in my library of The Jack Goldberg Comedy, Gambling, Jokes and Government Service Collection; and how Uncle Phil's book ultimately ended up on the second-hand bins for fifteen cents a copy.

Well, at least it ended up somewhere.

Speaking of my father, to my therapists, Dr. Gayle Lewis, Dr. Art Robbins, and to my psycho-pharmacologist, Dr. David Gandler.

To the great photographers, friends, and acquaintances who charged nominal fees or lent me fabulous photos to make this book a visual journey as well as a literary one. In a few cases—thirty years, four phone numbers, three lofts, apartments, houses, states, or countries later, I have learned more about rights than I ever wanted to know. As one Miami Danny Rose told me, "Doll, when I get the money, you get the money."

I thank also the New York Public Library for the Performing Arts at Lincoln Center that houses my archive, *Jane Goldberg's Wandering Shoes of tap(h)istory,*

Tip Top Tapes, Tapalogues, Tapology, and Tapperabilia" in The Gregory Hines Tap Collection. That branch hosted a "Fair Usage" panel, where I learned it was OK to use a picture of Fred Astaire with my photo plastered on top of "Ginger's," in the name of a "transformational" experience. To the New York Committee to Celebrate National Tap Dance Day for use of some footage for the DVD.

The seed of this book was planted in the fall of 1987 when I went up to Blue Mountain Center, an artist colony in the Adirondacks with my audiotapes and tap shoes. I spent valuable time also at Yaddo, The MacDowell Colony, and the Virginia Center for Creative Arts in Lynchburg, Va., and Auvillar, France.

To my friends, Romans, countrymen and women who have lent me their ears, and stayed in my corner concerning this book: Vivek Adarkar, Jan Albert, Stewart Alter, Angelo Ascagni, Cher Bertram, Lauren Carnali, Lorrie Fink, my high school English Teacher—Nancy Gallagher, Gary Giddins, Owen Gray, brother Arthur Goldberg, Allan Guggenheim, Peter Guralnick, Iris and Jason Lampel, Negrita Jayde, Deborah Jowitt, Marilyn Kallett, Bob Katz, Kirsten Kenny, Ann Kilkelly, Katherine Kramer, Pamela Koslow, Jeanette MacDougal, sister-in-law Hani Miletski, Melinda Mousouris, Jodee Nimerichter, Fred, Gabe, and Gregory Pinkney, Claudia Rahardjanoto, Craige Roberts, Sarah Safford, Barry Saperstein, Jamie Larowitz Sherman, Marcia Siegel, David Smith, Eric Stewart, Tao Strong, Uncle Sammy, Constance Valis Hill, Dorothy Wasserman, Danny Weitzman, Shay Youngblood, and Howard Zinn.

To shoemakers Gus Banks and Angel Villanueva. To the now defunct Morgan Taps makers, who made taps that could make a shoe ring and sing.

To those I have forgotten, it was not my intention. I did not have as much time to work on these acknowledgments as I did to write the book.

And finally, to all the hoofers, closet hoofers, and tap dancers I write about who ultimately make these memories mostly pleasant ones. ■

Appendix

"TALKING TAP" (AND SPORTS) ONE LAST TIME WITH GREGORY HINES

Though he looked very, very thin, Gregory Hines still had his beautiful smile when he stood outside to greet me on the narrow little path with his fiancée, Negrita Jayde. Our discussion covered a period of three different days, starting June 24 and ending July 6. This was his last interview. (He died of cancer August 9, 2003.)

DAY ONE
FRIENDS TO THE END

GREGORY HINES: Did I ever tell you my favorite Robert De Niro story? Treat Williams told it to me. He and Robert De Niro were doing a scene from *Once Upon a Time in America* where there is a carafe of wine and Treat's glass and De Niro's glass. Robert De Niro is supposed to take the carafe and pour some wine into Treat's glass and they were rehearsing and rehearsing and it just didn't feel right to De Niro.

De Niro kept saying, "Not enough wine in the carafe, I need more wine in the carafe." Finally De Niro gets comfortable with the carafe and he says, "This is it." So the director says, "Action," and De Niro passes the carafe over to Treat Williams. Now Treat, for a moment, almost said, "But I thought you were supposed to pour?"

But Treat said he was so acutely aware of who he was acting with, that he just picked the carafe up and poured for himself and he was never supposed to do that. But that's what happened and that's the way life is.

The "quarreling" twosome. Friends to the end.

I mean, you know Jane, you're in our home, so we're supposed to pour for you, we're supposed to get for you, but maybe just you being you, and you feeling it, you pick up something and pour it for me and say, "Hey, Negrita, hand me your glass." And that's the way life happens.

It was such a powerful lesson for me, because I hadn't done much acting and still haven't compared to somebody like Robert De Niro, and yet, it's the whole idea that it is coming out of real life into these characters so that sometimes the investment has to supercede what's on the [scripted] page. You know what I mean? The older I get, the more I'm impressed by the investment that people make into what they're doing, Jane. It doesn't have to be fanatical; it's what's happening, the investment they're making right then. It's interesting that with all the stories I could tell you about Savion Glover . . . when I think of him, sometimes, or when someone mentions his name, the thing I think about is sitting in a rehearsal hall on a break during the rehearsals of *Jelly's Last Jam*.

Ted Levy (a co-choreographer with GH of *Jelly's Last Jam*) and I were sitting and talking over on the side. I was invested in my conversation with Ted and I was enjoying listening to Savion and every now and then we'd say, *"O ho, yeah, ha ha ha ha hoooo, haha . . . "* But after awhile, it was like those movies where the young singer gets up and sings and everybody is talking and all of a sudden people start listening and "a star is born" because everyone hears her and that's how the story plays out. That always happens in movies like that. And we . . .

JG: Getting back to the De Niro thing. Was it him, or Treat Williams you were most impressed with?

GH: De Niro. But Treat Williams as well because it was Treat who could go with the moment. I was impressed with both of them, actually.

JG: Yeah, I saw a book in your living room, something in the title that said, "Stop Acting."

GH: That's the title of the book: *How to Stop Acting.*

JG: Maybe I could read it and then never learn how to act.

GH: That's the toughest thing, to not act. But what that is, Jane, it's "don't work so hard." That's the toughest thing to do, to just relax. Relax, and enjoy. I was thrilled to meet the long jumper, Bob Nieman, a broad jumper. Jesse Owens had set the record 30 years before. Nieman broke it by one and a half feet. I loved it, the competition . . .

JG: I remember once you told me in an email that I was competitive, but didn't feel comfortable with being competitive. And I always hear: "I'm competing with myself." I don't feel that at all. Do you think that's what Savion was thinking when he was practicing?

GH: No. I don't think competition is competing against yourself. Even when people say, "I'm not competing with anybody. I am competing against myself." No. I'm competing against the last condition I was in. You look at golf pros. They say they're competing against the course and yet there's a board up there and they keep their eye on it to see where they are on the board. Ever since Tiger Woods came on the scene, that's what they're looking for, to see where he is.

JG: You mean it doesn't have to be like competition one on one. It's "Whoever was the best last?"

GH: No, it's like "Who's in the lead—and how far am I away from him?"

JG: You once said Honi [Coles] was competing with John Bubbles.

GH: I feel differently about that now. I don't think Honi was competing with Bubbles. I think Honi was always trying to prove worthy of the level he had placed John Bubbles on. He told me he thought John Bubbles was the best.

JG: Yeah, I know you asked Honi on his death bed.

GH: On his death bed, I asked him who he thought was the best.

JG: I know. I can't believe you said that. People hear that you asked that, they can't believe it either.

GH: How come?

JG: Because it's so macho—so into that being-the-best head set.

GH: Uh huh. For me the Challenge has always been an important part of my development and my process.

JG: But you didn't have to grow up on the streets. You didn't have to challenge anybody.

GH: You don't have to grow up on the streets.

JG: Did you have that mentality as a kid?

GH: I can't say it was necessarily my mentality. It was just I was very sports oriented. I wasn't into politics. I wasn't into intellectual stuff. I was into sports.

JG: You are an intellectual even if you weren't into it.

GH: Yeah, but I wasn't into those kinds of pursuits. I was into sports and I had my teachers who said to me, "If your power of retention were as great with your school work in listing dates as it is with sports statistics, you'd be a tremendous student." I couldn't remember that stuff. It just didn't interest me at all. But how many carries Jim Brown had and how many yards he gained and how many years per game per carry and touchdowns and fumbles—no problem. I almost had a photographic memory.

JG: There must have been some attraction for you to sports other than playing them.

GH: I just loved sports. I loved watching them.

JG: You loved watching somebody tackle and beat up somebody else?

GH: No, no. I just loved watching people compete with each other and, you know.

JG: You do?

GH: There's nothing like it! Yeah, it's so exciting.

JG: But don't you think that's often what's divisive about tap dancers?

GH: I don't think that's the divisive thing in tap. I don't think The Challenge is divisive. I think that healthy respectful competition is a beautiful thing—when people go into it with respect for each other, for each other's ability, skills, and each other's love for the art, whatever that would be. You know I've seen boxing matches where they get up and try to beat each other in ten rounds. As soon as the bell rings for the tenth round, they embrace. As far as each of them is concerned, the respect is just at the highest level. I'm not saying there's not envy and jealousy involved in sports. Of course there is. Larry Bird bringing the ball down the court and then Magic Johnson comes up to defend him. This is it!—Magic against Bird. Also, there is a lot of success in sports.

Day Two
More Clarification on "The Challenge"

GH: I apologize for not being able to see you while you've been here, but I know that you're here (California), so I've been thinking about my feelings about different things. I remember that when I was introduced to The Challenge, the whole idea of it was that it wasn't necessarily the winning of it that was the challenge. The Challenge as I remember it was somebody would get out there and do eights or even sixteens and they'd go [he scats], "Geeet bop be ge bok, dah bak de dah a de dah, geed ka de bop, geeka do bo debo bo bo bo, be diddly boop, be deleboop, be deleboop a bidili boooo doo doo doo." And then when it was my time to come in, I would start off with "a billia boop, a billia boop, a billia doop dooo doo doo doot" and take it from there, which indicated that I was listening, and I could do it, what they just did.

That meant: "I'm going to show you how well I was listening, and I'm going to let you know I could do it by starting off my eights or sixteens with what you just finished doing." Because I've heard musicians do that. Musicians, when they're taking solos, they're doing fours. I've heard saxophone players finishing off their fours, [and] a trumpet player, starting off his fours with what the saxophone players did. That's what I remember about The Challenge. It wasn't so much that in the end everybody acknowledged, "That's the winner." No, the whole thing was impressive because people were able to show their ability to listen, their ability to keep time, their ability to do what another dancer did.

JG: But that's a certain kind of Challenge . . .

GH: That's a Challenge I remember being introduced to. I'm sure Challenges can be all kinds of things.

JG: How were you introduced to it?

GH: Sandman Sims.

JG: When you were little?

GH: Well, I was about ten, eleven.

JG: You were in a circle?

GH: No, just me and Sandman . . . I would do something and he would do what I just did, and I would think "Wow". . . It's not like I finished my thing and he took a few beats to figure out how he was going to do what I did. 'Cause he didn't necessarily have to make my sound doing exactly the footing I did. He could just reproduce it and I thought that was amazing. I thought that was really amazing.

And I was thinking how we talk so much about moving the art form forward, one dancer at a time, and the each-one-teach-one concept, that one of the ways tap has continued to survive is from one dancer to another.

And I started to think that that's one of the wonderful things about tap festivals . . . Leon Collins is not going to show one dancer who's going to show another. But Dianne [Walker] is going to show maybe a couple hundred people . . . and in addition to learning all this great stuff, the people who come to the festival get to spend time around Dianne Walker—or somebody like Dianne. Or I notice Fayard Nicholas is going to be at a festival, or Jimmy Slyde . . . I mean, you know it's a great opportunity. It's a great way for tap dancing to accelerate, for tap steps and tap consciousness and tap styles to move faster out into the tap community.

Yeah, you know [NY Tap Festival producer] Tony is interested in doing as much as he can in the time allotted . . . which I find very impressive. And he's also looking to reach back and acknowledge. That's been one of the most cherished aspects of tap dancing, how young dancers, well, every dancer, no matter how old, will reach back about dancers who impressed them. I got an email from Andrew Nemr (Tap Legacy Foundation) about Henry [LeTang]. And Henry is a freak of nature (smoking 'til he was ninety, etc.) . . . I remember Eubie Blake was such a great person and he knew a million stories. If there was a lull, Eubie could tell you a story that would just blow your mind. I mean, you know that phrase, "O man, it blew my mind. I couldn't believe it when I saw that and my mind was blown" Eubie Blake had stories that would blow my mind . . . and whenever I would see him, at some point in the evening, he would say, "Do you realize how close I am to being one hundred?" His wife meant everything to him. She was the one you had to talk to if you were going to talk to Eubie. She was everywhere and doing everything for him. When she died (at eighty-eight), everybody went into, "How are we going to tell Eubie? How is he going to react? Where should we tell him? Should we tell him and have a nurse?" I remember he said, "Everybody's dead"— everybody Eubie knew. Someone who spoke at his memorial said that Eubie was the ultimate showman, which he was, and he knew how to promote. Long before television or the Internet, he knew how to promote. If he was going to be appearing some place, Eubie knew how to promote it. *(Ed note: So did Gregory; he walked Eubie to the offices of Saturday Night Live, and got them both on that show in a beautiful segmet of the two of them singing.)*

JG: I remember I was with John Bubbles sitting with him in a nursing home when Eubie died.

GH: Was anybody else there?

JG: No. He had this far-off look.

GH: John?

JG: Yeah, Bubbles, his thing was all about competition. Everything was "a compete." He called it "a compete." People thought it looked like a spelling error, but that's what it was for him.

GH: Well, you know I went to him when he was still living in his house in Inglewood (Ca.) I called him up and told him I wanted to come up and talk to him about something 'cause I wanted to do his life story. It wasn't 'til later on, in retrospect, that I realized that he got a kick out of the idea that I wanted to do it, you know he didn't want anything to happen until he wrote a book, but he got a chuckle out of it because he definitely didn't think I was anywhere near the level as a tap dancer.

JG: Were you already a celebrity then?

GH: I wasn't that well-known, but I'd done a number of things. I'd done *Eubie*, I'd done *Coming Uptown*. So, I said, "I want to portray you in your life story." His chuckle was wonderful.

—⁓—

DAY THREE
ON THE CONTROVERSIAL NATURE OF TAP

JG: Do you think the festival is the right place to talk about the "isms" of racism, sexism, ageism, classism, to confront them?

GH: These "isms" are the toughest to deal with. Tap dancing is just a microcosm of our culture . . . We live in a racist, sexist, ageist culture—and hey, we've got something to say and we feel like we've been treated this way, and they get a little bit of media attention and it fades away because people don't want to talk about the isms. They don't. There is no way to go about talking about it. There really isn't.

It takes courage. It takes people who are willing to disagree. Out of the courageous ability to disagree, a lot of understanding can come. But a lot of times, bad feelings come first. Because, you know, it's very difficult for white folks to talk about racism without getting defensive. There are white people who have never

Tap dancing is just a microcosm
of our culture . . .

put down black folks, who all of a sudden, say, "We've got to talk about racism. We were doing so nice, we were talking about tap dancing and steps, and now we have to talk about the way women are treated . . . or the fact that there's a racist energy in tap dancing." That's heavy stuff for anybody, but it does take people who are willing to talk about it. It's tough. I'm telling you, it's tough. I know a lot of black people who don't want to talk about this.

But in these festivals, to incorporate a round table discussion for anyone who's interested in talking about these things. Not have it show up in an overall "Ain't it great that we're all tap dancers and we're all in the round table discussion and we're having a great time." But allocate a workshop or discussion for people who are interested in these problems that we have. Then the people who show up are the ones who want to talk about it, and we would be surprised to make some inroads about it, and we might be surprised at how many people would show up for that type of thing.

JG: I think there would be a lot.

GH: But knowing, going in, what the workshop or discussion will be about. [Being] ready for it. As opposed to having the topics just show up.

JG: You mean the audience would have to be required to say something?

GH: No, no, no—just that they would know going in that, "These are the topics" . . . We're not talking about stages, and volume, and amplification and wardrobe, and the cost of moving a floor and any of that stuff. We're talking about racist energy that exists in tap, sexism . . .

JG: You think ageism exists?

GH: You go see Savion Glover and the marquee says "Savion Glover and Friends" and a couple of those friends could be seventy-five years old, and people go and see . . . and there is this great reverence for these great dancers who will include Cartier Williams along with Jimmy Slyde and Buster Brown, and people have never seen this guy just slide across the stage. He's obviously not a teenager, and they get the opportunity to see that. Much like Mikhail Baryshnikov would tour with the White Oak company and do choreography by these young choreographers who would never get their work seen by all these packed houses without somebody like Mike to say, "Hey, I'm coming to town and this is what I'm coming to town with . . ." People line up and buy tickets, and they say, "Hey, that was an interesting . . ."

JG: Yeah, he really brought out Yvonne Rainer . . . and her choreography into public view.

GH: Yeah, right now he's out with Eliot Feld's choreography . . . So Savion

> # We're not talking about stages, and volume, and amplification and wardrobe, and the cost of moving a floor and any of that stuff. We're talking about racist energy that exists in tap . . .

has made a habit of doing a similar thing.

JG: But when I was working with those old veterans, that's what the audience wanted to see. They didn't want to see young people.

GH: You mean in the beginning? In the beginning there weren't a lot of young people who could really go . . . You know, there just weren't. Most of the people had gone to ballet or jazz or other dance forms that they had the potential to at least make a living at . . . It wasn't until tap started to become attractive again to younger people that they started studying it again . . . wanting to do it again.

The total effect of everything was going on in tap, all the different people who were doing it, all the different places it would pop up . . . It was really great.

I remember in 1983 they had Night of 100 Stars at Radio City Music Hall,

You never know where the seed is planted.

and I was called up and told, "We're doing a big tap number and we'd like you to be in it." They're reeling off all these people who are going to be in it: Christopher Walken, Ann Miller, and it turned out to be a great thing . . . They'd never had anything like that in The Night of 100 Stars . . . This was the fourth year of it. All of a sudden whatever viewing audience was there, saw a big tap number in the middle of this show!!!—With all these different people tap dancing . . . People would come out and they'd say, "Wow!" Christopher Walken would come out and do a great combination and my brother Maurice was in it and a whole bunch of people.

I remember someone was talking about Ruby Keeler, when she was in *No No Nanette*, and she could really go. And she was dancing. She was dancing! I don't know whether she was seventy-seven or seventy-six but whatever age she was, she could still go. And she was dancing in front of Broadway audiences, many of whom had never seen live tap dancing before .

JG: Who plants the seed?

GH: You never know where the seed is planted.

JG: Remember in 1992 when you said—after women had really done a lot of tapping—that they shouldn't be on the stage yet?

GH: I said, "Women *shouldn't* be tapping onstage?"

JG: Not shouldn't, but "Show me a woman who can get into my ballpark . . ."

GH: That's different. That's very different from "shouldn't be on the stage."

JG: How?

GH: Well, because anytime you have anything, any medium, whatever it might be, any discipline, you have to prove yourself. You have to. I mean you can talk it. You can talk it like crazy. I mean who talked it more than Muhammad Ali? But ultimately, you have to get in the ring and back that up! I'm fine with that.

JG: Jimmy Slyde once brought . . .

GH: Wait a minute, wait a minute. We're not talking about Jimmy now. We're talking about me—where I'm coming from. Yeah. Show me somebody who can juggle twelve balls in the air. Then when I see someone who can juggle twelve balls in the air, I say, "Wow," and they say, "O there's another guy who can juggle twelve balls in the air," and I say, "Oh really? I'd like to see it." Just because I've seen this one guy juggle twelve balls in the air, everybody could say they can juggle twelve. Do it! "And then when I see you do it, cool! There's a big juggling show that we're building and we want as many great jugglers as we can get!" Yeahhhhhhh. Ohhhhhhh. I don't mind proving myself. I've never minded that as long as I'm judged by the same standard as everybody else.

JG: The "same standard" to you is the feet. Remember in our arguing about feet, I said tap could also be a sensibility? Like this guy I know who has this great

I don't feel that I have to meet one other person in this world who feels about feet the way I do in order to continue to feel about feet the way I do. That's an important thing.

rhythm but not necessarily great feet . . . but great humor. He played The Frog Prince in one of my shows.

GH: Fine! I don't have any problem with that either. I don't feel that I have to meet one other person in this world who feels about feet the way I do in order to continue to feel about feet the way I do. That's an important thing. You know sometimes people . . . have you ever met somebody whose opinion is based on the last person they spoke with?

JG: Me.

GH: And you say "Jeeeze, you said this yesterday, and now you say this today." I'm not talking about change . . . because change is a really good thing. I mean the Lord above knows I have said some things ten or fifteen years ago that I feel differently about now. I have no compunction, I don't hesitate in saying how I feel now, knowing that it's different. That's a good thing.

JG: Is that true with tap?

GH: With tap? I mean, you know!!!!!!!!!!

JG: Was it always feet for you?

GH: I was always impressed by feet. Always . . . I feel that feet—it's like the great equalizer.

JG: So you're happy that a shuffle can make twenty sounds and you would work on tonation?

GH: I don't feel it in a specific sense . . . I know it when I see it and when I hear it. I know it when somebody's got great feet. And I know when somebody's got . . .

JG: Great musicality?

GH: It's in the feet. The time is in the feet. It's all there in the feet. I play drums. And I play OK drums. But I drag the time when I play drums. I've been told this by musicians I've played with . . . I've felt it from musicians I've played with. Maybe they didn't say I "dragged the time," but I could feel it . . . And there were times when I've been playing that I could feel myself dragging the time and I'm trying to get back to where the bass player is because he's got it and I'm dragging it . . . I just love watching a person who's got great feet and the time is impeccable. It's right there in the feet whether the music is playing or whether they're dancing a-capella. Impeccable. I just love it. They can be male, female . . .

Look, when I say "feet," I don't mean I'm oblivious to everything else that is happening, that my eyes and ears and whole consciousness are just riveted on the feet. I'm taking everything in. *But one of the great things that separates tap dancing from everything else is that you see the body move and you hear the body move.* If I'm watching somebody and their movements have a beautiful grace to them but their feet are not happening, I'm not saying that they're not good dancers. It's that feet are what really impress me the most.

I don't think we can explain these things. Hey, why are they trying to clone?

> But one of the great things that separates tap dancing from everything else is that you see the body move and you hear the body move.

Because they can't really explain how to do it, what steps need to be taken to make people great at something, or why this person is just so outstanding and nobody else seems to be able to touch them. No, there's no explanation for it. How do we explain Jackie Robinson? Do we say . . . "Well, he had a good education...he knew what he was up against; he knew what a great achievement it would be?" The fact that he knew he knew . . . he was bright . . . can't be explained . . . of what he was able to accomplish. You could never explain it. You can't explain Savion Glover. You can't boil it down to all these certain factors. No . . . You can't explain Muhammad Ali.

JG: What about Arthur Ashe?

GH: You can't explain it.

JG: Were those books by Ashe on African Americans in sports good?

GH: Yeah, it's like an encyclopedia of black achievement. It's impossible to explain these things. It's like this guy Cal Ripken (Jr.). You know, he's known as the Iron Man because he broke a record. Lou Gehrig played 2,130 consecutive baseball games. But Ripken played, I don't know, 2,500 or 2,450 games [final record: 2,632 consecutive games], and of all those games he played, and people say, "Wow, how could this guy play like he was never hurt?" And this guy said that he was always hurt. Always. Anytime you're an athlete and you play professional sports, you are going to hurt yourself. And if you're playing baseball, you don't have a whole lot of time to heal. You hurt yourself in a game on Monday, and you're playing Tuesday, Wednesday, and then you're traveling Thursday, and then you're playing on Friday—that's their life. So he was always hurt. But how do we explain how he could do it—and wanted to do it so badly?!

JG: Is it called second wind?

GH: No, I've had it happen when my knee hurt for a whole performance, or when I've hurt my heel and I put a piece of sponge in the shoe, but even then the heel hurt and then I'd have to compensate for the heel, and then the other knee starts to feel a little sore. There's no explanation. You know, I don't think there's an explanation for The Nicholas Brothers. There were live acts where they did splits and dives and jumps and leaps . . . but not like The Nicholas Brothers . . . Incomparable—completely incomparable. I don't know if I mentioned this already, but at one point they talked about doing the life story of The Nicholas Brothers on Broadway and I thought that was an admirable idea but impossible to really do it. Who are you going to find?

JG: That's what John Bubbles used to say about . . .

GH: Well, John—somebody could conceivably do John. Savion Glover could do John Bubbles.

(Gregory used to think about how Savion Glover was like Michael Jordan in skill level, but then he began thinking differently, about how Savion didn't have to be the greatest tap dancer to revolutionize the art of tap. Greg explains how, with Bill Russell shot-blocking, the basketball game changed.)

GH: Unlike previous shot blockers who would swat the ball off the court, just reject it out of bounds, Bill Russell would block it and keep it inbounds and often his players would get the rebound, get the block. Now by him blocking say five shots a game, that's potentially ten points for the other team that they don't get. By him keeping the ball in play those times, that's potentially ten points that

We live in a NEGATIVE culture. People want to see a reality show and they don't want to see necessarily a reality show to see who's gonna win it. They want to see all these people who are going to fail along the way.

his team gets cut in half, five points. You know how many basketball games are settled when one team wins 105 to 103. Bill Russell revolutionized the game. All of a sudden people were trying to draft shot blockers. They didn't care whether they could score points, they just wanted to get these guys who could block shots, but not block 'em like they wanted to kill the ball, block the shot so that it would stay inbounds.

Savion took tap dancing and *CHANGED IT* . . . changed how people saw it, changed how people wanted to learn it, learn how to do it, changed how people wanted to perform it . . . and put it to the degree that you have to see Savion, and if you want to see the progression, you have to see *Noise/Funk* LAST!!!!! You want to see *River Dance*, cool, you want to see *The Lord of the Dance*, you want to see *Tap Dogs*, you wanna see *Stomp*, see them first. Don't see *Noise/Funk* and then go to *Tap Dogs* . . . you can't do that. You have to see *Tap Dogs*, enjoy it for what it is: hunky guys dancing in various forms of undress, dancing on water, then you see (Savion) to see what tap dancing *IS*, where it *IS*, where he continues to take it.

Anyone who does this kind of stuff loses friends, and has a group of people who, while they don't pray for the person's failure, would enjoy it. If the person does not succeed or something bad happens to him along the way, that's just the way our culture is . . . and it's more so now than ever before.

More so now than ever, Jane. We live in a NEGATIVE culture. People want to see a reality show and they don't want to see necessarily a reality show to see who's gonna win it. They want to see all these people who are going to fail along the way. And then when they fail, they take that walk. And they fail when walking away. People want to see them fail. They have these reality shows now. You know I wouldn't look at a show like *American Idol*.

I would NEVER look at a show like that. Someone gets up and they audition and they are at their most vulnerable, people that are auditioning them get to say all these terrible humiliating things to them. "I can't believe you think you can sing! You can't even hold a tune! You need to get a job selling insurance . . . or jewelry. And they just take it.

I've auditioned. I've auditioned where people have said after the audition, "That was good. That was good. Thank you very much . . ." And it *killed* me. 'Cause I knew what that meant! *It hurt like hell. They didn't say, "You* call that tap dancing?" Then I might have collapsed on the floor. *This is an audition. I'm giving everything I have . . . I'm just trying to get this gig. I'm* putting it out there for you and you're going to say all these horrible things to me on *national television*?!

No. We live in a culture where when we get to the checkout line, we get all our groceries, and the *last* thing we see are the tabloids, trying to out-negative each other so we'll buy one of them. 'Oprah's secret love child on one' . . . 'Hillary has lesbian affair; Bill uh . . . knows about it' . . . Next one . . . 'Prince William his deep dark secret that the Queen is trying to keep it.' So now which one do we want? This thing about Prince William, he's a young up and comer, I bet he has some kind of deep dark . . . let me get this one: This is going to be my negative for today, this seems to out-negative the other two papers. This is our culture. And this is what people want.

So the most difficult thing for people to do WHO are in a field, who are in the art, is to look at somebody like Savion who is enjoying a massive success. Whether they realize it or not, paving the way for potential more work, for more recognition, more awareness of tap as an art form, and potentially achieving things as a tap dancer that we can *ALL* be proud of. That, no, let's root against him just a bit . . . it's too much . . . He's got too much going for him.

JG: You mean tap dancers are doing that, or general public or the dance critics?

GH: I don't think tap dancing is widely known enough for people in the general public to do it. So, I think it's more within the art form. I think there are plenty of people who adore him and who are not jealous and envious. Let's say, envious. I can understand the jealousy. How can you not be?

You know sometimes when I haven't seen Savion dance and I see him dance, I feel *jealous*. I think to myself, *damn* . . . How can he dance so fast and *clean* like that? I wish I could do that.

JG: And one reason you didn't feel angry at him . . . well one reason, when he left you out of the *Noise/Funk* mentoring part was because he was so good at it?

GH: No, nooooo . . . There was no way I felt I belonged in that because I never functioned principally as a mentor, as a tap mentor for Savion.

JG: You told me another reason years ago.

GH: Well, but I'm telling you NOWWWWWWWWWWW!

JG: OK . . . that's good, we're setting the record straight.

GH: RIGHT. Right . . . Because it's NOW. I'm sure because any question you asked me, you could draw up what I said years ago.

JG: Well, I was going to ask you if I can use some of the emails from years ago because—

GH: BECAUSE WHAT? Where's the value? . . . Let me finish.

JG: Because it's in my chapter on you.

GH: But let me finish.

JG: But where's the value is because it's a creative thing for me as a writer . . .

GH: YEAH, BUT this is not you as a writer. This is an interview!

JG: It's not an interview, it's a discussion!

GH: Oh, it's a discussion. So you could spend the whole discussion saying, "You know you once said, blah de blah de blah de blah de . . . blah." And I could say, "Yeah, I feel the same way now." And we could go on to the next thing.

JG: THAT'S NOT TRUE!

GH: Or I would say, "I've changed."

JG: That's great!

GH: No, it's only great because you're concerned with what happened years ago.

JG: And other people are, too!

GH: You're very interested in what people *SAID*!

JG: And so are a lot of other people!

GH: (yelling) I DON'T THINK SO! I COULD NOT BE LESS INTERESTED IN SOMEBODY SAYING TO SOMEBODY . . .

JG: OK, now we are talking in the present . . .

GH: OK, WAIT A MINUTE . . . LET ME JUST FINISH THIS THING WITH SAVION.

JG: Well, wait a minute.

GH: No, no, *you wait a minute! 'Cause I know you love going backward.*

JG: NO, I'M NOT GOING BACKWARDS!

GH: LET ME STAY RIGHT NOW . . . I KNOW IT'S HARD . . . LET ME STAY RIGHT NOW . . .

JG: *(giggling) Am I stressing you?*

GH: No.

JG: Good.

GH: I functioned as a father in a way . . . as an older brother, as a really good friend, as a supporter, as someone interested in him as a human being, and trying to get that kind of relationship going. I saw from the get go there was going to be no limit to how many people were interested in him as a tap dancer and helping him grow in that way. Sure, maybe I showed him a step or two, or you know, maybe we played around and maybe I encouraged him as a tap dancer, sure . . . but, as a parent—

JG: You thought of yourself as a parent?

GH: Right, as a parent, and looking at Yvette—

JG: *(interrupting)* Not as mentor . . . remember we talked about the difference between . . . oh, we haven't *done that yet, we haven't* talked about the difference between mothering and mentoring—

GH: Fathering!

JG: And fathering and mentoring.

GH: Looking at Yvette raising Abron, and Carlton, and Savion, by herself, I felt like maybe I could lend a hand where Savion is concerned. I didn't spend much time with Carlton, and hardly any time with Abron, but with Savion, because we were working together and tap dancing, I was able to spend that time. So, I wasn't looking for it to be "Buster, Lon, Jimmy, and Greg," No . . . not at all . . . and I think there were a few people who thought, "Oh he must be upset!" No, no. I thought this is beautiful . . . this is a beautiful tribute.

JG: So what do I do if I have the history of what you've said . . . before . . . it's not that I . . .

GH: What do you do? THROW IT AWAY!

JG: You mean, don't even read those e-mails?

GH: THROW IT AWAY!

JG: But I want to write a book about it!

GH: Well, hey, if you want to write a book, maybe you ought to take a look at this when we finish it and see where this leads you in terms of book writing.

JG: But you even said, "Don't you think this could be published, concerning our e's . . . ?"

GH: I know, I know . . . what I said. But now, we're actually in it now. We're doing something we used to do that we haven't done in a long time . . . And now maybe this feels more real and more current . . . and more right.

JG: Oh.

GH: You know I just bought a book, this guy interviewed Marlon Brando. And this guy said, "You once said". . . and Brando chewed him up!!!! He said, "Yeah, yeah, yeah." I don't know specifically what he said, I'll try to find it for you but in essence what he was saying was, "That's what interviewers are always saying to me. 'You once said.'"

JG: TO ME?

GH: What do you mean?

JG: Did he say, "You once said" to me?

GH: No no no, "You once said."

JG: Right, so he read it somewhere else. These e's are personal. These are things that I think about.

GH: But these are things that are GONE! You know—what was the hippie rule? Everything that's real is *right now*. There ain't nothing real about what's gone down before. Ain't nothing real about what's supposed to come next . . . This is what's real: RIGHT NOW! ■

HOOFIN'
By Jackie Raven

We need two sheets
Of masonite, 4x4 and a spot:
Columbus in front of Haagen Dazs;
Bleecker near the Bitter End;
Or West Broadway and Prince.
Soho's our favorite, iffy
In the '70s, but on a summer night,
After dinner at Raoul's, people
Want to hear tap dancing.

Always someone whom we love
Carries our boards and passes the hat.
Charles is hit by an egg one night
While we dance to Ray's sousaphone.
But tonight the money is good.
Joni Mitchell gives us $20 with a smile,
The crowd is going wild.

We dance for our hoofer heroes
Ralph Brown in his pink shoes,
Tall, thin prince of elegance, Honi Coles,
Our fearless tap mother, Brenda Bufalino,
Who has trained us with neurotic genius;
We are working this corner.
Our red shoes hit the boards hard.
Hands clap, we're all laughing.

Who sees the bucket coming?
Who feels the cold-water splash?
Who hears the sirens screaming?

Later, at a booth in Panchito's,
Over two tall pina coladas with extra rum,
We'll count the change we've made.
In piles, the quarters add up, as alcohol hits
And cools our aching backs and shins.

Dancing in the Streets: Katherine Kramer and Jackie Raven in their early tapping days. Ray Anderson behind them blowing the sousaphone.

Stewart Alter (right) as "The Frog Prince."

THE FROG PRINCE
By Stewart Alter

The Tap "Sensibility"

I'm the frog prince, but it's very strange,
It's not the kiss of a princess that will make me change.

Even though I know that's how the story goes
Kissing lips won't change me . . . only tapping toes.

When I hear the rhythm of that complex beat,
I want to transmutate, starting with my feet.

When I hear tap dancing, I don't want to clap,
I want to change from frog . . . to the Prince of Tap.

The ME you see is not who I am,
On the surface I seem nervous or a shameless ham.

Underneath, I seethe with daring ambition,
To be a frog no more but in transition.

From a water-logged loser with two left feet
To a rhythm master who controls the beat.

It's not impossible, for I've changed before.
I was a tadpole once—I want to change once more.

—ᴡᴡ—

"You'll never dance," my critics say.
My legs are weak, my ankles creak, and my knees give way.

My belly's jelly, and my spine's in a curve,
I may try to swing, but in the end I swerve.

I've heard it said, I've no dancing talents,
No sense of space, even no sense of balance.

No grace, no poise, and no untapped skill,
I'm at my dancing best when I just stand still.

—ᴡᴡ—

I've lost my friends, they all resent me.
But when they claim I want fame, they misrepresent me.

Why deny, they cry, my awkward frog-like ways,
Unless I'm out to prove I'm better than they?

Why don't I face my life and embrace my fate?
Do I despise them? Is it myself I hate?

Why do I often feel I'm an awful flop?
Because I'll never tap, but can only hop.

—ᴡᴡ—

Frog Prince: I LONG TO TRANSFORM.

   Tapper responds: THAT'S NOT THE NORM!

Frog Prince: I WANT TO CHANGE MY SHAPE.

   Tapper: THAT'S AN ESCAPE!

Frog Prince: I NEED TO METAPMORPHOSE.

   Tapper: THAT'S JUST A POSE!

Frog Prince: I AM A PRINCE!

   Tapper: WE'RE NOT CONVINCED!

———

Frog Prince: I still have hope.

   Tapper: Though, there's not much cause.

Frog Prince: I can't tap, but I'm not trapped.

   Tapper: You are by Nature's Laws!

Frog Prince: Why presume I'm doomed?

   Tapper: Because you'll never win!

Frog Prince: A frog can jump.

   Tapper: BUT NOT OUT OF YOUR SKIN!

Frog Prince: I WON'T be depressed . . .

Tapper: For you that's a task.

Frog Prince: I can be second best.

Tapper: Even that's a lot to ask!

———

Frog Prince: (now speaking slowly, expressing determination)
      I'm a sloppy jalopy, not a gyroscope.
      But I'll watch and copy . . .
      AND I'LL LEARN THE ROPES . . .

(Frog Prince taps briefly, then hops offstage in his flippers and crown and green frog suit.)

COLLAGE BY DOROTHY WASSERMAN

COLLAGE BY DOROTHY WASSERMAN

Dorothy Wasserman is a tapper and a visual artist. This collage is called, "You Remind Me of Me".
She put Gregory's picture in my sunglasses (which you can't see here, but you can in the original). I
wouldn't mind a cappuccino in hand in a café in Paris.

MY BROTHER, ARTHUR

ARTHUR GOLDBERG, SELF-PORTRAIT

My brother Arthur illustrated all of my flyers,
programs, and publicity material over the years.

The New York Times

SUNDAY, FEBRUARY 26, 1978

Jane Goldberg Taps With Hoofers

By JENNIFER DUNNING

Years after the golden days of tap in the 1920's, 30's and early 40's, the days of streetcorner competitions and the Hoofers Club in Harlem, a dancer named Jane Goldberg was bitten by the tap bug. During the last few years, she has absorbed a good deal of that vernacular form from teachers like Charles Cook, Bert Gibson and Jazz Richardson.

Friday at the Experimental Intermedia Foundation loft in SoHo, Miss Goldberg presented "It's About Time." an evening of tap. Her enthusiasm is infectious. This was one of the happiest get-togethers of many a season.

•

The three men were on hand to reminisce, clown and deliver some exhilarating dance. There was a "funny step" competition, time step demonstrations and, with Miss Goldberg, evocations of great hoofers like Pete Nugent, Bill Robinson and Baby Laurence. Mr. Cook, a slyly elegant exponent of the art, contributed a delicate number he described as Creole "gumbo or something," and his touching "Let's Be Buddies" number with Miss Goldberg was a compendium of tap rhythms and sounds that proved the subtle variety of a dance form that is not often given its due.

If the real joy of the evening was the rare chance to see these three very different hoofers in action, Miss Goldberg and Andrea Levine contributed some flavorful tapping of their own. A split-second-timed tap and drum duet for Miss Levine and Chris Braun was a high point of the program, as was a final "shim shammy shim" with the dancers, Ernest Brown, a surprise guest artist, and a throng of Miss Goldberg's tap students.

•

Mr. Brown and Sandman Sims were among several intent hoofers in the audience. It is one of the great mysteries—and tragedies—of cultural life in this city that there is no permanent home or at least deserved acclaim and encouragement for these great exponents of one of our richest and most idiomatic art forms. There are two more performances tonight. Break down the doors if you have to.

New York Times *review of my first show in 1978, "It's About Time—An Evening of Jazz Tap Dancing."*

By Word of Foot™, *1980. At the bottom of the Gate: John Bubbles talking to George Hillman. Joe Albany at piano, Major Holly, (back to us) on bass.* By Word of Foot Two *and* Three *were in 1982 and 1985.*

By Word of Foot

a historic documentary by:

Jane Goldberg

BY WORD OF FOOT: TAP MASTERS PASS ON THEIR TRADITION

We were out to show that this "self-taught on the streets" art *could* be taught and that it didn't have to be romanticized and eulogized and retrospected in museums. I had by 1980 gathered a good sized mailing list from touring the country in the late 1970s. Closet hoofers and live-wired pros came to New York from throughout the country and Canada in 1980 to check out the scene of seventeen masters teaching their art. There are now large and small scenes all over the country with festivals breeding professionals, usually in the summertime. This is the means of production, the way the art "jes grew" again, in the words of Ishmael Reed *(Mumbo Jumbo).*

A CAMPAIGN TO GET TAP RECOGNIZED
AS A UNIQUE AMERICAN ART FORM

Declaration of Tap Survival (circa 1978–79): Ellington and Basie alumni and other jazz greats signed my letter (right) to keep tap alive: Dizzy Gillespie, Paul Quinichette, Brooks Kerr, Russell Procope, Sonny Greer, Tiny Grimes, Betty (Bebop) Carter (who worked with Greg's favorite and totally unsung hoofer, Teddy Hale). Count Basie, Charles Mingus, Dexter Gordon, Dannie Richmond, George Wein and Max Gordon also signed this letter. I went to musicians I knew worked with hoofers at one time. Philly Joe Jones wrote his own letter (below) to the National Endowment for the Arts by hand.

Jazz/Folk/Ethnic Panel
National Endowment of the Arts
General Programs
Grants Office
Mailstop (500)
Washington, D.C. 20506.

To the members

This letter is sent to you, hoping to support Jazz Tap dancing, America's classic dance. We have had and still have the greatest exponents of this Art. As long as there is music this Art should be kept alive, they go together the same as male and female on this earth. We have been fortunate to have had such artist as Baby Laurence Jackson, L.D. Jackson, Teddy Hale whom have passed on.

Were also still fortunate to have such greats as Fred Astaire, Honey Coles, Stomp & Stumpy, Ladys like Eleanore Powell and many others. Ms Jane Goldberg is a lady whom I support. She is making a concrete effort to have the remaining dancers (Tap) pass on this tradition and insure its survival. She has studied with the dance masters and intends to continue setting up classes to go ahead in this field to create & preserve this Art form.

Sincerely
Philly Joe Jones (Percussionist)
and former tap dancer.

Jazz/Folk/Ethnic Panel
National Endowment of the Arts
General Programs
Grants Office
Mailstop (500)
Washington, D.C.   20506

To members of the Jazz/Folk/Ethnic panel:

This is a letter to support the fact that jazz tap-dancing is
the visual as well as aural form of jazz music and should be
kept alive as a tradition of America's classic dance, and an
important part of the jazz tradition.
As a musician who has worked with tap dancers I understand its
close relationship to jazz music and realize it is in danger of
becoming a lost art. As I understand it, Jane Goldberg has been
making a serious and conscientious effort to find the remaining
jazz tap dancers who can pass the tradition on. I support her
studies with the jazz dance masters, her desire to set up classes
between them and other jazz dance enthusiasts, and to preserve
as well as create in the jazz dance form.

Sincerely yours,

Jerry Potter (Drums)   *Russell Procope*

Sonny Greer   *Tiny Grimes*   *(Hal Ashby)*

Tiny Grimes

William Ireson   *Brooksteen*

Eddie Durham

Paul Trim Chitte

Dizzy Gillespie

Jerry Potter (Drums)   *Russell Procope*

Sonny Greer   *Tiny Grimes*

Tiny Grimes

Dannie Richmond
(DRUMS)

Charles Mingus

Dexter Gordon   *Count Basie*

STAN MACK'S REAL LIFE FUNNIES

NOT YET COPACETIC

ALL DIALOGUE GUARANTEED OVERHEARD

HOME AND WORKPLACE PLANNING DIFFICULT ORGANIZING PROBLEMS OUR SPECIALTY ★ CALL 212-313 6021 ☆ SPACE-PRO ☆

COME IN, I'VE JUST MOVED, COMBINED HOME AND WORK-SPACE, I'M GOING CRAZY!

WHAT SPACE-PRO DOES IS THERAPEUTIC.

MY DESK IS NEXT TO MY BED, MY PHONE IS IN THE SINK, MY THINGS ARE ALL AROUND...

YOU MUST CLAIM A SACRED SPACE WHERE YOUR WORK DOESN'T PULSE AT YOU.

CHANGING TIMES TAP DANCING COMPANY

THESE ARE MY FRIENDS: THE WHOLE HISTORY OF TAP, ORAL HISTORIES OF GREAT HOOFERS, MY DANCE COMPANY RECORDS...

...SEVEN TELEPHONE DIRECTORI MY PICTURE OF SID CAESA MY CARIBBEAN PAINTINGS, MY DIARIES SINCE I WAS NIN

WE'RE GONNA HAVE TAKE SOME BROAD BRUSH STROKES HERE

JANE GOLDBERG

TAI CHI

THE A OF FIL

I HAVE 500 BABY LAURENCE RECORDS, THE TABLE IS FROM AUNT BRENDA BELLE, I LOVE MY JOHN BUBBLES TAPES...

WEED YOUR GARDEN TO MAKE ROOM FOR FLOWERS.

I CAN'T PART WITH MY DESK. IT'S FROM GIMBEL'S, FULL OF MY MOTHER'S PHOTOS, MY BILL ROBINSON MEMORABILIA...

FIND SOME CALM IN THE MIDDLE OF YOUR WHIRLWIND.

ASTAIRE DANCING

THE VIDEOTAPES IN THIS CABINET ARE SYMBOLIC OF MY LIFE...THESE DANCE AND DEMON SCULPTURES ARE SPECIAL.

LEMONS

THERE IS STILL TIME

BUT WHERE SHOULD I PHONE, SLEEP, WORK, STORE MY THINGS....?

PUT A LAMP IN THE SINK, USE LOTS OF TENSION POLE (I DO), MOVE YOUR MOUNTAIN ONE SPOON AT A TIME

THERE'S TOO MUCH STUFF! GET RID OF THAT YELLOW FILE CABINET! YOU HAVE TOO MANY MIGRATORY THINGS!

CAN I KEEP THE DRAWERS...HOW ABOUT THIS LITTLE BLUE BOX?

PRETZELS

NO! THE WHOLE SHOOTING MATCH GOES! AND THE TCHOTCHKES, TOO! WE HAVE TO GET TO THE BOTTOM OF THIS!

PART OF ME WILL ALWAYS BE DANCING AT THE APOLLO.

♫TAP YOUR ♫TROUBLES AWAY

YOUR PLACE IS TOO HIGGLEDY-PIGGLEDY! STUFF YOUR STUFF IN YOUR CLOSETS AND CLOSE THE DOORS. FREE YOUR ENERGY... G'BY...

B-BUT MY PLACE IS STILL A MESS AND MY THERAPIST IS ON VACATION.

CLEAR THE DECK OF YOUR ALBATROS AND PRAY!

?

JANE IN THE ARCHIVES

I used to call this room "The Gloom Room." It was so messy. It still is. Some would say "it shows creativity in action."

Much of the archive is now at The New York Public Library for the Performing Arts at Lincoln Center. One day, people who do research on tap might have to decipher my handwriting. This photo covers only a tiny part of the entire home collection.

Opposite Page: I was the subject of three Stan Mack "Real Life Funnies" cartoons in The Village Voice. *This one is my favorite where I hired an organizer and she wanted me to get rid of my archives!*

©DOROTHY WASSERMAN

"If you can't liberate the world,
you must liberate the ground
upon which you stand."

—*Howard Zinn*—

About Jane Goldberg

Jane Goldberg is a *"rara avis"*: a dancer who is also a writer. She has been one of the most prolific voices in the tap dancing field for the past three decades.

In 1972, while a government major at Boston University, the dancing of Fred Astaire and Ginger Rogers infected her imagination, and the virus spread throughout her body. She began to study tap and write about dance for *Boston After Dark*, *The Boston Phoenix*, and when she moved to New York, *The Village Voice*. As one of the tap renaissance's pioneers, she set out to revive interest in the art by combining her muckraking and artistic talents.

Ferreting out many of the remaining entertainment greats of the 20th century, Goldberg apprenticed herself to them while at the same time interviewing the old time great hoofers and documenting their work. Today, her archive "Jane Goldberg's Wandering Shoes, Tap(hi)istory, Tip Top Tapes, Tapalogues, Tapology and Tapperabilia" lives at the New York Public Library's Lincoln Center for the Performing Arts, part of The Gregory Hines Tap Collection.

Goldberg has performed her comedy/tap act, *Rhythm & Schmooze*, which examines politics, sexuality, tap roots, career vs. family, cultural escapism, and other issue-oriented themes in countless venues in this country and abroad. She is the recipient of two Fulbright Scholarships to India where she performed her highly idiosyncratic "tap-a-logue" between voice and feet throughout the entire subcontinent including Mumbai, Calcutta, Bangalore, New Delhi, Darjeeling, Ahmedebad and Chennai (Madras).

She is the artistic director of Changing Times Tap, Inc., and has received numerous National Endowment for the Arts and New York State Council for the Arts grants. Her Flo-Bert Life Achievement Award, Mama Lu Parks Award and St. Denis Award for Creative Choreography proudly hang on her home archive walls.

She is the inventor of tap-a-gram,™ a tapping telegram service.

She lives in New York City with the painter Owen Gray. ∎